Global Concepts and Applications in Corporate Finance

Md. Kamrul Bari
Uttara University, Bangladesh

IGI Global
Scientific Publishing
Publishing Tomorrow's Research Today

Published in the United States of America by
IGI Global Scientific Publishing
701 East Chocolate Avenue
Hershey, PA, 17033, USA
Tel: 717-533-8845 | Fax: 717-533-7115
Website: https://www.igi-global.com E-mail: cust@igi-global.com

Library of Congress Cataloging-in-Publication Data

Names: Bari, Md Kamrul, 1985- editor.
Title: Global concepts and applications in corporate finance / edited by Md. Bari.
Description: Hershey, PA : IGI Global Scientific Publishing, [2026] | Includes bibliographical references and index. | Summary: "This book will aim to provide relevant frameworks and the latest developments in the area of corporate finance. It will be written for professionals, students, and researchers, who want to improve their understanding of the role of different corporate financial concepts in the context of a corporate firm operating with the objective of maximizing its shareholders' wealth"-- Provided by publisher.
Identifiers: LCCN 2024054471 (print) | LCCN 2024054472 (ebook) | ISBN 9798369382479 (hardcover) | ISBN 9798369382486 (paperback) | ISBN 9798369382493 (ebook)
Subjects: LCSH: Corporations--Finance.
Classification: LCC HG4026 .G6225 2025 (print) | LCC HG4026 (ebook) | DDC 658.15--dc23/eng/20250314
LC record available at https://lccn.loc.gov/2024054471
LC ebook record available at https://lccn.loc.gov/2024054472
British Cataloguing in Publication Data
A Cataloguing in Publication record for this book is available from the British Library.

Editorial Advisory Board

Table of Contents

Detailed Table of Contents

The alternative functioning measures against the worldwide financial constraints on SME growth have yet to either be initiated or are being exercised in limited form in the Bangladesh context. The Credit Bureau, one of such measures, is being applied here in a limited form where further technological advancement and sophistication are needed. Given the urge, the study employed a "phenomenological method of qualitative research" with the objective of developing a new pattern or phenomenon of a 'common online platform for credit bureaus' from the essence of earlier experiences both home and abroad in the credit reporting industry. In data collection, it used document analysis and in-depth interviews to supplement the findings. Compiling the existing and new concepts resulting from the research findings, the paper concluded with a 'model proposition'. Thus, the study contributes to the further sophistication of the conventional credit information-sharing mechanism of the country. The research might help develop feasibility studies in the future to assist policy executors in this regard.

Preface

INTRODUCTION

Corporate finance has long been a central pillar of modern economic systems, guiding how organizations allocate capital, manage risk, and create sustainable value. In an increasingly interconnected global economy, financial decision-making extends beyond traditional frameworks to incorporate technological innovation, regulatory change, sustainability considerations, and cross-border financial practices. These evolving dynamics demand a broader understanding of corporate finance that reflects both established theories and emerging global applications.

Over the past decade, digital transformation, financial innovation, and economic disruptions—such as the global pandemic and rapid technological advancement—have reshaped financial management practices. New tools such as financial analytics, mobile financial platforms, and digital reporting systems have enhanced the capacity of organizations to make informed decisions. At the same time, challenges related to fraud prevention, regulatory compliance, environmental responsibility, and financial inclusion continue to shape the strategic landscape of corporate finance across developed and emerging markets.

This edited volume brings together scholarly perspectives from researchers and practitioners across multiple regions, presenting contemporary insights into corporate finance theory, practice, and policy. The chapters address diverse topics, including digital finance, sustainable investment, corporate governance, financial planning, and capital management. Together, they provide readers with a comprehensive exploration of the evolving financial ecosystem and the mechanisms through which organizations navigate complex financial environments worldwide.

CHAPTER OVERVIEW

Chapter 1 – Mobile Financial Services (MFS) for Online and In-Store Purchases: Users' Experiences and Scam Vulnerabilities

This chapter investigates the adoption of mobile financial services in developing economies, with particular emphasis on user experiences and exposure to digital fraud. Through empirical data collected from users, the authors analyze the benefits and risks associated with mobile wallet technologies and highlight the need for stronger security frameworks and user awareness.

Chapter 2 – The Emergence of Green Venture Capital and Its Role in Financing Early-Stage Green Technology Companies

The chapter explores the rise of green venture capital as a specialized investment mechanism supporting environmentally sustainable innovations. It examines the funding structure, mentorship opportunities, and risks associated with investing in early-stage green technology firms while emphasizing the growing importance of sustainable finance.

Chapter 3 – The Impact of Digital Transformation on Corporate Financial Practices: A Global Perspective

This chapter discusses the ways in which digital technologies, such as artificial intelligence, blockchain, and cloud computing, are transforming financial management, reporting, and auditing processes. It highlights the efficiency gains and transparency benefits of digital finance while addressing regulatory, security, and workforce adaptation challenges.

Chapter 4 – Forensic Accounting: The Frontline Defence Against Corporate Frauds

This chapter explores the increasing importance of forensic accounting practices in detecting and preventing corporate fraud. It discusses investigative techniques ranging from financial statement analysis to digital forensics, and even data analytics, while emphasizing the role of forensic accountants in maintaining corporate transparency and accountability.

Chapter 5 – Competition Law and Corporate Finance in India: Evaluating a Decade of Leniency Program Impact and Challenges

This chapter analyzes the evolution and effectiveness of the leniency program under India's Competition Act of 2002. It examines the intersection between competition law and corporate finance, highlighting how regulatory frameworks influence corporate strategy, market competition, and financial governance.

Chapter 6 – Best Practices for Financial Planning and Analysis in the Context of COVID-19

This chapter examines how organizations adapted financial planning and analysis practices during the global COVID-19 crisis. It emphasizes the importance of dynamic forecasting, scenario planning, and risk management in navigating economic uncertainty and sustaining organizational resilience.

Chapter 7 – Navigating the Corporate Finance–Time Value of Money Nexus by Resilience of Capital Rationing in Ethiopia

The final chapter examines the relationship between corporate finance practices, capital rationing, and the time value of money in resource-constrained organizations. Using quantitative analysis, the study demonstrates how effective financial management practices influence investment decisions and long-term value creation.

Chapter 8 – Enhancing SME Finance in Bangladesh through an Integrated Online Credit Bureau Platform

This chapter examines the financial constraints faced by small and medium-sized enterprises (SMEs) in Bangladesh and proposes the development of an integrated online credit bureau platform. Using qualitative research methods, the authors explore how improved credit information sharing can enhance financial transparency, expand lending opportunities, and strengthen the country's financial infrastructure.

CONCLUSION

The contributions in this volume collectively demonstrate the evolving nature of corporate finance in a rapidly changing global environment. From digital financial platforms and sustainable investment models to forensic accounting and regulatory governance, the chapters highlight the diverse factors shaping financial decision-making across industries and regions. Together, they illustrate how theoretical concepts in corporate finance continue to adapt in response to technological innovation, market dynamics, and global economic challenges.

Equally important is the recognition that corporate finance does not operate in isolation. It intersects with broader domains including law, technology, sustainability, and organizational management. The studies presented in this book underscore the importance of interdisciplinary approaches in addressing complex financial issues such as financial inclusion, digital security, fraud prevention, and strategic investment planning.

As the editor, I hope that this book will serve as a valuable resource for researchers, students, policymakers, and practitioners seeking to understand both the foundational principles and contemporary applications of corporate finance. By presenting global perspectives and diverse research approaches, this volume contributes to ongoing discussions about how financial systems can evolve to support sustainable economic growth and responsible corporate governance in an increasingly interconnected world.

Md. Kamrul Bari

Uttara University, Bangladesh

Introduction

This introductory chapter offers a relevant background for the readers to understand the contexts in which the book's chapters are written. The necessity to revisit corporate financial concepts, applications, and theories is highlighted in this chapter with necessary arguments and analogies as and when needed. This chapter starts with discussions of the basic concept of corporate finance and lays a foundation for the reader to understand that today's dynamic world continuously reshapes the ways in which business operations are conducted, affecting both risks and cash flows of a firm, and hence the corporate firm's ability to generate value. The chapter then goes on to the discussions of the evolution of corporate finance, the rationale for understanding the key concepts of corporate finance in the VUCA world, the need for contemporary research in the field of corporate finance, the effect of technological advancements on corporate finance, the dynamism of the legal and regulatory environments in which a corporate firm operates and their effects on corporate finance as a discipline, and finally the interplay of financial needs and financial planning in an evolving world.

1. THE BASIC CONCEPTS OF CORPORATE FINANCE

Corporate finance is a discipline that looks into THREE basic corporate decisions, namely capital budgeting, capital structure, and working capital management decisions, with the sole objective of maximizing firm value or the value of its existing shareholders' wealth (Brealey et al., 2019). Capital budgeting involve decisions related to identifying, evaluating, and selecting the best long-term investment decisions, while capital structure decisions are concerned with choosing the optimum mix of debt and equity to maximize firm value. Working capital decisions, on the contrary, look into the optimum management of short-term or day-to-day balance of current assets and current liabilities of a corporate firm (Berk & DeMarzo, 2019). Inherently, the financial managers of corporate firms are tasked with weighing investments that improve long-term cash generation ability against the distribution of surplus income to shareholders through dividends or share repurchases, since these choices are linked by the ultimate goal of improving firm value. The primary tasks of the corporate managers can thus be expressed as follows:

a. Take investment decisions in a manner so that the cash generated by the investment opportunities exceeds initial (and/or later) investments, and
b. Take financing decisions in a manner so that the firm can return a larger amount of cash back to the financial markets (or fund providers) compared to their investments

The goal of value addition is said to be attained by (a) taking corporate decisions to generate positive net cash flows while keeping the risk constant, (b) taking corporate decisions in manners, which reduce risks while keeping cash flows constant, or (c) taking corporate decisions in ways that increase cash flows and reduce risks at the same time. The challenges surrounding value addition, therefore, come from estimating cash flows, estimating, mitigating, and incorporating risks in corporate decisions. Topics such as discounted cash flow analysis, the capital asset pricing model for determining cost of equity, and weighted average cost of capital computations that act as hurdle rates for investment choices are all part of the corporate finance analytical toolset helping managers to attain their objectives (Damodaran, 2015).

With the recent evolution in technological advancements, changing legal and regulatory landscapes, evolving stakeholder expectations, gradual importance of sustainability concerns, and adoption of innovative measures by financial criminals to deceive systems and related stakeholders have certainly affected the cash flows and the risks of different corporate firms affecting their value generation capabilities. Therefore, a detailed understanding of the implications of the aforementioned issues is critical to enable managers of the corporate firms to take prudent corporate decisions to add value to the shareholders' wealth.

2. EVOLUTION OF CORPORATE FINANCE AND RELATED DISCIPLINES

The origination of corporate finance as a discipline can be traced back to the mercantile commerce in Europe and Italian city-states back in the fifteenth century (Goetzmann & Rouwenhorst, 2005). The Dutch East India corporation, as the first publicly traded corporation to retain fixed capital stock and pay dividends on a regular basis, made a significant contribution to the establishment of joint-stock organizations and public securities markets throughout Europe. By the early nineteenth century, London had become a global hub for corporate finance, creating novel investment and lending tools to support industrial growth. The rise of managerial capitalism and the dominance of common stock finance during the 20th century were accompanied by theoretical advancements, including Modigliani and Miller's capital structure irrelevance propositions (commonly known as the MM proposition), which profoundly altered scholarly and professional understanding back in the days when no one could offer any effective mathematical model of capital structure to address its link(s) to firm value (Modigliani & Miller, 1958).

Corporate finance became more entwined with venture capital, private equity, and investment management in the second half of the 20th century, and the rise of behavioral finance called into question presumptions of rational decision-making, which had magnified since Allan Greenspan's (former Chairman of the Federal Reserve) use of the famous phrase 'Irrational exuberance' (Shefrin, 2001). In light of growing public expectations for corporate responsibility, corporate finance has lately broadened to include environmental, social, and governance aspects along with the behavioral aspects mentioned above (Eccles et al., 2014).

3. THE RATIONALE FOR A DETAILED UNDERSTANDING OF THE EVER-CHANGING CORPORATE FINANCE LANDSCAPE

Scholars, practitioners, and policymakers must pay constant attention to the rapidly changing corporate finance landscape. In addition to creating new risks and opportunities that were unthinkable ten years ago, technological advancements like distributed ledger systems, artificial intelligence, and data analytics are radically changing how financial decisions are made and carried out (Goldstein et al., 2019). E-invoicing has been made mandatory across the globe, new governance mechanisms are also being put in place, including but not limited to improved disclosure requirements as a response to the technological advancements along with societal expectations (Armour et al., 2018). The evolution of green finance on the horizon added additional challenges to the researchers and practitioners in the field of corporate finance, since it mandates analytical exploration of the issues associated with controlling climate-related finance risks and environmental evaluation, and channeling funds to environmentally sustainable projects (Giglio et al., 2021). Additionally, the reform agenda intended to improve investor protection and market integrity has also been concurrently prompted by corporate failures of large firms, and the requirements of fraud prosecutions caused the enhancement of scrutiny of the financial governance along with accountability processes (Coffee Jr, 2020). Finance professionals, whose goal is rational value maximization, are now tasked with the responsibilities for managing uncertainty, ensuring organizational resilience, and generating sustainable value in a VUCA (Volatility, Uncertainty, Complexity, and Ambiguity) world, needing the comprehension of the overlapping processes and aligning these newer developments towards the overall corporate goal through meaningful and effective adoption of the advanced technological and environmentally friendly solutions into their regular decision making agenda.

4. ADDRESSING THE NEED FOR CONTEMPORARY CORPORATE FINANCE RESEARCH

The evolution of the newly added challenges and to grab the opportunities created by the modern corporate financial tools, the need for rigorous research has become imperative, particularly to understand the ways in which corporate finance is changing and how it must adapt to be relevant in light of the evolution of disruptive technologies, regulatory reform agenda, and environmental imperatives. Stakeholder expectation is also continuously being reshaped and unprecedented environmental risks have been taunting the researchers and practitioners alike turning traditional financial theories and practices obsolete primarily due to their initial developmental landscape (which often assumed a perfect world with frictionless economy, and almost no market imperfections, and an environment with no exponential technological and environmental shifts on the horizon) face fundamental challenges (Zingales, 2022). Therefore, research surrounding a dynamic financial and environmental context addresses a number of vital purposes, including documenting new practices and identifying those with real potential for value creation, assessing whether current regulatory frameworks are still sufficient to regulate new financial instruments and business models, and creating analytical tools that can capture the complexities brought about by digitization, artificial intelligence, and climate risk (Thakor, 2020). Additionally, the moderation and/or the interaction effects of technology, regulations, and sustainability with corporate financial environments, theories, and tools possess the potential to identify systemic risks that could result from the uncoordinated adoption of new practices or from a mismatch between regulatory oversight and financial innovation (Philippon, 2016). Gradual cointegration of financial markets and the cross-border presence of modern corporate firms amplify these concerns, since the practices developed in one jurisdiction now may generate consequential spillover effects into national regulatory boundaries. Without rigorous and contextually grounded research, today's policymakers may be at risk of devising interventions based on outdated assumptions, while practitioners may adopt innovations without adequate or any understanding of their potential risks.

5. TECHNOLOGICAL ADVANCEMENTS AND CORPORATE FINANCE

5.1 Fintech and Corporate Finance

Financial technology has become a disruptive force in the modern era. It is continuously changing the ways businesses operate (for example, the processes through which businesses obtain capital, tackle liquidity concerns, and carry out financial transactions). Fintech solutions are being incorporated into corporate financial operations in a large number of areas. For example, the creation and execution of financial contracts simultaneously, introducing automated lending platforms, and implementing digital payment systems through the utilization of groundbreaking technologies (such as blockchain-based instruments). These technologies provide added capabilities for real-time monitoring, improved transparency, and lower transaction costs while addressing the inefficiencies in financial intermediation (Chen et al., 2019). Fintech solutions now provide treasurers with highly sophisticated capabilities for managing currency exposures and exchange rate risks, interest rate risk, and counterparty credit risk across more complicated global organizational structures, as well as better insights into global liquidity situations.

The availability of financing choices has also become really interesting and diverse. Alternative financing channels like peer-to-peer lending platforms, invoice trading marketplaces, and tokenized asset offerings are consistently challenging the efficacy and the existence of conventional banking channels. In many cases, banks are following the 'if you cannot beat them, join them' philosophy and using these evolutionary service platforms as supplements to their regular service offerings. It is also turning the fund transfer process into an efficient one while reducing financial frictions. Additionally, these channels are also offering new sources of capital for small and medium-sized businesses, which often encounter difficulties obtaining conventional financing (Cornelli et al., 2023). Earlier research also shows that fintech innovations enhance efficiency and transparency of financial markets, particularly in nations with strong technology infrastructure and sophisticated regulatory frameworks (Frost et al., 2019). Fintech solutions can ensure easy and quick access to finance by making sophisticated risk pricing a reality through their ability to improve the capacity of a firm to handle enormous amounts of data and offering automated credit assessment reports. However, the emerging markets are yet to adopt a number of these solutions, questioning the efficacy of the corporate financial practices of the financial managers in that part of the world.

With the added efficiency of the aforementioned technological solutions, additional challenges surrounding data privacy, cybersecurity, and operational resilience have emerged through the incorporation of such advanced solutions into corporate finance. While dependence on third-party technology causes larger risk concentration, which might be insufficiently captured by the conventional risk management frameworks, the digitalization of financial processes expands attack surfaces for malicious actors. Regulators across the globe are not reacting proportionately to the fintech innovations, making it difficult for international firms to comply with regulations, and may allow regulatory arbitrage that compromises the goals of financial stability. Research on the connection between fintech adoption and corporate financial performance is still ongoing, and early findings indicate that the advantages depend on organizational capacity, the technology infrastructure already in place, and the regulatory framework in which businesses operate (Gaibulloev et al., 2025; Iatzaz Ul Hassan et al., 2025). When assessing fintech adoption decisions and creating policy measures meant to maximize societal benefits while limiting possible hazards, these factors highlight the need for an overarching as well as context-specific analysis.

5.2 Artificial Intelligence and Corporate Finance

Artificial intelligence (AI) has gone beyond the prediction of human imagination and now possesses the capabilities to offer seamless optimization, meaningful prediction, and decision-support mechanisms across a range of business operations, including the financial domain. Forecasting, credit risk assessments, fraud detection, investment analysis, cost optimization, business system automation, and even decision-making (in different contexts) have now become AI-driven tasks. These capabilities are enhanced through the application of a plethora of technological solutions, including but not limited to machine learning algorithms, natural language processing systems, and predictive analytical tools, catalyzing data processing and data interpretation tasks associated with the financial operations of an organization. Machine learning techniques can also offer complex forecasts analyzing a variety of data sources, such as unstructured information from news headlines, social media sentiment, and supply chain indicators, which eventually improves future performance of the concerned firm (Souma et al., 2019; Zhang et al., 2025). These abilities have certainly offered firms with better working capital management, more precise valuation estimations, and more informed investment decisions, while lowering the frequency of value-destroying investment mistakes and increasing overall capital allocation efficiency.

However, Significant concerns about accountability, governance, and the future of human judgment in financial decision-making have all been questioned in view of the incorporation of AI into corporate financial decisions. Auditability issues associated with the machine learning techniques' opacity are also suspected to go against stakeholder desires for openness and regulatory requirements (Černevičienė & Kabašinskas, 2024; Choowan & Daovisan, 2025; Evite et al., 2026; Lakshminarayanachar et al., 2024). In addition, concerns related to the fairness and equal access to financial services are magnified given the possibility that the inappropriate applications of training data could lead to biases while implementing AI. Therefore, it is only imperative that the pace of research and applications is simultaneously and equally paced with the growth potential of the AI technologies and their increased implementations across the globe. This requires an integrated approach towards tackling the aforementioned challenges from academia, industry, and governments or regulators across the globe.

5.3 Green Finance and Technology

Over the past decades, green finance has gradually emerged as a separate discipline. Today's discussions of green finance expand to issues surrounding green bonds, sustainability-linked loans, carbon credits, environmental impact investments, and even green venture capital, with the aim aims to provide funds to businesses and initiatives that produce favorable environmental results (Flammer, 2021). Technology also plays a significant role within this ecosystem. Starting from supporting the invention of new financial instruments, promoting the growth of markets for environmental commodities, and ending with the very act of catalyzing the process of data collection and verification, are now significantly controlled by advanced technologies.

In addition, technology has also enabled the development of new green finance instruments and market processes that were previously impractical due to coordination and information-related challenges. Tokenized carbon credits stored on distributed ledgers have the potential to enhance carbon market liquidity along with transparency, facilitating price discovery as well as successful emissions reduction tactics (Sorensen, 2023). Smart contracts, in contrast to their primitive predecessors, now incorporate automated verification of environmental performance data, effectively ensuring a close match of financial incentives with environmental goals by triggering rewards or penalties based on effective and meaningful outcomes.

Technological advancements are offering more complex analysis of climate-related financial risks and are accelerating the incorporation of climate issues into mainstream corporate finance. Therefore, it is now imperative that skills are developed in the concerned and overlapping areas of green finance and modern technology, which can only be made possible through additional research and development in these fields of study. This book is a step towards achieving that goal as well.

6. REGULATORY AND INSTITUTIONAL MECHANISMS AND CORPORATE FINANCE

6.1 Corporate Law, Competitiveness, and Corporate Finance

Corporate legal frameworks are influenced and can also influence corporate financial practices of the corporate firms. Development of new financial instruments and transaction structures frequently pushes the limits of current legal regulations, which may eventually lead to judicial or legislative clarification that broadens the parameters of acceptable behavior. Legal systems built on classic corporate structures and conventional securities face issues as new kinds of finance arise, such as special purpose acquisition firms, digital asset offers, and decentralized autonomous organizations. Which financing arrangements thrive and which countries profit economically from financial innovation will be greatly influenced by how the corporation law responds to these developments. In addition, the competitive landscape of the global firms is also heavily influenced by the effective crafting of policies with appropriate implementation strategies across the globe. Therefore, the interaction among policy formulation, implementation, competitiveness, fairness, and financial consequences must be rigorously studied to understand how they are affecting business as well as the financial operations of a corporate firm.

6.2 Corporate Frauds and the Role of Corporate Finance

With the advancements of technology, fraud detection and prevention have also become an immediate challenge to address for all corporate firms across the globe. Designing an efficient fraud detection and prevention tool necessitates a thorough understanding of how corporate fraud could relate to corporate financial practices. One could define corporate fraud as the breach of financial integrity with major consequences for investors, workers, and the stakeholders as a whole. Fraudsters often exploit financial vulnerabilities of financial controls, governance frameworks, and incentive systems through their carefully crafted fraudulent strategies for financial misreporting, asset theft, and corruption schemes (Dyck et al., 2024). The responsibilities of the finance departments of global corporations are enormous, since they are at the core of both committing and stopping fraud because of their involvement in preparing financial statements, managing cash, and executing transactions with utmost sincerity, integrity, and contractual commitments to their principals (shareholders). Therefore, along with the researchers in the field of corporate finance, the practitioners must also possess sufficient knowledge and skills to devise effective fraud prevention strategies (such as improved control settings), whistleblower protections, and accountability systems that raise the expected costs of wrongdoing,

The above discussions have certainly established a rationale for the aforementioned parties to explore the contexts, realities, problems, and offer solutions through new research-based strategies. In fact, the exponential growth of technology has also mandated that corporations implement a practice of action research, the beginning of which can be a thorough understanding of the process of corporate frauds. This book certainly sheds light on these matters.

7. ADDRESSING FINANCING NEEDS AND FINANCIAL PLANNING IN CORPORATE FINANCE TODAY

7.1 Evolving Financing Requirements in a Tech-Driven Economy

Technology companies have unique financing needs, such as large initial investment requirements, protracted periods of negative cash flow during growth phases, and a great deal of uncertainty regarding ultimate commercial viability. By combining equity investment with active governance engagement and phased funding commitments that balance investor and entrepreneur incentives, venture capital has developed as a specialized financing type tailored to these features (Gompers et al., 2021). Technology innovation in a variety of geographical settings has been made possible by the expansion of venture capital markets worldwide, but the concentration of investment in significant innovation hubs raises concerns about the geographical distribution of entrepreneurial possibilities.

Beyond conventional cost of capital optimization, corporate finance strategies in technology-intensive industries are increasingly incorporating strategic concerns. Beyond the immediate profits from capital rounds, access to outside funding may convey confidence in business models to suppliers, clients, and other partners. Investor relationships may give you access to networks, knowledge, and reputation that help you expand in the future. These factors necessitate more sophisticated frameworks for assessing financing options that take into account strategic advantages and signaling effects, and they complicate straightforward financial models that are solely concerned with reducing funding costs (Davila et al., 2003).

7.2 Financial Planning in Today's Corporate World

Modern corporate financial planning operates in a setting that challenges conventional methods based on yearly budgeting cycles and static predictions due to increased uncertainty, rapid change, and increased stakeholder expectations. As organizations deal with disruption from technological change, geopolitical volatility, and environmental pressures that make historical relationships unreliable indicators of future performance, the limitations of traditional financial planning methodologies have become more apparent. Financial planning is being rethought by forward-thinking companies as a dynamic, ongoing process that incorporates adaptive resource allocation, real alternatives thinking, and scenario analysis. The global contingencies, such as the COVID-19 pandemic, had also altered the ways in which corporate financial planning was done during the pre-COVID days. Instead of subscribing to single-point predictions, scenario-based planning has developed as a useful method for managing uncertainty in financial planning, allowing firms to construct strategic responses across several probable futures. In view of these, it is only rational to dig deeper into the discussions of financial planning with a special focus on global contingencies.

CONCLUDING REMARKS

Technological advancements, environmental concerns, ever-changing legal and regulatory frameworks, global contingencies, sustainability concerns, tremendous developments in the global entrepreneurial landscape, global reform expectations in terms of transparency and accountability, and continuous need of funding with the challenges of value creation have all created a new version of the reality in the world of corporate finance, which is hardly discussed in the conventional theoretical settings in the past. Therefore, it is essential that the researchers and practitioners take meaningful initiatives to untangle the mysterious interplay of risk and return with a focus on addressing the global needs of the stakeholders while ensuring that the task of sustainable value creation for corporate firms is tackled with utmost sincerity through the actions of risk mitigation while enhancing both efficiency and effectiveness of the business operations of the underlying corporate firms. This book is an initiative that brings together global knowledge that sheds light on different aspects of these global challenges and opens the door for further research to ensure a more comprehensive understanding of the evolving global concepts and applications in the field of corporate finance.

REFERENCES

Armour, J., Enriques, L., Ezrachi, A., & Vella, J. (2018). Putting technology to good use for society: The role of corporate, competition and tax law. *Journal of the British Academy*, *6*(s1), 285–321. https://ora.ox.ac.uk/objects/uuid:d5c9ea7a-61a2-46bd-96b7-6d035a77bfcb. DOI: 10.5871/jba/006s1.285

Berk, J., & DeMarzo, P. (2019). *Corporate Finance* (5th Global Edition). E-Learning with e-Book, MyLab Finance.

Brealey, R., Myers, S., & Allen, F. (2019). *Principles of Corporate Finance* (13th ed.). McGraw-Hill Education.

Černevičienė, J., & Kabašinskas, A. (2024). Explainable artificial intelligence (XAI) in finance: A systematic literature review. *Artificial Intelligence Review*, *57*(8), 216. DOI: 10.1007/s10462-024-10854-8

Chen, M. A., Wu, Q., & Yang, B. (2019). How valuable is FinTech innovation? *Review of Financial Studies*, *32*(5), 2062–2106. DOI: 10.1093/rfs/hhy130

Choowan, P., & Daovisan, H. (2025). Artificial Intelligence in Data Governance for Financial Decision-Making: A Systematic Review. *Big Data and Cognitive Computing*, *10*(1), 8. DOI: 10.3390/bdcc10010008

Coffee, J. C., Jr. (2020). *Corporate crime and punishment: The crisis of underenforcement.* Berrett-Koehler Publishers. https://books.google.com/books?hl=en&lr=&id=13znDwAAQBAJ&oi=fnd&pg=PP1&dq=Coffee,+John+C.+2019.+Corporate+Crime+and+Punishment:+The+Crisis+of+Underenforcement.+Oakland,+CA:+Berrett-Koehler+Publishers.&ots=cgjmGKFEgr&sig=vH5BO5cf2BV7GZS1DbODkrWYtTI

Cornelli, G., Frost, J., Gambacorta, L., Rau, P. R., Wardrop, R., & Ziegler, T. (2023). Fintech and big tech credit: Drivers of the growth of digital lending. *Journal of Banking & Finance*, *148*, 106742. DOI: 10.1016/j.jbankfin.2022.106742

Damodaran, A. (2015). *Applied corporate finance* (4. ed). Wiley.

Davila, A., Foster, G., & Gupta, M. (2003). Venture capital financing and the growth of startup firms. *Journal of Business Venturing*, *18*(6), 689–708. DOI: 10.1016/S0883-9026(02)00127-1

Dyck, A., Morse, A., & Zingales, L. (2024). How pervasive is corporate fraud? *Review of Accounting Studies*, *29*(1), 736–769. DOI: 10.1007/s11142-022-09738-5

Eccles, R. G., Ioannou, I., & Serafeim, G. (2014). The Impact of Corporate Sustainability on Organizational Processes and Performance. *Management Science*, *60*(11), 2835–2857. DOI: 10.1287/mnsc.2014.1984

Evite, P. M., Svetlova, E., & Bucur, D. (2026). *Trade-offs in Financial AI: Explainability in a Trilemma with Accuracy and Compliance* (arXiv:2602.01368). arXiv. https://doi.org//arXiv.2602.01368DOI: 10.48550

Flammer, C. (2021). Corporate green bonds. *Journal of Financial Economics*, *142*(2), 499–516. DOI: 10.1016/j.jfineco.2021.01.010

Frost, J., Gambacorta, L., Huang, Y., Shin, H. S., & Zbinden, P. (2019). BigTech and the changing structure of financial intermediation. *Economic Policy*, *34*(100), 761–799. DOI: 10.1093/epolic/eiaa003

Gaibulloev, K., Mirzaei, A., Moore, T., & Saad, M. (2025). The effect of fintech financing on firm performance: Evidence from emerging economies. *Journal of International Financial Markets, Institutions and Money*, *103*, 102201. DOI: 10.1016/j.intfin.2025.102201

Giglio, S., Kelly, B., & Stroebel, J. (2021). Climate Finance. *Annual Review of Financial Economics*, *13*(1), 15–36. DOI: 10.1146/annurev-financial-102620-103311

Goetzmann, W. N., & Rouwenhorst, K. G. (2005). *The origins of value: The financial innovations that created modern capital markets*. Oxford University Press., https://books.google.com/books?hl=en&lr=&id=-oi7Osz2Ss0C&oi=fnd&pg=PR5&dq=Goetzmann+and+Rouwenhorst+2005&ots=DtuPW2Xphu&sig=ZI2jZW8DTavoTFf2U-2WAFc3a9k DOI: 10.1093/oso/9780195175714.001.0001

Goldstein, I., Jiang, W., & Karolyi, G. A. (2019). To FinTech and beyond. *Review of Financial Studies*, *32*(5), 1647–1661. DOI: 10.1093/rfs/hhz025

Gompers, P., Gornall, W., Kaplan, S. N., & Strebulaev, I. A. (2021). Venture capitalists and COVID-19. *Journal of Financial and Quantitative Analysis*, *56*(7), 2474–2499. DOI: 10.1017/S0022109021000545

Iatzaz Ul Hassan, M., Wu, M., Lu, J., Sohu, J. M., Ali, S., Anjum, H. N., & Bilal, M. (2025). Financial technology and banking performance in developing countries: Evidence from an advanced quantile regression approach. *Humanities & Social Sciences Communications*, *12*(1), 1455. DOI: 10.1057/s41599-025-05571-8

Lakshminarayanachar, R., Chattopadhyay, R., Ph.D, D. K. G., & Sreeravindra, B. B. (2024). Navigating Ethical and Governance Challenges in AI: Finance. *International Journal of Global Innovations and Solutions (IJGIS)*. DOI: 10.21428/e90189c8.da2c2ed6

Modigliani, F., & Miller, M. H. (1958). The cost of capital, corporation finance and the theory of investment. *The American Economic Review*, *48*(3), 261–297.

Philippon, T. (2016). *The fintech opportunity*. National Bureau of Economic Research. https://www.nber.org/papers/w22476

Shefrin, H. (2001). BEHAVIORAL CORPORATE FINANCE. *The Bank of America Journal of Applied Corporate Finance*, *14*(3), 113–126. DOI: 10.1111/j.1745-6622.2001.tb00443.x

Sorensen, D. (2023). Tokenized Carbon Credits. *Ledger*, *8*. Advance online publication. DOI: 10.5195/ledger.2023.294

Souma, W., Vodenska, I., & Aoyama, H. (2019). Enhanced news sentiment analysis using deep learning methods. *Journal of Computational Social Science*, *2*(1), 33–46. DOI: 10.1007/s42001-019-00035-x

Thakor, A. V. (2020). Fintech and banking: What do we know? *Journal of Financial Intermediation*, *41*, 100833. DOI: 10.1016/j.jfi.2019.100833

Zhang, Y., Zhu, Y., & Linnainmaa, J. T. (2025). Man versus Machine Learning Revisited. *Review of Financial Studies*, *38*(12), 3768–3790. DOI: 10.1093/rfs/hhaf066

Zingales, L. (2022). *Regulating big tech*. Bank for International Settlements, Monetary and Economic Department. https://www.bis.org/publ/work1063.pdf

Section 1
The Evolving Role of Technology-Driven Financial Innovation in Reshaping the Corporate Financial Landscape

Chapter 1

Mobile Financial Services (MFS) for Online and In-Store Purchases:

Users' Experiences and Scam Vulnerabilities

Md.Khaled Amin
http://orcid.org/0000-0002-3929-3088
American International University-Bangladesh, Bangladesh

Vichayanan Rattanawiboonsom
Naresuan University, Thailand

Md. Kamrul Bari
http://orcid.org/0000-0001-5325-2779
UCSI University, Bangladesh

ABSTRACT

This study aims to explore the usage patterns, users' experiences, and scam vulnerabilities associated with Mobile Financial Services (MFS) in developing countries like Bangladesh. While the notion of m-wallet

DOI: 10.4018/979-8-3693-8247-9.ch001

is getting much more popular, it also poses some risk of digital fraud. The study used primary data collected from one hundred and ten users employing a standard questionnaire. The link to the questionnaire, which was designed with MS Form, was distributed among the users by email and instant messaging service. The study highlights several challenges and scams that may deter users from using the service. To fully use the potential of MFS technology, it is essential to address the challenges by incorporating robust security measures, designing user-friendly interfaces, and providing widespread education. This study also stresses the urgent need for stronger authentication protocols, enhanced data encryption, and comprehensive user education initiatives to secure m-wallet platforms that support sustainable digital financial inclusion in strengthening the economy.

INTRODUCTION

Advancements in science and technology are eventually speeding up the evolution of the various mobile-based applications by which the transaction process is getting easier, faster, enjoyable, and reliable. As such, various Mobile Financial Services (MFS), including mobile banking, mobile payments, and mobile wallets, are introduced where one can avail the service via hand-held devices virtually. MFS has gained substantial interest from consumers in an emerging market where access to traditional banking is limited and costly (Jack & Suri, 2011).

Some of these are truly application-oriented, in which the service can only be rendered on various apps (Donner & Tellez, 2008). Mobile apps are mainly regarded as a form of embryonic self-service technologies (SSTs) that have highly impacted the development and establishment of e-commerce (Robertson et al., 2016). The SSTs, which include ATMs, online banking, mobile banking, self-check machines, online shopping, and online bill payment, emerged as an interactive platform by which customers can avail of desired products and services online or in person while in store (Shahid Iqbal et al., 2018).

To speed up the transaction process, many e-wallet services are being highly incorporated and valued by consumers; concurrently, these are much appreciated by the vendors, though the services are accepted by a limited number of vendors. Various functional aspects of a mobile app positively influence customer satisfaction (Iyer et al., 2018). As a result, consumers are highly connected to various self-service technologies, such as e-wallets, automated telephone banking, and online ticketing (Newman et al., 2018). Numerous studies have been conducted to find out the behavioral factors or components influencing consumers' behavioral intention to adopt e-wallets as an alternative method of buying goods and services online or in-store.

To meet the growing demand and provide hassle-free services, various e-wallet apps have been launched by the e-wallet service provider in Bangladesh. The users perceive these apps mainly as software programs that can be downloaded from the Android market and installed on a mobile device, and these are introduced to accomplish purchases online and offline conveniently (Rakestraw et al., 2013). Over time, researchers have found numerous factors influencing the use of MFS across the globe.

The service offers both convenience and accessibility. Research by Bagla and Sancheti (2018) found that attractive cashback, rewards, ease of use, perceived usefulness, and transaction security were the factors responsible for the growing use of digital wallets. The continuation of MFS usage hinges on perceived usefulness, trust, and security (Dahlberg, Guo, & Ondrus, 2015). The adoption behavior is found to be influenced by some demographic factors, such as age, education level, and digital literacy (Oliveira, Thomas, Baptista, & Campos, 2016). In terms of usage, higher satisfaction is shown by comparatively younger people, while the old-timers may encounter challenges in grasping the technicalities (Thakur, 2013).

As of late, mobile payment platforms, which are declared to be the most successful mobile service, have gained limited attention from researchers in developing countries (Slade et al., 2015). In Bangladesh, mobile-based cash transactions, commonly known as e-wallets, mobile wallets, remote mobile platforms, mobile payment, mobile commerce, and digital wallet services were first introduced by the BRAC bank and eventually admired by the local people since it was proven to be quite useful, safe, and hassle-free. Due to its diverse benefits, in Bangladesh, the number of users has reached fifty million to date.

Scholars have extensively studied the phenomena incorporating their local context, but not much attention has been drawn by the local scholars. Scholars have placed much emphasis on the adoption and acceptance behavior of mobile phones and mobile wallets, but the adoption and continued use of e-wallet apps in buying products from non-store retailers have not been studied extensively. In addition, scam issues were neglected at the early stage of m-wallet adoption as the focuses were primarily centered on measuring users' experience to improve service level, leaving the challenges behind. This lack of emphasis on security led to literature gaps in fraud detection and prevention measures, inviting scholars to investigate the phenomenon. Furthermore, addressing those issues and formulating preventive measures has become indispensable.

The usefulness of the M-wallet was widely documented in the literature, highlighting several visible benefits for users and merchants, including ease of transaction, ubiquity, security, incentives, etc. It has also been seen that m-wallets are gaining much popularity in in-store purchases in parallel with online purchases. The functionality of contactless payment, payment made through QR codes, etc., has doubled the shopping experience. Despite several visible benefits, concerns over data privacy, trust issues, and technicalities shrank the widespread acceptance (Jain & Singla, 2022); the scam issues were highly overlooked. Existing literature drafted in the local context mostly filled the gaps of adoption and acceptance issues, but did not pinpoint challenges and barriers. Knowing the obstacles and challenges to adoption by analyzing local data and cases could significantly contribute to the body of knowledge. The chapter also sheds light on scam vulnerabilities and protective measures in the context of a developing country. The findings have theoretical and practical implications, particularly for providing better customer service and mitigating pitfalls.

LITERATURE

The adoption of m-wallet faced multiple challenges that prevented users from using the service further. Greater adoption of MFS depends on perceived ease of use, perceived usefulness (Zhou, 2012). User experience in MFS is shaped by trust and perceived security (Shaikh & Karjaluoto,

2015). In the context of developing countries, a higher user experience relies mostly on convenience, cost-effectiveness, and the ability to conduct transactions without visiting a bank (Donovan, 2012). However, developing countries' users may suffer from inconsistent network coverage, low smartphone penetration, and low digital literacy (Jack & Suri, 2011). Furthermore, in some Asian countries, customer service quality, ease of navigation, and service availability are closely linked to user satisfaction (Chawla & Joshi, 2017). The users also suffer from several issues. The issues are categorized as security, technology, and regulatory. Fear of fraud, data breaches, cyberattacks, and identity theft were found to be the primary concerns that eventually deterred the users from using the system (Upadhyay, Upadhyay, Abed, & Dwivedi, 2022); because m-wallet requires personal data to be stored on a server, causing a high risk of data breaches (Shankar & Kumari, 2019). In a developing country, users' willingness to adopt m-wallet was affected by trust, where people were skeptical about the technology providers due to low financial literacy and a lack of knowledge about digital transactions (Hussain, Gupta, & Bhardwaj, 2024; Liu et al., 2019). Users may get frustrated with the user experience and platforms, which may prevent them from using the system continuously (Chawla & Joshi, 2020). In underdeveloped regions, m-wallet adoption was disrupted by poor network connectivity and accessibility issues, which may fall under technological barriers (Kapoor, Sindwani, & Goel, 2024). It has been communicated on digital media that the use of an m-wallet does not require technical knowledge, but, in reality, the perceived complexity of using an m-wallet may dissuade people from adopting an m-wallet (Slade, Williams, Dwivedi, & Piercy, 2015). The associated technicalities may reduce the appeal as users face complexity and unfamiliarity (Rana, Dwivedi, Lal, Williams, & Clement, 2017). In a developing country, the government often imposes regulations to control fraud and detect illegal activities, such as money laundering, which may create a barrier for legitimate users, causing a serious hamper on adoption (Oliveira et al., 2016). The limited merchant acceptance, due to transaction fees and operational complexity, may jeopardize the use of m-wallets (Agrawal & Yadav, 2024). Finally, the literature also sheds light on socioeconomic challenges, such as low income and low literacy may further restrict the use of m-wallets (Dass & Pal, 2011). In line with the challenges discussed earlier, integrating local data, the next parts of the chapter portray the phenomena of urban areas in other developing countries. Despite a tremendous adoption rate in Asian countries, MFS is prone to various vulnerabilities, such as phishing attacks, SIM swap fraud, identity theft, social engineering scams, etc. A weak regulatory, lack of awareness among users are responsible for the vulnerabilities in the low-income regions (Kshetri, 2013). Cybersecurity threats, which may arise from the lack of standardized authentication protocols and reliance on SMS-based transactions, are particularly concerning for users in low-income countries, as they are more vulnerable to interception and fraud (Kshetri, 2013).

DATA COLLECTION TECHNIQUES

The study adopted a descriptive research method with which a group of users, i.e., 110, were drawn purposively and surveyed using a structured questionnaire. The study covered only those users who were currently dwelling in urban areas and actively using various mobile wallet apps to buy products (e.g., fashion products, groceries, home decor, etc.) from non-store retailers, such as online E-commerce, F-commerce, online selling, etc. The survey used structured questionnaires including statements largely adopted from prior studies. The headings of the tables used in the paper summarize the items presented in the questionnaire; therefore, the full questionnaire was not included in the chapter.

The link to the questionnaire was posted on various social media platforms or sent via e-mail for possible quantitative responses. Finally, all responses were coded for initial inspection and estimating descriptive statistics, i.e., frequency and percentage. Throughout the phase of data collection, ethical considerations were kept in mind as no benefits in any form were provided to the respondents.

USAGE PATTERN OF M-WALLET APPS IN A DEVELOPING COUNTRY

There are approximately eighteen financial institutions in Bangladesh offering mobile financial services to the citizens. A few of these are highly admired by the urban community, but many of these have failed to position in the minds of the users. The market is very mature as the total transactions exceeded Tk 10,75,990 crores in 2022 (Hasan, 2024). Before we delved into the use pattern of m-wallet apps in an urban area, we first tried to know the types of services preferred by the users in solving financial issues. As shown in Figure 1, the majority opted for the bkash app, which is the pioneer in this industry in Bangladesh, followed by Nagad, a service initiated by the Bangladesh Post Office, a government agency providing postal services to the nation. Few prioritized Rocket, a service introduced by a private bank known as Dutch-Bangla Bank PLC. In other words, bKash is leading the market, yielding the maximum market share, followed by Nagad, a challenger striving to be the leader of the market. Rocket is competing head-to-head to become the challenger.

Figure 1. Distribution of m-wallet usage among different brands

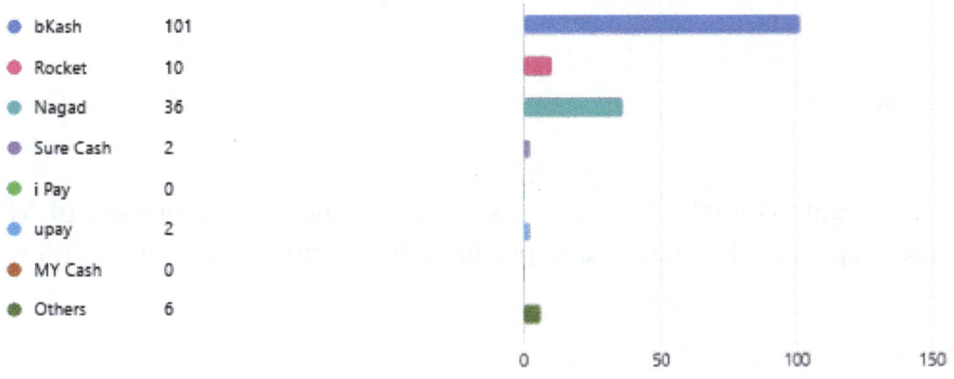

Source: Survey data

Figure 2 shows the areas in which the money has been disbursed. The use of m-wallets has been extremely popular in buying products and services online and in-store. The users often withdraw funds from their m-wallet account. Topping up a mobile balance is also a common use. People use a wallet for bill payment and shopping.

Overall, this data reveals that cash withdrawals, mobile recharges, and bill payments are the primary uses, while donations, education fees, and remittances are less common. The two services, peer-to-peer and savings, have shown moderate demand. Donations and education fees are on the list of less common practices. Remittance is the least popular and has the lowest usage. Overall, this data reveals that cash withdrawals, mobile recharges, and bill payments are the primary uses, while donations, education fees, and remittances are less common.

Figure 2. Primary usage

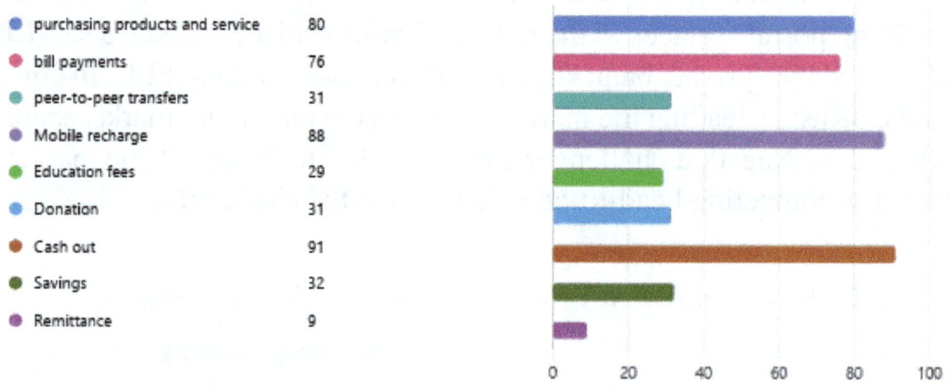

Source: Survey data

The figure (Figure 3) showcases survey data on the frequency of M-wallet app usage for purchasing products from online and store retailers.

Figure 3. Frequency of M-wallet app usage

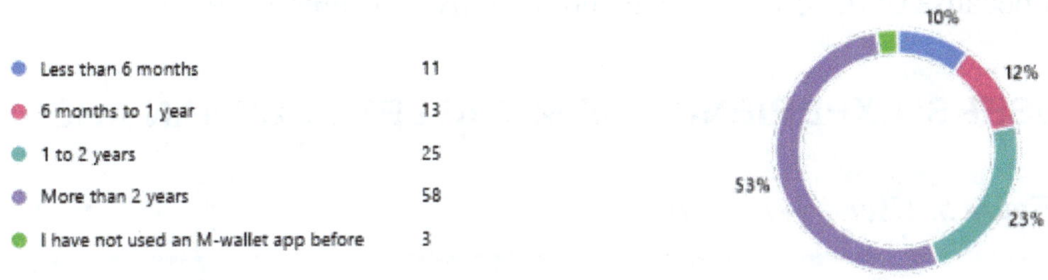

Source: Survey data

Almost half of the users used the m-wallet several times a week. One-third considered using it once or twice a month. One-fourth utilized it once a week. Little used it daily or multiple times a day. As shown in Figure 4, it can be seen that the majority shared that they adopted the service because it was handy for them. Almost half of the users were induced by the incentives offered to them.

Figure 4. Initial reasons behind the use

Source: Survey data

One-third of the users were found to be innovators as they adopted m-wallets because they were curious about the service. A few were enticed by their peers within the community.

In conclusion, three mobile financial service brands gained much popularity in urban areas, holding the major market share. Urban users mainly use MFS for four reasons: purchasing products online, paying bills, recharging mobiles, and withdrawing cash from local agents or ATMs, and the service is demanded several times a week. Most of the users adopted it because of the convenience and incentives offered to them.

USERS' EXPERIENCE OF M-WALLET IN URBAN AREAS

Figure 5. Users' perception

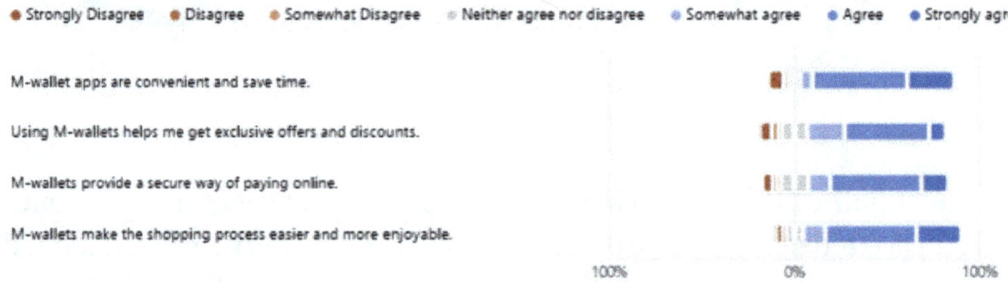

Source: Survey data

Figure 5 depicts users' perception of m-wallets in urban areas. To measure users' perceptions, we asked four questions of the respondents on a Likert scale. M-wallet apps are handy and save time, as agreed by most of the respondents, as they help them get exclusive offers and discounts. M-wallet ensures security while transacting online, which makes the shopping experience easier and more enjoyable for the users, as shared by most of the respondents. To clarify the incentives and security, we further asked two specific questions about different sales. Figure 6 shows the survey result for the question, “Do you think m-wallet offers better promotions or cashback offers than other payment options?” A majority (61%) of respondents perceive that m-wallets provide better promotions or cashback offers compared to other payment options. Twenty-eight percent of respondents are not sure about the difference, which could imply a lack of awareness of the service.

Figure 6. Users' perception of incentives

Source: Survey data

Figure 7 shows survey results for the question, "How secure do you feel when using M-wallets for purchases online?" Half of the users (56%) felt very secure using the m-wallet for online purchases. A considerable proportion of users (37%) felt neutral, followed by a small minority (7%) who felt insecure, raising little concern over security.

Figure 7. Users' perception of security

Source: Survey data

We further asked questions related to security issues, such as fraud, to know their experience. Figure 8 shows survey results for the question, "Have you ever experienced security issues, such as fraud, while using an m-wallet?" 42% of the users raised serious concerns over security as they experienced fraudulent activities, which may have caused them inconvenience. A respectable number (58%) of users denied the security concerns, suggesting they may have a low level of awareness. To gauge the level of awareness, we asked another question about the potential risk associated with the use.

Figure 8. Users' experience with security issues

Source: Survey data

Figure 9 shows survey results for the question, "How aware are you of the potential fraud risk associated with m-wallet apps?" The result confirmed that 13% of the users were not aware of the potential fraud risk.

Figure 9. Awareness level of potential fraud risks

Source: Survey data

In conclusion, most of the responses are skewed toward agreement across the statements, forming a positive attitude towards m-wallet in terms of convenience, security, and shopping experience. Most respondents expressed optimism about the incentives provided, though a small group voiced concerns about security issues. Despite being aware of potential fraud risks, these concerns could slightly hinder m-wallet adoption. Knowing the potential challenges may aid the industry in finding a remedy to the issues.

CHALLENGES CONFRONTED BY THE USERS IN URBAN AREAS

Figure 10 illustrates the challenges confronted by users in urban areas while using the m-wallet. The users were asked the following questions: "What challenges have you encountered while using m-wallet apps?" Data show that technical issues are the most reported issues the study found, and it was shared by most of the respondents. One-fourth of respondents indicated poor support service as one of the challenges. One-third of respondents noted significant concern over data safety and privacy issues. Issues related to scams were also marked by 25% of the respondents. A few respondents mentioned the issues, such as limited acceptance among the vendors and complexity in use.

Figure 10. Challenges

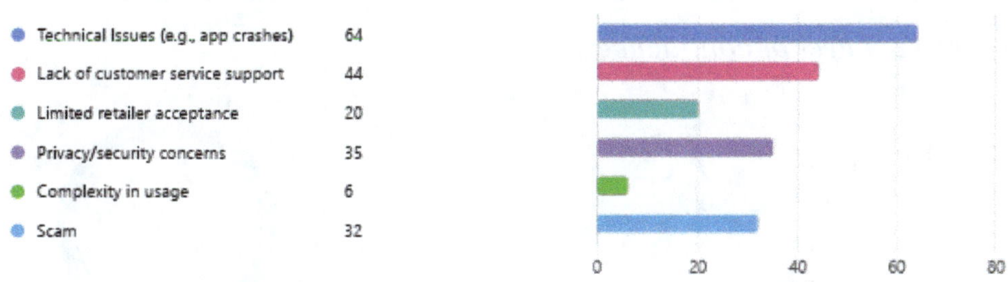

Source: Survey data

The users showed concern over some issues, which are portrayed in Figure 11. Users were asked to rate their level of concern for various challenges that are depicted in Figure 10. The respondents were extremely concerned about the security of personal information, network issues, and fraud management, which raised our interest in knowing more about issues related to security and fraud management.

Figure 11. Level of concern for the challenges mentioned

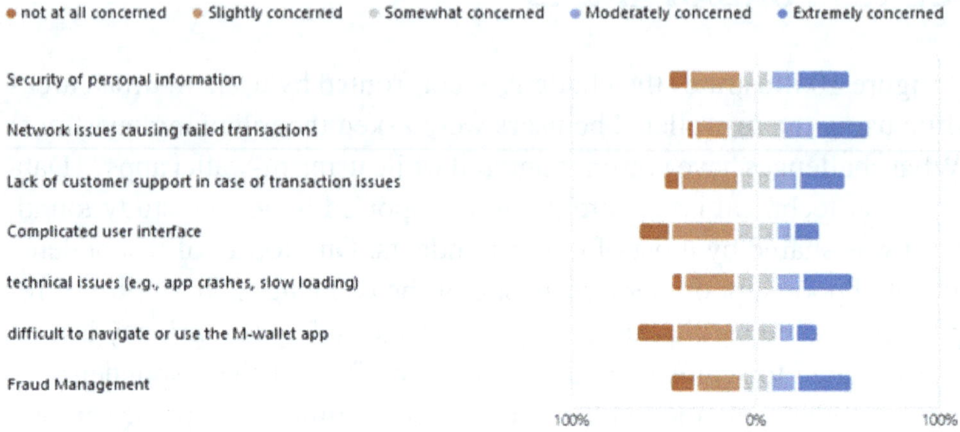

Source: Survey data

Figure 12. Level of confidence

Source: Survey data

Figure 12 presents users' confidence levels about the security of their M-wallet accounts against fraud and unauthorized access. One-fourth of the users felt confident that their accounts were secure against scams. A few users were not confident about the security. One-third of the users were uncertain about the situation. Concerning this, questions were asked to find out the factors that may deter them from using the m-wallet in the future, and the result is depicted in Figure 13. Data show that 47% of the users identified security concerns as an obstacle, labeling it as the most significant factor for consideration. One-third of the users noted connectivity problems as the second most common challenge to be aware of. Thirty-three percent of the users had serious concerns over fraud or scam issues, preventing them from using the system. Twenty-nine percent of the users were discouraged by fees and additional charges related to transactions. Technical issues with app performance were marked by 23% of the users. Lack of sufficient information to feel comfortable using m-wallets and limited acceptance of m-wallets among the retailers were also on the list shared by 15% and 10% of the respondents, respectively.

Figure 13. Factors may prevent users from using the system

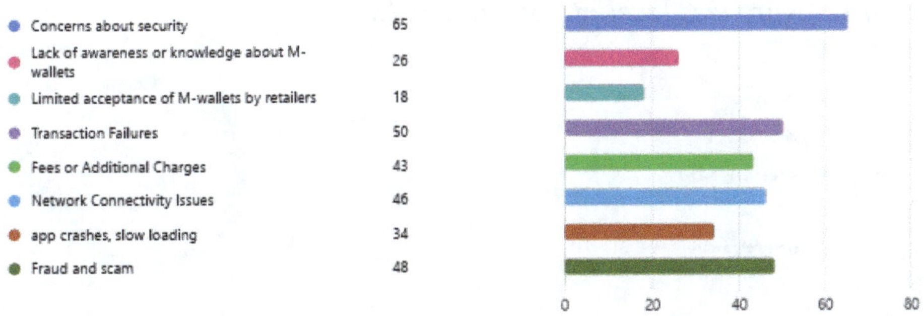

Source: Survey data

In summary, the main challenges with M-wallet apps are technical issues, lack of customer support, and privacy/security concerns. Users are most concerned about security, network issues, lack of customer support, and fraud management. The main factors discouraging more frequent M-wallet usage are security concerns, transaction failures, fraud risks, and network connectivity issues. This is true for many users, that security and reliability to be the critical factors influencing their willingness to use m-wallets in urban areas.

FACTORS THAT MAY PREVENT USERS FROM USING THE SYSTEM

Before we talk about the roles that need to be played by the service providers, we wanted to know how aware the users are of potential risks and scams in m-wallets. As shown in Figure 14, most of the users (87%) were aware of the risks at various levels because they (87%) were informed about attempts at phishing and fraud attempts, e.g., Figure 15. Conversely, a small proportion of users (13%) were not aware of the risks associated.

Figure 14. Awareness level of potential risks

Source: Survey data

Figure 15. Knowledge about scams

Source: Survey data

Figure 15 shows that most respondents have been educated or informed about phishing or scam attempts related to M-Wallet usage.

Figure 16. Frequency of receiving updates and notifications about safe use practice

Source: Survey data

Figure 17. Factors that may prevent users from using the system

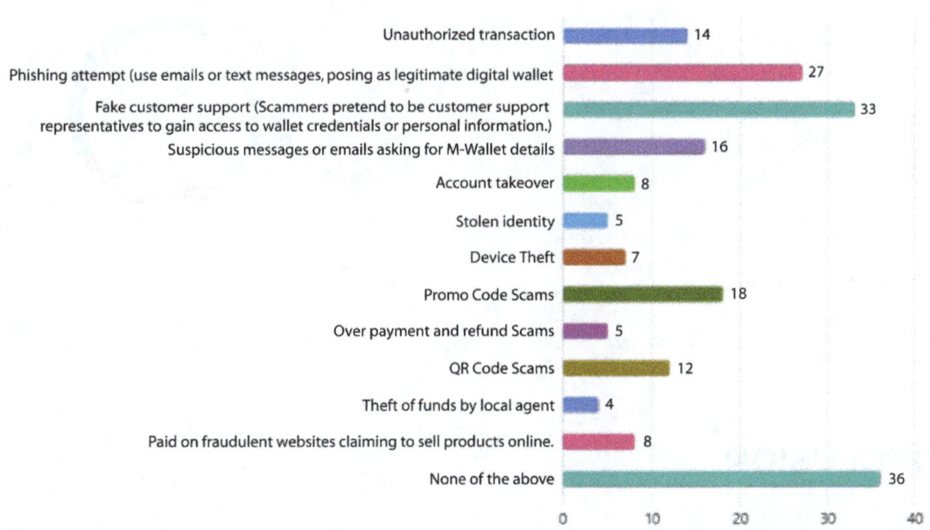

Source: Survey data

Users were asked to name the types of scams they encountered lately. Figure 17 highlights various scams that the users have faced so far. Out of the scams listed above, 'Fake customer service' is the most common type of scam, with 30% of the users experiencing it, followed by 'Phishing attempts' with 24.5%, and 16.4% of respondents noted them respectively. Phishing attempts are a type of scam where fraudsters approach through text messages or emails, persuading victims to click on malicious links or download fake applications. Another type of scam, which has been highlighted, is 'Fake customer support' in which scammers pretend to be official customer support representatives to gain access to wallet credentials or personal information, such as passwords or PINs. On the other hand, a substantial number of users have experienced any of the scams listed above. We also wanted to know how likely respondents are to report a suspicious transaction in their m-wallet apps. As shown in Figure 18, most respondents 88% are likely to report a suspicious transaction, with a few users (12%) being unlikely to report them.

Figure 18. Likelihood of reporting a suspicious transaction

Source: Survey data

CONCLUSION

The community of Bangladesh has been truly fortunate to reap the benefits of Mobile Financial Services (MFS), which brought blessings to the people in dealing with small transactions. This notion has transformed the transaction process online and in-store, mitigating the hassle and offering convenience and accessibility. However, the shift exposed users to significant scams, such as phishing, SIM swapping, QR code scams, etc., due to inadequate security measures, and the level of awareness to deal with the vulnerabilities, which made the users prone to various forms of digital fraud. From the experience of a developed country, service providers mitigate these challenges by prioritizing robust authentication systems, advanced encryption, and comprehensive user education. By improving these areas, we can boost user trust, safeguard transactions, and propel the sustained growth of M-wallet adoption in Bangladesh. However, the study also put forward some policies to foster adoption and mitigate fraud.

1. Users need to be educated about common scam techniques, such as phishing and QR code manipulation, to better protect themselves. Interactive content highlighting various scams can be posted on various social media platforms to raise awareness.
2. Regulatory bodies are encouraged to establish concrete guidelines for M-wallet providers to advance security measures and conduct regular audits of their systems.
3. Incorporating AI-driven fraud detection systems that monitor transaction patterns, flag suspicious activities, and block accounts in real time can help prevent scams.
4. Setting default daily or transaction limits on m-wallets for suspicious accounts, especially for new or unverified accounts, can safeguard against large-scale fraud.
5. Government bodies can partner with educational institutions, such as schools, universities, and community centers, to work jointly to offer digital literacy programs to the community that make people aware of cybersecurity.
6. Large-scale campaigns through television and other broadcast media outlets can educate the public on safe practices and contemporary scams, helping users stay informed.
7. Setting up an online dispute resolution mechanism for fraud cases, allowing victims to report cases easily and recover losses more efficiently.
8. A dedicated helpline can be offered to the users for scam-related queries and collaboration with authorities for faster resolution.
9. Setting up a scam alert system on m-wallet, eliminating fraudster agents, and enhancing the experience of using m-wallet.
10. Enhancing user support and offering more rewards or incentives would induce the users to increase their continuity.

11. Expanding partnerships with more retailers and providing access to Wi-Fi free of cost within the retail outlet may enhance the continuity of use.
12. One-stop and dedicated customer support would improve the overall experience.
13. Cash-out and other transaction fees should be reduced.
14. A mechanism to enable NID information for both the vendors and users is necessary.

REFERENCES

Agrawal, R., & Yadav, M. (2024). Enablers for Usage of the Mobile Wallet by Msmes in Rural India: Using the Interpretive Structural Modelling Approach. *Financial Internet Quarterly*, *20*(2), 26–40. DOI: 10.2478/fiqf-2024-0010

Bagla, R. K., & Sancheti, V.BAGLA. (2018). Gaps in customer satisfaction with digital wallets: Challenge for sustainability. *Journal of Management Development*, *37*(6), 442–451. DOI: 10.1108/JMD-04-2017-0144

Chawla, D., & Joshi, H. (2017). Consumer perspectives about mobile banking adoption in India–a cluster analysis. *International Journal of Bank Marketing*, *35*(4), 616–636. DOI: 10.1108/IJBM-03-2016-0037

Chawla, D., & Joshi, H. (2020). The moderating role of gender and age in the adoption of mobile wallet. *Foresight*, *22*(4), 483–504. DOI: 10.1108/FS-11-2019-0094

Dahlberg, T., Guo, J., & Ondrus, J. (2015). A critical review of mobile payment research. *Electronic Commerce Research and Applications*, *14*(5), 265–284. DOI: 10.1016/j.elerap.2015.07.006

Dass, R., & Pal, S. (2011). A meta analysis on adoption of mobile financial services. *Indian Institute of Management Ahmedabad*, *2*(1), 1–26.

Donner, J., & Tellez, C. A. (2008). Mobile banking and economic development: Linking adoption, impact, and use. *Asian Journal of Communication*, *18*(4), 318–332. DOI: 10.1080/01292980802344190

Donovan, K. (2012). Mobile money for financial inclusion. *Information and Communications for Development*, *61*(1), 61–73.

Hasan, M. (2024, January 28). Changing landscape of mobile money in Bangladesh. Retrieved November 6, 2024, from The Daily Star website: https://www.thedailystar.net/supplements/mfs-and-financial-inclusion-bangladesh/news/changing-landscape-mobile-money-bangladesh-3530006

Hussain, S., Gupta, S., & Bhardwaj, S. (2024). Determinants inhibiting digital payment system adoption: An Indian perspective. *Qualitative Research in Financial Markets*. Retrieved from https://www.emerald.com/insight/content/doi/10.1108/QRFM-09-2023-0223/full/html

Iyer, P., Davari, A., & Mukherjee, A.IYER. (2018). Investigating the effectiveness of retailers' mobile applications in determining customer satisfaction and repatronage intentions? A congruency perspective. *Journal of Retailing and Consumer Services*, *44*, 235–243. DOI: 10.1016/j.jretconser.2018.07.017

Jack, W., & Suri, T. (2011). *Mobile money: The economics of M-PESA*. National Bureau of Economic Research. Retrieved from National Bureau of Economic Research website: https://www.nber.org/papers/w16721

Kapoor, A., Sindwani, R., & Goel, M. (2024). Assessing inhibitors to adoption of m-wallet: A BWM approach. *International Journal of Business Excellence*, *32*(4), 433–455. DOI: 10.1504/IJBEX.2024.137567

Kshetri, N. (2013). *Cybercrime and cybersecurity in the global south*. Springer. Retrieved from https://books.google.com/books?hl=en&lr=&id=SepWfACNTgQC&oi=fnd&pg=PP1&dq=Kshetri,+N.+(2016).+Cybercrime+and+cybersecurity+in+the+global+South.+Palgrave+Macmillan.&ots=BFIGqbCHZW&sig=vssMzKotSTeNFvnwJPssIoTUFW0

Liu, Y., Wang, M., Huang, D., Huang, Q., Yang, H., & Li, Z. (2019). The impact of mobility, risk, and cost on the users' intention to adopt mobile payments. *Information Systems and e-Business Management*, *17*(2-4), 319–342. DOI: 10.1007/s10257-019-00449-0

Newman, C. L., Wachter, K., & White, A.NEWMAN. (2018). Bricks or clicks? Understanding consumer usage of retail mobile apps. *Journal of Services Marketing*, *32*(2), 211–222. DOI: 10.1108/JSM-08-2016-0289

Oliveira, T., Thomas, M., Baptista, G., & Campos, F. (2016). Mobile payment: Understanding the determinants of customer adoption and intention to recommend the technology. *Computers in Human Behavior*, *61*, 404–414. DOI: 10.1016/j.chb.2016.03.030

RAKESTRAW, T. L., EUNNI, R. V. & KASUGANTI, R. R. (2013). The mobile apps industry: A case study. *Journal of Business Cases and Applications*, *9*, 1.

Rana, N. P., Dwivedi, Y. K., Lal, B., Williams, M. D., & Clement, M. (2017). Citizens' adoption of an electronic government system: Towards a unified view. *Information Systems Frontiers*, *19*(3), 549–568. DOI: 10.1007/s10796-015-9613-y

Robertson, N., McDonald, H., Leckie, C., & McQuilken, L.ROBERTSON. (2016). Examining customer evaluations across different self-service technologies. *Journal of Services Marketing*, *30*(1), 88–102. DOI: 10.1108/JSM-07-2014-0263

SHAHID IQBAL, M., UL HASSAN, M. & HABIBAH, U. (2018). Impact of self-service technology (SST) service quality on customer loyalty and behavioral intention: The mediating role of customer satisfaction. *Cogent Business & Management*, *5*, 1.

Shaikh, A. A., & Karjaluoto, H. (2015). Mobile banking adoption: A literature review. *Telematics and Informatics*, *32*(1), 129–142. DOI: 10.1016/j.tele.2014.05.003

Shankar, A., & Kumari, P. (2019). A study of factors affecting mobile governance (mGov) adoption intention in India using an extension of the technology acceptance model (TAM). *South Asian Journal of Management*, *26*(4), 71–94.

Slade, E., Williams, M., Dwivedi, Y., & Piercy, N. (2015). Exploring consumer adoption of proximity mobile payments. *Journal of Strategic Marketing*, *23*(3), 209–223. DOI: 10.1080/0965254X.2014.914075

Slade, E. L., Dwivedi, Y. K., Piercy, N. C., & Williams, M. D.SLADE. (2015). Modeling consumers' adoption intentions of remote mobile payments in the United Kingdom: Extending UTAUT with innovativeness, risk, and trust. *Psychology and Marketing*, *32*(8), 860–873. DOI: 10.1002/mar.20823

Thakur, R. (2013). Customer Adoption of Mobile Payment Services by Professionals across two Cities in India: An Empirical Study Using Modified Technology Acceptance Model. *Business Perspectives and Research, 1*(2), 17–30. DOI: 10.1177/2278533720130203

Upadhyay, N., Upadhyay, S., Abed, S. S., & Dwivedi, Y. K. (2022). Consumer adoption of mobile payment services during COVID-19: Extending meta-UTAUT with perceived severity and self-efficacy. *International Journal of Bank Marketing, 40*(5), 960–991. DOI: 10.1108/IJBM-06-2021-0262

Zhou, T. (2012). Understanding users' initial trust in mobile banking: An elaboration likelihood perspective. *Computers in Human Behavior, 28*(4), 1518–1525. DOI: 10.1016/j.chb.2012.03.021

KEY TERMS AND DEFINITIONS

Cashless Transactions: Financial transactions are conducted without the use of physical money, often involving digital wallets, mobile banking apps, or contactless payments.

Digital Literacy: The ability to use information and communication technologies in a full range to find, evaluate, create, and communicate on digital platforms.

Financial literacy: An understanding of financial components, such as investing, financing, taxation, or skills that allow an individual to make smart financial decisions in managing money.

Mobile Financial Services (MFS): A broad category of financial services accessible through mobile devices, including mobile banking, mobile payments, and mobile wallets.

Mobile Wallet (M-Wallet): A type of mobile financial service that allows users to store payment information and conduct digital transactions via a mobile device.

Scam Vulnerability: An unauthorized and unethical attempt to trick or manipulate people with fraudulent activities.

Self-Service Technologies (SSTs): Technological interfaces, such as ATMs, online banking, and mobile devices, which enable customers to produce services independent of direct service employee involvement.

Chapter 2
The Emergence of Green Venture Capital and Its Role in Financing Early-Stage Green Technology Companies

Manjit Kour
http://orcid.org/0000-0003-1043-3187
Chandigarh University, Mohali, India

Harman Kaur
MCM DAV College, Chandigarh, India

ABSTRACT

Green venture capital is one of the emerging funding options for early-stage green technology companies. GVC is one of the venture capitals, majorly invested in companies that are developing innovative technologies aimed at reducing environmental impacts and promoting sustainable development. In doing this, this chapter provides an overview of GVC, its uniqueness, and how it differs from other conventional venture capital. The chapter deals with GVC involvement in financing early-stage green

DOI: 10.4018/979-8-3693-8247-9.ch002

technology companies. It talks about GVC investments, including the kind of source of capital, mentorship, and expertise the early-stage companies need to progress and grow their business. Implications and risks of GVC investments are also analyzed. High returns among other benefits and having an extensive network of resources, making GVC investments worthwhile. Besides, the chances to make a difference in the environment are excellent. The risks involved relate to uncertainties from the commercialization of green technologies and effects of any regulatory change for the industrial sector.

INTRODUCTION

There is more awareness on the crucial role that green technology is going to play in finding solutions to the many acute environmental problems facing humanity and creating a sustainable future. The urgency to transition into a low-carbon economy and to undo the adverse effects of human activities on the environment accelerates with time because issues such as climate change, depletion of resources, and pollution keep piling up. Therefore, it is at this juncture that this breakthrough green technology developed by early-stage businesses will prove instrumental in it.

One of the investments targeted towards start-up businesses in the research, development, and commercialization of advanced green technologies is green venture capital. It is targeted towards start-ups that undertake activities including research, development, and the commercialization of advanced green technologies to better serve new environmental challenges, promote sustainability, and reduce negative impacts of human activity on the environment (Marra et al., 2017). Green venture capital, in most instances, has been beneficial to the companies that are involved in various operations, such as clean transportation, waste management, sustainable agriculture, and renewable energy. The emergence of green venture capital may be pegged from the fact that there was an enhanced awareness concerning the immediate need for sustainable solutions to environmental problems (Demirel et al., 2019). Governments, organizations, and citizens have been actively seeking ways to facilitate the development and utilization of clean technologies, with such concerns over climate change, resource depletion, and pollution. Companies involved in early-stage green technologies received specific challenges since these technologies had protracted lead times to develop, were very expensive upfront, and market environments surrounding their products were uncertain. Traditionally, financing strategies had not worked well for companies like these. Green venture capital has recently emerged as a niche investment strategy that responds to early-stage green technology startups in need of financing.

This fund source will not only avail cash support to small businesses but also networks, mentorship, and strategic advice critical for the survival of small businesses, a view attributed to Beck et al. in 2008. Green venture capitalists have now realized that these new technologies hold much promise and could solve sustainability problems at the same time as building profits. This is the chapter where the discussion of green venture capital will consider the definition of green venture capital and standard investment and value proposition to be discussed. As such, this chapter shall discuss what factors made this form of investment recognized, including shifting market dynamics in increasing environmental awareness and favorable statutory frameworks. In this chapter, discussions of the challenges and opportunities that face the green venture capitalists as well as the ventures themselves shall be provided.

Figure 1. Venture capital process

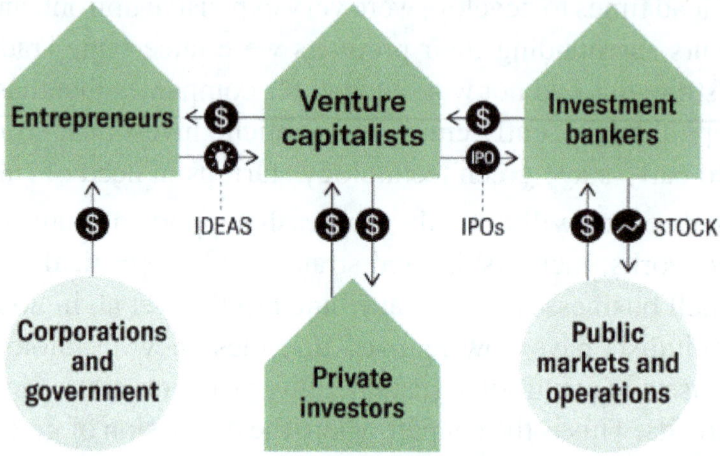

Source: Harvard Business Review (https://hbr.org/1998/11/how-venture-capital-works)

GREEN TECHNOLOGY AND THE NEED FOR FINANCING

Definition of Green Venture Capital

Green venture capital is a type of venture capital used to fund start-up companies that produce environmentally friendly products and services. It is a subset of venture capital focused on companies in clean tech, sustainable agriculture, waste, renewable energy, and energy efficiency (Croce & Bianchini, 2022). Green venture capital differs from mainstream venture capital in emphasizing both financial returns and environmental impact. Green venture capital firms invest in companies that proffer advanced solutions to pressing environmental issues in order to accelerate transition to a low-carbon sustainable economy.

Characteristics of Green Venture Capital Organizations and Investors

Many unique features distinguish green venture capital companies and investors from other venture capital participants. Some of these features include:

Impact on environment: Green venture capital companies lean much on environmental matters. They opt for more investments on businesses that solve the environmental problems and boost sustainable growth (Tran et al., 2020). Sometimes these firms are mission-oriented and manage to reap profit while at the same time have positive impacts on the environment.

Sector skills: There are companies that have invested in green technology and industry, bringing with them a special kind of knowledge and expertise. They can offer strategic guidance and assistance to portfolio firms because they know the exact challenges and opportunities which exist in a certain industry such as renewable energy, energy efficiency, and sustainable transportation.

Value-added services: Besides finance provision, green venture capitalists offer other value-added services. They offer mentorship, strategic counseling, and access to networking by offering their portfolio firms knowledge and experience in the understanding and operation of the uncertainty of the green technology sector (Holtslag et al., 2021). The purpose is that this should catalyze the growth and prosperity of green technology new ventures.

Long term: Investors in green venture capital mainly think long-term. They become aware of the fact that the development, research, and process for adapting such green technology in mass happens after a rather long time. In this respect, they are ready to invest slowly and help businesses through several rounds of investments so as to make them successful in the long run.

Environmental impact: An important emphasis by green venture capital firms is measuring environmental impact alongside financial performance. They measure and report the environmentally positive impacts created by their portfolio companies through measurements and frameworks (Croce & Bianchini, 2022). A type of impact measurement helps investors monitor the performance and effectiveness of their investments toward sustainable change.

Types of Green Venture Capital Investments

Depending on the stage of the firm as well as the type of technology being used, green venture capital investments may vary in their forms. Generally, green venture capital investments are conducted in these forms:

Seed financing: Seed funding refers to financing offered to startup ventures during the concept or proof-of-concept stage. Green venture capitalists specializing in such type of venture capital investment may invest in start-ups having concepts of novel green technologies and aid them in developing prototypes, conducting research, and refining their business plans (Alunni, 2019).

Early-Stage Funding: It is funding for businesses that have moved past the start-up phase but still need financing to develop innovation and market products. Green venture capital firms offer this type of funding as they support product development, validate a product in a market, and make an initial entry into a market (Debrah et al., 2022).

Figure 2. Types of Green venture capital investments

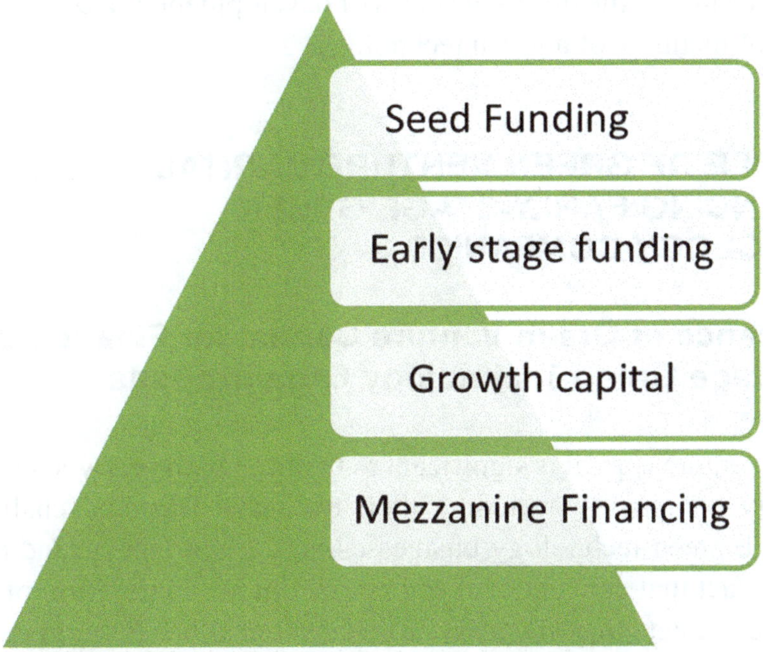

Growth Capital: Growth capital is invested in firms that have already provided evidence of market traction and revenue growth. Such an amount that a business requires to scale up to new markets, to product/service development, to the operation scaling is offered by green venture capital firms.

Mezzanine Financing: In mezzanine financing, funds are advanced to the companies with the intention of offering an IPO or M&A (Taşkın, 2021). Mezzanine finance can further assist companies in the final phase of growth while avoiding further loads when transitioning to public markets. Such companies may include green venture capital firms.

Green venture capital is one of the kinds of venture capital firms and investors who invest in the newly established companies, which design green products and technology. Some features of green venture capitalists involve environmental care and know-how concerning industries, and such investment holds a long-term view. In addition to financial investments, ventures provide value-added services and supports to their portfolio companies. It may assume a wide range-from seed finance to mezzanine financing and many forms in between-from green venture capital investments according to the different stages of development of a company and the level of maturity of a given technology.

THE ROLE OF GREEN VENTURE CAPITAL IN FINANCING EARLY-STAGE GREEN TECHNOLOGY COMPANIES

Significance of Green Venture Capital for Financing Early-Stage Green Technology Organizations

Green venture capital is significant to facilitating the early-stage green technology companies overcome their exclusive financial challenges. Early-stage green technology businesses very often face a funding gap due to the fact that conventional sources of finance in the form of banks and public markets may shy away from investment because of perceived risks and uncertainties associated with the development of green technologies (Cowling & Liu, 2021). Green venture capital addresses the gap through the provision of funding required for undertaking research, development, and subsequent commercialization efforts. Green venture capital companies are specialists who comprehend the very specific risks and dynamics of a green innovation market. They invest in detailed due diligence and risk analysis, thereby reducing the unknowns surrounding start-up businesses in green technology (Sanz-Prieto at al, 2021). Green venture capital firms can help such companies reduce their risk profile and make them much more attractive to follow-on investors through infusing cash as well as expertise.

Green venture capitalists have a deep industry knowledge and capabilities in green technologies and areas. Since they are well-versed with the industry, they can identify new technology, assess market opportunity, and can offer portfolio firms strategic direction (Cowling & Liu, 2021). The connections and industry-specific knowledge that early-stage green technology businesses have become an overcome tool for many of them and enhance the possibility of achieving success. In addition to providing finance, green venture capital firms also provide value-added services to portfolio companies. Value-added services from these firms may encompass company development support, networking, or even introduction to clients or business associates. Green venture capitalists use their contacts and business savvy to help early-stage green technology ventures grow and succeed.

Successful Case Studies of Green Venture Capital Investments

A large number of case studies suggests that, as a whole, green venture capital has played a strong role in the success of early-stage ventures in this space. For example, the following are just two examples:

Tesla: Tesla, the world's finest electric car producer raises seed capital investments from VC firms such as Draper Fisher Jurvetson and Valour Equity Partners (Andersson, 2020). Such funds provide Tesla with enough capital to construct its electric vehicle technology and brand using the latest technology. Green venture capital funding transformed Tesla into a great company to become an industry leader in electric cars.

SunCity: VC firms such as DBL Partners and Mayfield Fund have invested highly with SunCity, in the sales of solar power systems, and services. Green venture finance was central to the cause of the company to ensure it goes prominent in the market. The deployment of Solar energy also paced heavily.

Bloom Energy: Early funding for Bloom Energy-which ranks among the developers of the solid oxide fuel cell technology in an efficient yet clean power-generation process-was guaranteed by the company of Kleiner Perkins and New Enterprise Associates (Lerner & Nanda, 2020). These funds were successfully developed and matured the 'fuel cell' technology to be commercially viable so it can be utilized for reliable sources of clean energy. Green venture finance had quite greatly assisted in the uptake of fuel cell technology and the decarbonization of the electricity sector.

Green Venture Capital Faced Challenges in Financing Early-Stage Green Technology Companies

Although green venture capital is the main component in the provision of finance for early-stage companies developing green technology, there is also some challenge facing green venture capital. Some of them include:

- *High Risk:* Technological as well as super market risks get involved while involving early-stage green technology startups. Their risk profile becomes magnified due to long cycles involved in development, uncertainties from regulations as well as existing market restrictions associated with green technologies (Cowling & Liu, 2021). Such risks, pertinent to the availability of funds, must be adequately judged and controlled by green venture capital companies.
- *Scarse Exit Opportunities*: the commercialization and market uptake of green technology investment is relatively longer than those that come with traditional sectors investment. Due to this characteristic, firms that invest in green ventures may have limited options as far exit events are concerned. This characteristic could limit their capacity to produce returns on investment at the expected time. Consequently, to successfully cut through the unique dynamics of the industry from the green technology side, for investors in green ventures, they need to be candid, patients and have long-run orientations.
- *Political scenario*: Politics may play an important role in shaping the business climates for firms developing green technologies. Changes in incentives, subsidies, and other changes in market rules may change the financial viability of green initiatives and their market potential. Investment choices may become complex because the green venture capital firms need to monitor and respond to policy environments in flux (Polzin et al., 2017).
- *Scarce Availability of Capital*: Green venture capital is scarcer than traditional venture capital, in general. To the extent that more funding is being demanded by early-stage green technology start-ups, so much is still not yet available for use in this industry. The availability of limited capital may make the search for finance challenging in terms of discovering funders for early-stage green technology start-ups.

Green venture capital is crucial in funding the start-up green technology business venture. It fills the funding gap that enables small businesses to expand and succeed by overcoming risks and offering value-added services and industry experience. Case studies can clearly view how green venture capital will foster innovation and market uptake of sustainable solutions. The high-risk nature of green technology, restricted availability of finance, legislative and regulatory issues, and the very limited exit opportunities pose a difficult hurdle to green venture capital. Full exploitation of the potential of green venture capital for financing early-stage green technology startups will occur subsequent to surmounting these barriers.

BENEFITS AND RISKS OF GREEN VENTURE CAPITAL INVESTMENTS

Benefits of Green Venture Capital Investment

Green venture capital investment enjoys numerous economic and environmental advantages. While green venture capital investments emphasize environmental impact over anything, such investments could also yield high financial returns (Bocken, 2015). Green technology companies can be scaled rapidly and achieve profitability, which means giving massive returns on investment to venture capitalists. Venture capitalists can also enter new markets and industries that have high growth potential by investing in highly promising green technologies.

Figure 3. Benefits of green venture capital investments

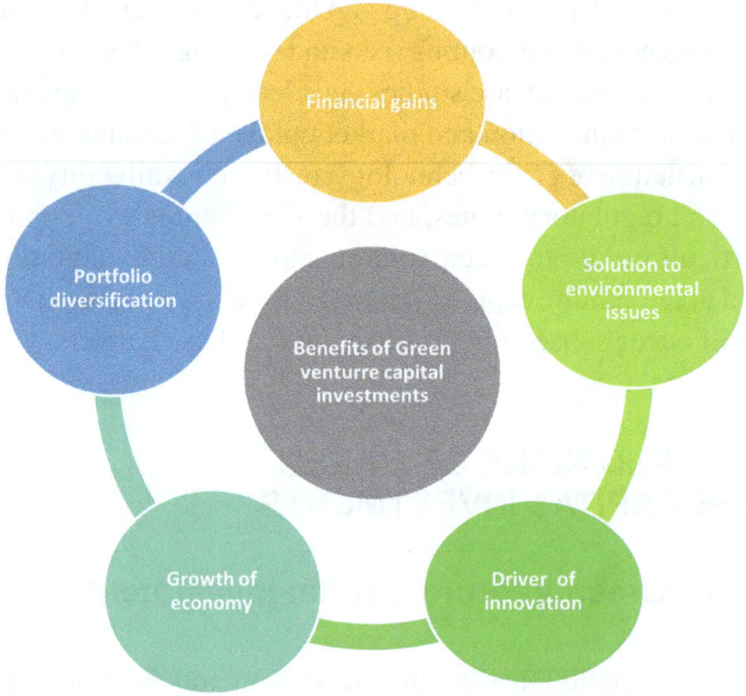

Green venture capital investments address urgent environmental issues. Venture capitalists play a crucial role in hastening the development and utilization of sustainable solutions because they provide early-stage finance to green technology start-ups (Lin, 2022). Transition to a low-carbon economy, reduction of greenhouse gas emissions, the conservation of resources, and damage caused to the environment is minimized due to these investment activities. In reality, successful green enterprises make an enormous difference long into the future by contributing significantly to the environment. Innovation and technological growth are triggered by the investments put forward in the green technology sector by venture capital (Croce & Bianchini, 2022). Venture capitalists assist these small developing companies by providing access to finance as well as support. Finance and support lay down the foundation upon which innovations emerge that alter the game and new solutions to problems of the environment are developed. These investments make possible the creation of new, sustainable goods and services and business models.

Green venture capital investments contribute to economic development and employment opportunities. Employment is generated in areas such as renewable energy, building efficiency, waste reduction, and environmentally friendly transportation due to job scaling and expansion of nascent green technology companies. These investments increase the economic competitiveness in the field of green technology and encourage more investment. Further growth of new industries is further encouraged. Investments in green venture capital offer a chance for diversification of portfolios for venture capitalists. Venture capitalists may easily distribute their resources in various firms in different industries thus reducing the risk and increasing the balance of their portfolios upon making investment in green technologies. Investments in green technology expose investors to developing markets and industry trends while reducing total investment risk.

Risks and Challenges of Green Venture Capital Investments

While there are several benefits associated with the green venture capital investment, there are also specific dangers and difficulties. Such include;

The green technologies are often in the early stages of development, which poses both technological as well as market concerns. These technologies must be effectively commercialized and taken up in the market so that green venture capital investments pay off. Many uncertainties exist, for example, concerning technology feasibility, market acceptance, and even those concerning competition, which in themselves could pose problematic problems concerning an investment's ability to generate profitability. Yet another concern would be governmental laws and regulations regarding change, affecting success in green venture capital investments. Changes in the incentives, subsidies, and market restrictions can affect the potential for financial viability and competitiveness of businesses dealing in green technologies. Developing and investment targets in making market forecasts can be highly challenging when dealing with policy uncertainties and changes.

Green technology development and market penetration can sometimes be long and capital intensive (Malek et al., 2014). Green initiatives can create capital intensity, which may become expensive for financial resources of the companies and venture funders. The longer periods needed for returns may also impact liquidity and the exit strategies for investors. Developments in their business may not come easy for early-stage green technology firms because of the barriers existing in the market. Such businesses will face limited growth prospects and poor financial performance due to small market, extreme competition in the industry, and an expensive cost of acquiring customers. Commercialization of green technology is rather complex and time-consuming and depends on the combination of expertise and effective teamwork.

The options in exit for green venture capital investment are not as vast as in the traditional venture capital. The IPO and acquisitions maybe less probable to occur within the industry and hence cannot be obtained through venture capital investments also. Besides, limited alternative options in exit can prolong the duration in holding of an investment and result in lack of liquidity in the portfolios on aggregate.

Some key benefits to this type of investment are the financial returns, environmental impact positives, innovations, new employment opportunities, and diversification of one's portfolio. However, it is equally important to weigh in on a few risks related to it: technological and market risks, regulatory uncertainty, capital intensity, market and commercialization risks, and the lack of quick access to an exit route. Venture capitalists invest in green technology with thorough risk assessment and management, backed by that industry's know-how to the investor and strategic support to maximize potential rewards while reducing obstacles associated.

FUTURE OUTLOOK FOR GREEN VENTURE CAPITAL

There is a bright future for the greening of capital venture. This is because the imperative to care for the environment and support initiatives for sustainability grows every passing day. The next section discusses potential future trends, opportunities, and issues that could restrict the growth of green venture capital.

Further Prospects and Developments for Green Venture Capital

Sustainable Solutions: This will give the market ample attention in this world, catapulting it to new heights for cutting-edge green technologies; growing demand for these sustainable solutions is of paramount importance to investors in early-stage business solutions for renewable energy, clean transportation, circular economy, and other areas that fall under environmentally sustainable sectors.

Technology Development: Green venture capital investment opportunities would mushroom with rapid developments in technology, which would shape energy storage and smart grids applications, water purification technologies, and other sustainable material options. Hence, there would be big investments in novel solutions that boost productivity and gains in productivity, cut down on emissions, and improve resource management.

Convergence of Technologies: The very best green technology disruption opportunities would arise through the convergence of green technology with some of the emerging areas, such as artificial intelligence, the internet of things, and blockchain. Such synergies could result in really creative and scalable solutions, giving rise to even more green venture capital investments in the area.

Figure 4. Future Developments and Prospects for Green Venture Capital

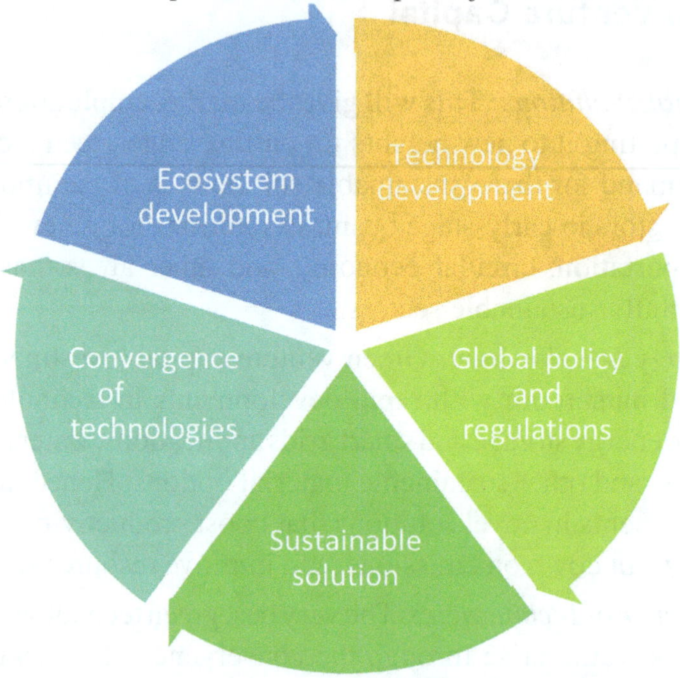

Ecosystem Development: The above will result in the green venture capital growth significantly due to the building of a complete ecosystem that will also aid in creating, communicating, and developing green technology startups. Such ecosystems will act as a means of communication regarding business owners with investors, the academic institution, and policymakers. Supportive ecosystems would push early-stage businesses to scale up faster and can even spur innovation in the green technology area.

Global Policy and Regulation: Going to be an excellent environment for green venture capitals with the establishment of good frameworks and regulation by global policies to reduce and combat climate change and support sustainable development. Various countries have formulated targets, incentives, and subsidiaries to invest in green technologies and can be a good opportunity for venture capitalists to fund businesses driving such policies.

Challenges and Challenges Facing Future Growth of Green Venture Capital

Access to Funds: Even though the demand for green venture capital increases, the funding for green ventures will remain at levels below it ought to be. Because the financing needed for early-stage green technology companies increases, the money that is set aside specifically for green venture capital shall have to be increased too.

Risk Perception and Mitigation: Green technologies are perceived to be riskier than conventional investment risks since they are triggered mainly by such uncertainties concerning the technology itself and regulatory difficulties. For green venture capital initiatives to expand into the future, a sense of greater risk needs to be removed along with effective measures for mitigating risks.

Exit opportunities: Exit opportunities from the green venture capital investments are poor and not workable. Poor IPOs and acquisitions in the green technology sector likely undermine the investors' prospects of an exit whereby they will be able to obtain a positive return and extract their returns from the investment. It can be solved by building new routes to exit, including secondary markets or specifically dedicated platforms for buying green technology.

Scaling Up and Market Adoption: Early-stage green technology companies often face challenges while seeking scaling up their businesses and mass consumer acceptance. To bridge the gap between the development/pilot phase and commercial-scale deployment, access to additional finance, strategic partnerships, and favorable market dynamics are necessary. This is how green venture capital firms can be very important providers of the needed support and guidance.

Policies: Rampant policy and regulatory changes might fuel uncertainty in the future prospects of green technology enterprises. Further, the development of policies regarding subsidies, incentives, and carbon pricing mechanisms might also create additional complexity and risks to be managed over green venture capital. This would involve constant updates regarding policies and adjustments in the strategy for investment accordingly.

Besides, growing global demand for sustainable solutions, technological growth, technological convergence, development of an ecosystem, and supportive global regulations will pave the way forward for green venture capital in the future. However, for further expansion of green venture capital, restricted availability of capital, perception of risk, formulation of an exit plan, scaling up, and uncertainty about legislation, among other things, are to be addressed. Green venture capital can thus play the central role of funding and accelerating the development of leading-edge green technology, which in turn can lead to a more sustainable future when these obstacles are overcome and the resulting opportunities exploited.

CONCLUSION

In this chapter, we discuss an in-depth case of green venture capital and its developments as related to the performance of funding support for green technology startups. What is it? What is so different? What type of investments do these companies carry out and much more. The case studies were framed around the significance of green venture capital at the very early stages of green technology start-ups and portrayed how this could be a positive aspect.

Green venture capital brings wide benefits consisting of potential returns, environmental impacts, innovation, new employment sources, and portfolio diversification. Investments in early-stage green technology companies will reciprocate with accelerating the solution to pressing environmental problems and igniting new technologies for the transformation into a low-carbon economy. There is tremendous scope for spins that would narrate success stories based on green venture capital investments, which will both create environmental benefits and yield economic benefits. Still, there are dangers and difficulties concerning the investment of green venture capital. Challenges to venture capitalists range from market and commercialization to legislative uncertainties, capital intensity, and restricted exit choices. Tremendous risk management, specific knowledge, and flexibility to change with the dynamics of the market will help overcome these issues.

With more and more emphasis on sustainable solutions, technological advancement, convergence of technologies, development of ecosystems, and benevolent global laws, the green venture capital is likely to grow and mushroom even more in the near future. The immediate challenges looming that these firms have to surmount include relatively less money available for investment, perceived risk, lack of exit options, scaling up, and policy uncertainty; these must be overcome before green venture capital can continue on a path of growth and prosperity.

Therefore, green venture capital is at the heart of support for innovation, accelerated transition to a sustainable future, and early-stage financing of green technology companies. Green venture capitalists facilitate the building and diffusion of clean technologies through funding, knowledge, and other assets. A seemingly promising green venture capital market; however, to achieve its fullest potential in molding a society sustainable it will require joint efforts from investors, politicians, and entrepreneurs in overcoming existing barriers.

REFERENCES

Alunni, A. (2019). *Innovation finance and technology transfer: Funding proof-of-concept*. Routledge. DOI: 10.4324/9780429278778

Beck, T., Demirgüç-Kunt, A., & Maksimovic, V. (2008). Financing patterns around the world: Are small firms different? *Journal of Financial Economics, 89*(3), 467–487. DOI: 10.1016/j.jfineco.2007.10.005

Bocken, N. M. (2015). Sustainable venture capital–catalyst for sustainable start-up success? *Journal of Cleaner Production, 108*, 647–658. DOI: 10.1016/j.jclepro.2015.05.079

Cowling, M., & Liu, W. (2021). Access to Finance for Cleantech Innovation and Investment: Evidence from UK Small-and Medium-Sized Enterprises. *IEEE Transactions on Engineering Management.*

Croce, A., & Bianchini, R. (2022). The role of environmental policies in promoting venture capital investments in cleantech companies. *Review of Corporate Finance, 2*(3), 587–616. DOI: 10.1561/114.00000024

Debrah, C., Chan, A. P. C., & Darko, A. (2022). Green finance gap in green buildings: A scoping review and future research needs. *Building and Environment, 207*, 108443. DOI: 10.1016/j.buildenv.2021.108443

Demirel, P., Li, Q. C., Rentocchini, F., & Tamvada, J. P. (2019). Born to be green: New insights into the economics and management of green entrepreneurship. *Small Business Economics, 52*(4), 759–771. DOI: 10.1007/s11187-017-9933-z

Holtslag, M., Chevrollier, N., & Nijhof, A. (2021). Impact investing and sustainable market transformations: The role of venture capital funds. *Business Ethics, the Environment & Responsibility, 30*(4), 522–537. DOI: 10.1111/beer.12371

Lerner, J., & Nanda, R. (2020). Venture capital's role in financing innovation: What we know and how much we still need to learn. *The Journal of Economic Perspectives, 34*(3), 237–261. DOI: 10.1257/jep.34.3.237

Lin, L. (2022). Venture capital in the rise of sustainable investment. *European Business Organization Law Review, 23*(1), 187–216. DOI: 10.1007/s40804-021-00238-8

Malek, K., Maine, E., & McCarthy, I. P. (2014). A typology of clean technology commercialization accelerators. *Journal of Engineering and Technology Management, 32*, 26–39. DOI: 10.1016/j.jengtecman.2013.10.006

Marra, A., Antonelli, P., & Pozzi, C. (2017). Emerging green-tech specializations and clusters–A network analysis on technological innovation at the metropolitan level. *Renewable & Sustainable Energy Reviews, 67*, 1037–1046. DOI: 10.1016/j.rser.2016.09.086

Polzin, F., Sanders, M., & Täube, F. (2017). A diverse and resilient financial system for investments in the energy transition. *Current Opinion in Environmental Sustainability, 28*, 24–32. DOI: 10.1016/j.cosust.2017.07.004

Sanz-Prieto, I., de-la-Fuente-Valentín, L., & Rios-Aguilar, S. (2021). Technical Due Diligence as a Methodology for Assessing Risks in Start-up Ecosystems. In ICEIS (2) (pp. 421-428). DOI: 10.5220/0010521704210428

Taşkın, D. (2021). Financing Strategies for New Product Development and Innovation. Engines of Economic Prosperity: Creating Innovation and Economic Opportunities through Entrepreneurship, 79-92. Andersson, T. L. (2020). Tesla: a sequence of belief (Doctoral dissertation).

Tran, T., Do, H., Vu, T., & Do, N. (2020). The factors affecting green investment for sustainable development. *Decision Science Letters, 9*(3), 365–386. DOI: 10.5267/j.dsl.2020.4.002

Chapter 3
The Impact of Digital Transformation on Corporate Financial Practices:
A Global Perspective

Vishal Jain
http://orcid.org/0000-0003-1126-7424
Vivekananda Institute of Professional Studies, India

Archan Mitra
http://orcid.org/0000-0002-1419-3558
Amity School of Communication, Amity University Mumbai, India

ABSTRACT

Digital transformation has revolutionized corporate financial practices globally, introducing advanced technologies like AI, blockchain, and cloud computing to enhance efficiency, accuracy, and decision-making. This paper examines the impact of these innovations on financial management, reporting, and auditing, focusing on automation, real-time analysis, and transparency. While digital tools offer significant advantages, challenges such as regulatory compliance, data security, and the need for workforce

DOI: 10.4018/979-8-3693-8247-9.ch003

reskilling remain prevalent. Through a comparative analysis of global sectors, this study highlights both the opportunities and risks associated with the integration of digital technologies in corporate finance.

1. INTRODUCTION

Background

The advent of digital transformation marks a pivotal shift in how industries operate, communicate, and manage their resources. This transformation, characterized by the adoption of digital technologies across various sectors, is fundamentally reshaping traditional business processes. Digital transformation is defined as the integration of digital technologies, such as artificial intelligence (AI), cloud computing, blockchain, and big data analytics, into all areas of business, fundamentally altering how companies deliver value to customers and how they operate internally (Vial, 2019). In corporate finance, this transformation is particularly influential, offering new avenues for enhancing financial management, reporting, and decision-making.

Historically, corporate financial practices were driven by manual processes, legacy systems, and extensive human intervention. These traditional financial frameworks, while reliable, are increasingly seen as inefficient in today's fast-paced, data-driven business environment. The rapid proliferation of digital tools has allowed organizations to automate financial operations, improve accuracy, and make more informed, real-time financial decisions (Kashyap, 2020). The growing influence of technologies such as AI and blockchain is transforming financial reporting, auditing, and forecasting, offering corporations opportunities to streamline processes and improve their competitive edge.

In the context of corporate finance, digital transformation is not merely about automating existing processes but also about rethinking financial operations in a way that aligns with the broader goals of efficiency, transparency, and agility (Deloitte, 2020). By leveraging digital tools, corporations are finding new ways to manage risks, optimize resource allocation, and enhance decision-making. However, this shift also comes with significant challenges, such as the need for regulatory adaptation, data security, and organizational restructuring to fully integrate digital solutions into corporate financial systems.

Problem Statement

As the global business environment becomes increasingly competitive and complex, the need for corporations to adapt their financial practices to a rapidly evolving digital landscape is more pressing than ever. Companies that fail to embrace digital transformation risk falling behind competitors who leverage technology to enhance efficiency and decision-making capabilities. In particular, the financial function of corporations is under immense pressure to transition from traditional methods to digitally driven frameworks to keep pace with market demands and global trends.

One of the critical challenges facing corporate finance is the ability to integrate digital technologies while ensuring compliance with regulatory standards, safeguarding data privacy, and maintaining operational efficiency. The transition to digital financial practices is further complicated by the need to reskill finance professionals and adapt to the changing technological landscape (Accenture, 2021). Corporations are grappling with questions about how best to incorporate digital tools into their financial operations, how to manage the risks associated with these tools, and how to maximize the benefits of digital transformation.

The problem, therefore, lies in understanding how digital transformation can be successfully implemented within corporate finance, what technologies are most impactful, and what challenges and opportunities exist for organizations on a global scale. This paper seeks to address these issues by examining the ways in which digital transformation is reshaping corporate financial practices.

Research Questions

The study is guided by the following research questions:

1. How is digital transformation reshaping corporate financial practices globally?
2. What are the key digital technologies influencing financial management?
3. What are the potential risks and benefits associated with digital transformation in finance?

Objectives

The primary objectives of this paper are as follows:

- **To explore the impact of digital technologies on corporate financial operations**: This objective focuses on understanding how specific digital technologies are transforming traditional financial processes. Technologies such as AI, blockchain, cloud computing, and data analytics are central to the discussion, as they offer new capabilities for financial forecasting, reporting, and auditing.
- **To examine how organizations are integrating digital solutions into financial decision-making and reporting**: This objective seeks to investigate the practical applications of digital tools in the corporate finance sector. By analyzing real-world case studies and financial reports, the paper will explore how corporations are utilizing digital technologies to enhance their financial decision-making processes and improve accuracy in financial reporting.
- **To assess the challenges and opportunities presented by digital transformation in corporate finance on a global scale**: The final objective addresses both the benefits and potential pitfalls of digital transformation. While digital tools offer significant advantages in terms of efficiency, transparency, and decision-making, they also present challenges such as data security risks, regulatory compliance issues, and the need for workforce reskilling. This section will provide a balanced assessment of the opportunities and risks associated with digital transformation in finance.

Impact of Digital Technologies on Corporate Financial Operations

The transformation of corporate financial operations is largely driven by the adoption of digital technologies that automate, streamline, and enhance financial processes. Technologies such as AI and machine learning enable more accurate forecasting, fraud detection, and real-time decision-making by analyzing large datasets in ways that were previously impossible (PwC, 2020). AI-powered tools are capable of detecting patterns and anomalies in financial data, improving the accuracy and speed of financial reporting.

Blockchain, another key technology, is revolutionizing the way financial transactions are recorded and verified. Its decentralized and immutable nature ensures transparency and security in financial operations, reducing the likelihood of fraud and enhancing trust in financial reporting (Kshetri, 2021). Similarly, cloud computing allows corporations to store and access financial data in real-time, facilitating more agile financial decision-making processes and reducing costs associated with traditional IT infrastructure.

Integration of Digital Solutions in Financial Decision-Making and Reporting

Corporations are increasingly integrating digital solutions into their financial decision-making and reporting processes. For instance, AI-powered predictive analytics tools help financial managers make more informed decisions by analyzing historical data and forecasting future trends. These tools provide insights that are more accurate than traditional methods, enabling companies to better manage risks and optimize resource allocation (Ernst & Young, 2021).

In financial reporting, digital tools such as robotic process automation (RPA) are automating routine tasks such as data entry and report generation, reducing human error and increasing efficiency. Additionally, blockchain technology is enhancing the transparency of financial reporting by providing a tamper-proof ledger of all transactions, which is particularly useful for auditing purposes (Deloitte, 2020).

Challenges and Opportunities of Digital Transformation in Corporate Finance

While the benefits of digital transformation in corporate finance are clear, the transition also presents several challenges. Data security is a significant concern, as the increasing use of digital tools exposes corporations to the risk of cyberattacks. Ensuring the privacy and security of financial data is crucial, especially as regulations surrounding data protection become more stringent (Accenture, 2021).

Additionally, the successful integration of digital technologies requires significant investments in infrastructure and workforce training. Corporations must reskill their finance professionals to work with new digital tools and adapt to changing financial practices. Despite these challenges, the opportunities presented by digital transformation are substantial. Organizations that embrace digital tools can improve their operational efficiency, enhance decision-making, and gain a competitive advantage in the global market (Kashyap, 2020).

Digital transformation is reshaping corporate financial practices on a global scale. By integrating digital technologies such as AI, blockchain, and cloud computing, corporations are able to enhance their financial operations, improve decision-making processes, and increase transparency in financial reporting. However, the transition to digitally driven financial practices presents challenges such as data security risks and the need for workforce reskilling. As organizations continue to adapt to the evolving digital landscape, the benefits of digital transformation will become increasingly evident, offering new opportunities for efficiency and innovation in corporate finance.

2. LITERATURE REVIEW

Overview of Digital Transformation in Finance

Digital transformation refers to the adoption of digital technologies that radically change traditional business processes, creating new business models and revenue streams. In the financial sector, this transformation has led to profound changes, reshaping how corporations manage, report, and analyze their financial data. Foundational theories and models, such as the Technology Acceptance Model (TAM) and the Diffusion of Innovations Theory, have provided frameworks for understanding the integration of technology within corporate financial environments (Davis, 1989; Rogers, 2003). These theories explain how technological innovations are adopted by individuals and organizations, highlighting factors such as perceived ease of use and usefulness in driving the adoption of new technologies.

Digital transformation in finance has been propelled by key technological innovations, including cloud computing, artificial intelligence (AI), blockchain, and data analytics. Cloud computing has revolutionized data storage and accessibility, enabling real-time financial reporting and global access to financial data (Mitra & Das, 2024). It offers scalability, flexibility, and cost efficiency, allowing companies to streamline operations and reduce costs associated with maintaining traditional IT infrastructures.

Artificial intelligence is another transformative technology, reshaping financial management through automation and advanced data analysis. AI-driven algorithms enhance decision-making by processing vast amounts of data with speed and precision, enabling real-time insights into market trends, investment strategies, and risk management (PwC, 2020). Moreover, AI-based systems are now used for fraud detection, auditing, and financial forecasting, increasing efficiency and accuracy in financial operations.

Blockchain technology has emerged as a disruptive force in financial services, offering secure, decentralized, and transparent solutions for financial transactions and record-keeping. Blockchain eliminates the need for intermediaries in transactions, reducing costs and increasing transaction speeds while ensuring security through cryptographic methods (Kshetri, 2021). The potential of blockchain to revolutionize auditing, financial reporting, and compliance processes has garnered significant attention from corporate finance leaders globally.

Data analytics, particularly big data, plays a crucial role in digital transformation by providing corporations with actionable insights based on vast amounts of financial data. Advanced analytics tools enable organizations to detect patterns, assess risks, and make data-driven decisions, leading to more efficient financial planning and performance monitoring (Mitra & Jain, 2024). Together, these technologies are reshaping the landscape of corporate finance by improving efficiency, enhancing decision-making, and driving competitive advantages in the global marketplace.

Global Trends in Corporate Financial Practices

The digital transformation of financial practices is a global phenomenon, with corporations across developed and developing economies adopting digital tools to enhance their financial operations. In developed economies, such as the United States and Europe, digital technologies are widely integrated into financial management systems, enabling real-time reporting, automated audits, and advanced data analytics (Accenture, 2021). These regions benefit from strong digital infrastructure, regulatory frameworks that support innovation, and a workforce with high levels of digital literacy.

In developing economies, such as those in Asia and Africa, the adoption of digital technologies in finance has been slower, primarily due to challenges related to digital infrastructure, regulatory barriers, and workforce readiness. However, developing economies are increasingly recognizing the importance of digital transformation in finance to improve transparency, reduce costs, and increase financial inclusion (World Bank, 2022). For example, in India, digital financial platforms such as Paytm and the Unified Payments Interface (UPI) have revolutionized the way financial transactions are conducted, increasing access to financial services in rural and underserved areas (Das & Mitra, 2024).

Regional differences in the adoption of digital technologies are also influenced by varying regulatory landscapes. In Europe, the General Data Protection Regulation (GDPR) and other regulatory frameworks ensure strict controls on data privacy and security, creating a more cautious approach to the implementation of certain digital tools, such as AI and blockchain (Deloitte, 2020). In contrast, regions like Asia are experiencing rapid growth in digital finance, with less stringent regulatory frameworks allowing for faster innovation and adoption of new technologies.

Despite these regional differences, the global trend toward digitization in corporate finance is clear. Across the world, corporations are leveraging digital tools to enhance their financial reporting, improve decision-making, and gain a competitive edge in increasingly data-driven markets.

Challenges and Opportunities

While digital transformation presents numerous opportunities for enhancing corporate financial practices, it also poses significant challenges. One of the most pressing challenges is the issue of cybersecurity. As corporations rely more heavily on digital platforms to store and manage financial data, they become more vulnerable to cyberattacks and data breaches. Protecting sensitive financial information from hackers and ensuring compliance with data privacy regulations, such as the GDPR, is a top priority for organizations undergoing digital transformation (Accenture, 2021).

Another challenge is the regulatory environment. The rapid pace of technological innovation often outstrips the ability of regulators to create appropriate frameworks for governing the use of new technologies in finance. For example, while blockchain offers significant benefits in terms of transparency and security, its decentralized nature presents challenges for regulators who are tasked with ensuring compliance and preventing illegal activities such as money laundering (Kshetri, 2021). Corporations must navigate these regulatory complexities while adopting digital tools that comply with existing laws and regulations.

Workforce reskilling is another major challenge posed by digital transformation. As financial operations become increasingly automated, the demand for traditional financial skills is declining, while the need for expertise in digital tools and data analytics is growing. Corporations must invest in training and reskilling their finance teams to ensure they can effectively use new digital tools and adapt to the changing financial landscape (Mitra & Sachdeva, 2023). Failure to do so can result in a skills gap, where finance professionals are unable to fully leverage the benefits of digital technologies.

Despite these challenges, the opportunities presented by digital transformation in finance are significant. One of the most compelling opportunities is the potential for enhanced decision-making. Digital tools such as AI and big data analytics allow corporations to analyze vast amounts of financial data in real-time, providing insights that were previously unavailable through traditional financial methods (PwC, 2020). This enables organizations to make more informed decisions, reduce risks, and improve financial performance.

Another key opportunity is the ability to improve cost efficiency. Digital technologies such as cloud computing and RPA reduce the need for manual processes and physical infrastructure, lowering operational costs and increasing scalability (Deloitte, 2020). For corporations operating in global markets, the ability to access financial data in real-time from anywhere in the world is a critical advantage, enabling faster and more efficient decision-making.

Finally, digital transformation offers opportunities for greater transparency and accountability in financial reporting. Blockchain, in particular, provides a secure and transparent ledger of financial transactions that can be audited in real-time, reducing the risk of fraud and improving trust in financial reporting (Kshetri, 2021). This is particularly important in a global financial environment where transparency and accountability are key drivers of investor confidence and regulatory compliance.

3. METHODOLOGY

Research Design

This study adopted a mixed-methods research design to investigate the evolving impact of digital transformation on corporate financial practices. The objective was to integrate quantitative breadth with qualitative depth to capture not only patterns of digital adoption but also the nuanced experiences of professionals navigating this transformation. This methodology allowed for a comprehensive analysis of technological, operational, and strategic dimensions of finance in the digital era.

The research design followed a convergent mixed-methods framework, wherein both quantitative and qualitative data were collected in parallel and then integrated during the analysis phase. This approach was selected to triangulate findings from different sources, thereby enhancing the validity of the results. Quantitative data offered insights into general trends, adoption levels, and perceived impacts, while qualitative data illuminated the context-specific experiences of financial professionals dealing with the implementation of digital technologies in various industries.

Purposive sampling was employed to ensure that participants possessed relevant professional experience and were actively engaged in corporate finance functions during the ongoing digital transformation. The study targeted Chief Financial Officers (CFOs), senior finance managers, and digital transformation officers working in mid-sized to large corporations across sectors such as banking, manufacturing, IT services, retail, and telecommunications. A total of 120 professionals completed the structured survey distributed via email and professional networks. The inclusion criteria ensured that all respondents had a minimum of five years of experience in corporate finance and had been exposed to at least one digital transformation initiative within their organizations.

To enrich the data set and provide contextual interpretation, qualitative interviews were conducted with a subsample of 15 professionals drawn from the survey cohort. Participants for interviews were selected based on their leadership roles and direct involvement in digital strategy implementation within finance departments. The interviews were semi-structured to provide consistency while allowing flexibility for participants to elaborate on their specific experiences and perceptions. Interview questions focused on digital tools adopted, strategic decision-making, perceived benefits and barriers, and the future outlook for digital finance. Interviews were conducted using secure video conferencing platforms and lasted between 30 to 45 minutes. All interviews were recorded with participant consent and transcribed verbatim for analysis.

Survey data were collected over a three-month period from January to March 2024. The structured questionnaire included 25 closed-ended questions divided into four thematic sections: types of digital tools adopted, extent of integration into financial processes, perceived operational and strategic benefits, and challenges encountered. Questions were framed using a five-point Likert scale to capture the degree of agreement or frequency related to each item. Data from the surveys were analyzed using SPSS software. Descriptive statistical techniques, including mean, standard deviation, and frequency distribution, were used to summarize the responses. Cross-tabulation was conducted to identify correlations between variables such as industry type and perceived benefits or challenges of digital adoption.

Qualitative data analysis followed Braun and Clarke's (2006) six-phase framework for thematic analysis. The first phase involved familiarization with the data through repeated reading of interview transcripts. In the second phase, initial codes were generated manually and through the use of NVivo software. Codes were then grouped into potential themes such as efficiency gains, resistance to change, regulatory uncertainty, and human capital implications. In the third phase, themes were reviewed and refined to ensure coherence and distinctiveness. Subsequently, themes were clearly defined and named in alignment with the research objectives. The final phase involved weaving the themes into a narrative that complemented and contextualized the quantitative findings, thereby enriching the overall analysis.

To ensure the reliability of the research instruments, the survey questionnaire was pre-tested with five finance professionals from different sectors. Their feedback led to the refinement of several questions for clarity and relevance. For example, ambiguous terms like "automation tools" were replaced with specific examples such as "robotic process automation (RPA)" to enhance respondent understanding. Reliability of the survey instrument was further tested using Cronbach's alpha, which yielded a score of 0.84, indicating acceptable internal consistency. In the qualitative strand, reliability was enhanced through inter-coder agreement. A second researcher reviewed 20 percent of the transcripts to verify coding accuracy and consistency.

Validity was established through multiple methods. Content validity of the survey and interview guides was ensured by consulting academic experts and industry practitioners during the instrument design phase. Face validity was checked by sharing the instruments with peer reviewers. Triangulation between quantitative survey data and qualitative interview findings further strengthened the study's internal validity by cross-verifying emerging patterns. Moreover, member checking was conducted with a subset of interview participants, who were invited to review a summary of the thematic findings to confirm accuracy and resonance with their perspectives.

Ethical considerations were central to the research process. All participants received an information sheet outlining the study's objectives, scope, and voluntary nature. Informed consent was obtained prior to participation in both the survey and interviews. Participants were assured that all data would be kept confidential, anonymized during analysis, and used solely for academic purposes. Data were stored securely on password-protected servers accessible only to the research team. The study was approved by the Institutional Research Ethics Committee and adhered to the ethical standards outlined in the Declaration of Helsinki.

This methodological approach was well-suited to the complex and evolving nature of digital transformation in corporate finance. By combining quantitative generalizability with qualitative depth, the research design enabled a robust exploration of how organizations adapt to technological changes and how finance professionals perceive and experience those changes. The integration of both data strands facilitated a more holistic understanding of digital transformation's implications—ranging from operational efficiencies and reporting accuracy to governance challenges and talent development. Furthermore, the mixed-methods design allowed the study to capture sector-specific nuances, organizational scale considerations, and regional disparities, all of which enriched the relevance and applicability of the findings.

In sum, the methodology adopted for this study was rigorous, ethically grounded, and strategically designed to address the multidimensional nature of digital transformation in corporate financial practices. The results generated through this approach form the empirical foundation for the discussions and recommendations presented in the following chapters.

Data Collection

To comprehensively explore how digital transformation impacts corporate financial practices globally, this study will gather both primary and secondary data. This dual approach ensures that the research is grounded in real-world experiences while also drawing on existing knowledge from industry reports, academic publications, and financial statements.

Primary Data Collection

Primary data will be collected using two key methods: surveys and interviews. Surveys will target financial managers and executives from various sectors, including banking, retail, and manufacturing. These surveys will be designed to capture quantitative data on the adoption of digital tools in financial management, the perceived benefits and challenges of these tools, and their impact on financial performance (Kothari, 2004). The survey will include both closed-ended questions to gather measurable data and open-ended questions to allow respondents to elaborate on their experiences with digital transformation.

The survey will cover key areas such as:

- The types of digital tools and technologies currently being used (e.g., AI, blockchain, cloud computing, and data analytics).
- The extent to which these tools have replaced traditional financial management practices.
- The perceived advantages of adopting digital technologies in financial management, including improved accuracy, efficiency, and decision-making.
- The challenges encountered during the digital transformation process, such as regulatory compliance, data privacy concerns, and the need for workforce reskilling.
- The overall impact of digital transformation on financial performance indicators such as profitability, cost reduction, and return on investment (ROI).

In addition to the surveys, semi-structured interviews will be conducted with financial executives and managers from selected corporations across different regions. These interviews will provide qualitative insights into how digital transformation is being implemented at the organizational level, the strategic decisions involved, and the long-term effects on corporate financial practices. The semi-structured nature of the interviews will allow for in-depth exploration of specific issues while providing respondents with the flexibility to express their views in detail (Smith, 2015).

Secondary Data Collection

Secondary data will be gathered from a variety of sources, including financial reports, industry case studies, academic publications, and market research reports. These documents will provide valuable context for understanding how digital transformation is affecting corporate financial practices on a global scale. Specifically, financial reports and case studies will offer examples of how organizations have integrated digital tools into their financial management processes and the outcomes of these efforts. Industry publications will provide insights into emerging trends, best practices, and potential future developments in digital finance.

Moreover, academic literature on digital transformation in corporate finance will be reviewed to identify key theoretical frameworks and models that underpin the adoption of digital technologies. This literature review will help contextualize the primary data within the broader academic discourse and provide a foundation for analyzing the research findings.

Sample Size and Selection

To ensure that the research captures a diverse and representative sample of global corporate financial practices, the study will focus on three key sectors: banking, retail, and manufacturing. These sectors were chosen because they represent a broad cross-section of industries with varying degrees of exposure to digital technologies and differing levels of complexity in their financial operations.

- **Banking**: The banking sector has been at the forefront of digital transformation, with widespread adoption of FinTech solutions such as blockchain, AI, and big data analytics. The study will include financial institutions in both developed and developing economies to examine how digital tools are reshaping banking practices globally.

- **Retail**: The retail sector has experienced significant digital disruption in recent years, particularly in terms of e-commerce and digital payment systems. The study will assess how digital tools are being used in financial management, inventory control, and customer relationship management (CRM) in retail companies.
- **Manufacturing**: The manufacturing sector is traditionally slower to adopt digital technologies, but digital transformation is gradually taking hold through the use of AI for supply chain optimization, robotics for automation, and data analytics for financial forecasting. The study will explore how digital transformation is influencing financial practices in this sector.

Geographically, the study will focus on four regions: North America, Europe, Asia, and Africa. These regions were selected to provide a diverse and comprehensive perspective on global trends in digital finance. North America and Europe are home to many of the world's leading financial institutions and tech companies, while Asia is experiencing rapid growth in digital financial services. Africa, while still in the early stages of digital adoption, presents an important case for understanding how digital transformation is impacting financial inclusion and corporate finance in developing economies.

The sample size for the survey will consist of 200 financial managers and executives across the three sectors and four regions. This sample size is large enough to provide statistically significant results while being manageable within the scope of the study (Fowler, 2014). In terms of interviews, approximately 20-30 executives will be selected based on their roles in implementing digital transformation within their organizations.

Data Analysis

Data analysis will involve both quantitative and qualitative methods. For the quantitative data collected through surveys, statistical tools such as regression analysis will be employed to assess the correlation between digital adoption and financial performance. Regression analysis will help identify key variables that influence the success of digital transformation in finance, such as the type of technology adopted, the sector in which the organization operates, and regional factors (Field, 2013).

The analysis will focus on key financial performance indicators, such as return on investment (ROI), cost efficiency, and profitability, to determine whether companies that have adopted digital tools are experiencing improved financial outcomes compared to those that have not. Statistical software such as SPSS or R will be used to conduct the regression analysis and generate descriptive statistics.

For the qualitative data collected through interviews, thematic analysis will be employed to identify common themes and patterns in the responses. Thematic analysis is a method for identifying, analyzing, and reporting patterns within data, providing a rich and detailed account of the findings (Braun & Clarke, 2006). This approach will allow the researcher to interpret the experiences and insights of financial managers and executives, shedding light on the challenges and opportunities associated with digital transformation in corporate finance.

By combining both quantitative and qualitative data, this study aims to provide a comprehensive analysis of how digital transformation is reshaping corporate financial practices globally.

4. RESULTS AND DISCUSSION

Analysis of Global Financial Practices

The findings from this study highlight the varying degrees to which different regions and sectors have successfully integrated digital technologies into their financial operations. The adoption of digital transformation in corporate finance varies across regions, depending on the level of technological infrastructure, regulatory frameworks, and cultural openness to innovation. The data collected from surveys and interviews with financial managers and executives across key sectors—banking, retail, and manufacturing—reveals significant differences in how digital tools are being utilized for financial management, reporting, and decision-making.

Regional Analysis

In **North America**, particularly the United States and Canada, corporations have been at the forefront of adopting digital financial technologies. Companies in this region are leveraging AI-driven analytics, blockchain, and cloud computing to streamline financial reporting and improve decision-making processes. Financial institutions in North America, such as JPMorgan Chase and Citigroup, have integrated AI into their risk management strategies, using advanced algorithms to predict market trends and identify potential risks (Kashyap, 2020). Additionally, the retail and manufacturing sectors in this region have embraced robotic process automation (RPA) to automate routine financial tasks, such as invoicing and reconciliation, thereby reducing manual errors and increasing efficiency.

Europe has also seen significant advancements in the digital transformation of corporate finance, particularly in the banking and financial services industry. However, the adoption of digital technologies in finance is more cautious in Europe due to stringent regulatory frameworks such as the General Data Protection Regulation (GDPR) (Deloitte, 2020). Despite these regulatory challenges, European companies are actively investing in AI and blockchain to enhance transparency and ensure compliance with financial reporting standards. For example, the UK-based Barclays Bank has implemented blockchain technology to streamline cross-border transactions, reducing transaction times from several days to minutes (Kshetri, 2021).

In **Asia**, the pace of digital transformation in finance has been rapid, particularly in countries like China, Japan, and Singapore. The widespread adoption of digital payment platforms, such as Alibaba's Alipay and Tencent's WeChat Pay, has revolutionized financial operations in the retail and banking sectors (Das & Mitra, 2024). Moreover, Japanese corporations have integrated AI-driven forecasting tools to enhance their financial planning and budgeting processes. However, the digital divide remains a challenge in developing Asian economies, where limited access to digital infrastructure hampers the widespread adoption of advanced financial technologies.

Africa presents a mixed picture of digital transformation in corporate finance. While financial institutions in countries like South Africa and Nigeria are increasingly adopting digital tools to enhance financial inclusion and streamline operations, many African economies still face significant barriers to digital adoption. Limited access to high-speed internet, regulatory challenges, and a lack of digital literacy among finance professionals are key obstacles that slow the integration of digital technologies into financial practices in this region (World Bank, 2022). Nevertheless, mobile banking platforms like M-Pesa in Kenya have demonstrated the potential for digital solutions to improve financial inclusion and enable real-time financial reporting in underdeveloped markets.

Sectoral Analysis

The **banking sector** has been the most proactive in integrating digital technologies into financial operations. Banks around the world are leveraging AI-driven financial forecasting, blockchain for secure transactions, and cloud-based systems for real-time reporting. Financial institutions are increasingly using AI algorithms to analyze vast datasets, identify market trends, and assess credit risk (PwC, 2020). In addition, blockchain technology has enabled banks to improve the security and transparency of cross-border transactions, reducing the reliance on intermediaries and cutting transaction costs.

The **retail sector** has also made significant strides in digital transformation, particularly in the use of AI and data analytics for financial forecasting and inventory management. Retail companies such as Amazon and Walmart are using RPA to automate financial processes such as order-to-cash, accounts payable, and expense reporting, leading to increased efficiency and accuracy in financial management (Mitra & Jain, 2024). However, smaller retail firms in developing regions face challenges in adopting these advanced technologies due to limited financial resources and a lack of access to digital infrastructure.

In the **manufacturing sector**, digital transformation in financial practices has been slower compared to banking and retail. However, there is growing adoption of AI-driven financial tools for supply chain optimization and financial planning. Manufacturing firms are increasingly using AI to forecast demand, optimize pricing strategies, and streamline procurement processes. For instance, companies like Siemens and General Electric are leveraging digital tools to enhance financial decision-making, particularly in budgeting and resource allocation (Accenture, 2021).

Technological Innovations Impacting Financial Practices

Several technological innovations have had a profound impact on corporate financial practices, transforming traditional approaches to financial management, reporting, and decision-making. The key technologies driving this transformation include AI-driven financial forecasting, blockchain for secure transactions, and RPA for financial operations.

AI-Driven Financial Forecasting

Artificial intelligence has become a critical tool in corporate finance, particularly in financial forecasting and risk management. AI algorithms are capable of analyzing large datasets in real-time, identifying patterns and anomalies that traditional financial tools might overlook (PwC, 2020). This has led to more accurate financial forecasting, enabling corporations to predict market trends, assess risks, and make data-driven decisions with greater confidence. For instance, companies are using AI to analyze historical financial data, identify correlations between market variables, and forecast future revenue streams and expenses.

AI is also being used in fraud detection and prevention. Machine learning algorithms are able to detect unusual patterns in financial transactions, flagging potentially fraudulent activities in real-time. This has greatly enhanced the ability of financial institutions to protect their assets and reduce financial losses due to fraud (Kashyap, 2020). Moreover, AI-driven tools are being integrated into enterprise resource planning (ERP) systems, providing financial managers with real-time insights into financial performance and enabling more agile decision-making.

Blockchain for Secure Transactions

Blockchain technology has revolutionized the way financial transactions are conducted, offering a secure, decentralized, and transparent ledger for recording financial transactions. In corporate finance, blockchain is being used to streamline processes such as cross-border payments, asset tracking, and contract management (Kshetri, 2021). By eliminating intermediaries in financial transactions, blockchain reduces transaction costs and increases the speed of financial operations.

One of the most significant applications of blockchain in corporate finance is in auditing and compliance. The decentralized nature of blockchain ensures that all financial transactions are recorded in an immutable ledger, making it easier for auditors to verify the accuracy of financial statements and ensuring compliance with regulatory standards (Das & Mitra, 2024). Furthermore, blockchain's transparency improves trust between corporations and their stakeholders, as it provides a verifiable record of financial transactions.

Robotic Process Automation (RPA) for Financial Operations

RPA is increasingly being adopted in corporate finance to automate routine financial tasks, such as accounts payable, accounts receivable, and financial reconciliation. RPA tools mimic human actions by interacting with digital systems, automating repetitive tasks, and reducing the need for manual intervention (Mitra & Jain, 2024). This not only increases operational efficiency but also reduces the risk of human error in financial processes.

For example, corporations are using RPA to streamline the order-to-cash process, from invoicing to payment collection, reducing the time it takes to process transactions and improving cash flow management. RPA also plays a critical role in financial reporting, where it automates the consolidation of financial data from multiple sources, ensuring that financial reports are generated quickly and accurately (Accenture, 2021). As a result, financial managers are able to focus on higher-value tasks such as strategic planning and decision-making.

Challenges Faced in the Digital Transition

While digital transformation presents numerous benefits for corporate financial practices, the transition also brings with it significant challenges. The data collected from surveys and interviews with financial managers and executives highlighted several key challenges, including regulatory frameworks, cultural resistance, data privacy concerns, and the need for upskilling finance professionals.

Regulatory Frameworks

One of the primary challenges facing corporations in the digital transition is navigating the complex regulatory environment. As digital technologies such as AI, blockchain, and cloud computing become more integrated into financial operations, regulators are struggling to keep pace with the rapid pace of innovation. In regions such as Europe, the stringent requirements of the GDPR pose significant challenges for corporations adopting digital technologies, as they must ensure that their use of financial data complies with data privacy and security standards (Deloitte, 2020). Failure to comply with these regulations can result in hefty fines and reputational damage.

Moreover, the decentralized nature of blockchain technology presents unique regulatory challenges. While blockchain offers enhanced security and transparency, its use in financial transactions can make it difficult for regulators to monitor and enforce compliance with anti-money laundering (AML) and know-your-customer (KYC) regulations (Kshetri, 2021). Corporations must work closely with regulators to develop frameworks that balance innovation with regulatory compliance.

Cultural Resistance

Cultural resistance to digital transformation is another significant barrier to the successful integration of digital technologies in corporate finance. Many organizations face resistance from employees who are reluctant to adopt new technologies, particularly those who have spent their careers working with traditional financial systems. This resistance is often rooted in fear of job displacement, as automation tools such as RPA threaten to replace routine financial tasks that were previously performed by humans (PwC, 2020).

To overcome this resistance, corporations must invest in change management strategies that encourage employees to embrace digital tools and provide training programs that equip them with the skills needed to work in a digital environment. Upskilling finance professionals to work with AI, blockchain, and data analytics tools is critical to ensuring that they can leverage these technologies to enhance financial operations.

Data Privacy and Security

As corporations increasingly rely on digital platforms to store and process financial data, concerns about data privacy and security have become more pronounced. Cybersecurity threats, including data breaches and hacking, pose significant risks to corporations that handle sensitive financial information. Ensuring the privacy and security of financial data is paramount, particularly as regulators impose stricter data protection requirements (Accenture, 2021).

In addition to cybersecurity risks, corporations must also address the challenge of managing large volumes of financial data. The rise of big data analytics has enabled organizations to process vast amounts of financial data in real-time, but this also creates challenges in terms of data governance and ensuring the accuracy and integrity of financial data.

Opportunities for Future Growth

Despite the challenges, digital transformation offers significant opportunities for corporations to enhance their financial practices and drive future growth. One of the most compelling opportunities is the potential for enhanced operational efficiency. By automating routine financial tasks with AI and RPA, corporations can reduce costs, increase accuracy, and free up finance professionals to focus on more strategic initiatives (Mitra & Jain, 2024).

Better risk management is another key opportunity presented by digital transformation. AI-driven risk management tools enable corporations to analyze market trends, assess risks, and make data-driven decisions in real-time, improving their ability to navigate volatile financial markets (PwC, 2020). These tools also enhance the accuracy of financial forecasting, helping organizations to anticipate potential risks and take proactive measures to mitigate them.

Real-time financial reporting is another area where digital transformation offers significant benefits. Cloud-based financial systems enable corporations to generate financial reports in real-time, providing stakeholders with up-to-date information on the company's financial performance. This not only improves transparency but also enables more agile decision-making, as financial managers can quickly respond to changes in the business environment.

Finally, digital transformation offers improved access to global markets. Digital financial platforms such as blockchain and AI enable corporations to conduct cross-border transactions more efficiently, reducing the barriers to international trade and expanding their reach in global markets (Kshetri, 2021). As corporations continue to embrace digital technologies, they will be well-positioned to capitalize on the opportunities presented by the global economy.

5. CONCLUSION

Summary of Findings

The study on the impact of digital transformation on corporate financial practices has revealed significant insights into how digital tools and technologies are reshaping global financial operations. Across regions and sectors, the integration of artificial intelligence (AI), blockchain, cloud computing, and robotic process automation (RPA) has fundamentally changed the way corporations manage, report, and make financial decisions.

The findings highlight that developed economies, particularly in North America and Europe, have been leaders in adopting digital tools for financial management, leveraging these technologies for more accurate financial forecasting, improved risk management, and streamlined reporting mechanisms. In regions like Asia and parts of Africa, the pace of digital adoption varies, with mobile banking platforms and digital payment systems playing a prominent role in financial transformation, especially in sectors such as retail and banking.

The study also uncovered that certain sectors, such as banking and retail, are at the forefront of digital adoption, while industries like manufacturing are gradually integrating digital tools to optimize financial planning and resource allocation. Overall, the global corporate landscape is seeing a shift from traditional financial practices to digitally driven frameworks, with significant improvements in operational efficiency, real-time reporting, and decision-making processes.

However, alongside these advancements, corporations are facing considerable challenges. Regulatory frameworks, data privacy concerns, cultural resistance, and the need for reskilling finance professionals are major hurdles in the path of full digital transformation. Despite these challenges, the opportunities for future growth, including enhanced transparency, better financial forecasting, and increased global market access, indicate a positive outlook for organizations that successfully embrace digital transformation in finance.

Theoretical and Practical Implications

The findings of this study contribute to the existing body of knowledge on digital transformation and corporate finance in several ways. From a theoretical standpoint, the study supports and extends existing models of technology adoption, such as the Technology Acceptance Model (TAM) and Diffusion of Innovations Theory (Rogers, 2003). These models emphasize that factors such as perceived usefulness, ease of use, and social influence play a critical role in the adoption of digital tools within corporate environments. The research further validates these models by illustrating how these factors manifest in corporate financial practices across different regions and sectors.

Moreover, this study contributes to the emerging literature on the impact of specific digital technologies, such as AI, blockchain, and cloud computing, on corporate finance. By focusing on real-world applications and providing sectoral and regional analysis, the research adds depth to the academic discourse on how digital tools are transforming financial management processes. The integration of these technologies into finance is not only reshaping operational efficiency but also influencing strategic financial decision-making and the broader governance of financial data.

From a practical perspective, the findings provide critical insights for financial managers and corporate leaders looking to leverage digital tools to enhance their financial operations. The results show that adopting technologies such as AI-driven financial forecasting and blockchain for secure transactions can yield tangible benefits in terms of accuracy, transparency, and cost efficiency. Financial managers should focus on aligning these technologies with their organization's strategic objectives to improve decision-making, mitigate risks, and optimize financial performance.

However, the practical implications of digital transformation also point to the need for a structured approach to managing the challenges that accompany technological adoption. Issues such as regulatory compliance, data privacy, and workforce upskilling must be addressed proactively to ensure that corporations can reap the full benefits of digital transformation. Furthermore, financial leaders must work closely with technology providers, regulators, and internal stakeholders to create an ecosystem that supports continuous innovation while safeguarding the integrity of financial operations.

Recommendations

For organizations looking to successfully navigate digital transformation in their financial practices, several strategies can be employed to minimize risks and maximize the benefits associated with adopting digital tools.

1. Invest in Workforce Upskilling and Change Management

One of the critical challenges identified in this study is the cultural resistance to digital transformation and the need for upskilling finance professionals. Organizations should prioritize training and development programs that equip their finance teams with the skills needed to work with AI, blockchain, data analytics, and other digital tools. Moreover, companies should implement change management initiatives to encourage a culture of innovation and continuous learning. By addressing resistance and fostering a digitally literate workforce, organizations can ensure that their finance teams are well-prepared to leverage new technologies effectively.

2. Focus on Regulatory Compliance and Data Privacy

As digital transformation accelerates, so too do the challenges related to regulatory compliance and data privacy. To navigate the complex regulatory environment, particularly in regions with stringent data protection laws such as Europe, organizations should work closely with legal and compliance teams to ensure that their use of digital tools adheres to all relevant regulations. This includes implementing robust data governance frameworks that prioritize data security and privacy. Companies should also adopt blockchain technology to enhance transparency and security in financial transactions, thereby mitigating the risks of non-compliance and data breaches.

3. Adopt a Phased Approach to Digital Transformation

While the benefits of digital transformation are clear, organizations should avoid adopting a one-size-fits-all approach to integrating digital tools. Instead, companies should develop a phased approach that starts with identifying key areas of financial operations that can benefit the most from automation and digitalization. For example, automating routine tasks through RPA or adopting AI for financial forecasting can provide quick wins in terms of operational efficiency and accuracy. Over time, organizations can scale their digital transformation efforts to include more complex applications, such as blockchain for auditing and compliance or AI-driven decision support systems.

4. Leverage Data Analytics for Informed Decision-Making

Data analytics is a powerful tool that can transform financial decision-making processes. Organizations should prioritize investments in big data analytics and AI-driven insights to enhance their financial forecasting, risk management, and performance monitoring capabilities. By leveraging data analytics, companies can make more informed and data-driven decisions, which will improve their ability to navigate market volatility, optimize resource allocation, and enhance profitability. Additionally, integrating AI-based analytics into enterprise resource planning (ERP) systems can provide real-time insights into financial performance, enabling more agile and strategic financial management.

5. Collaborate with Technology Partners and Innovator

Digital transformation is an ongoing process that requires continuous innovation and adaptation. To stay ahead of the curve, organizations should collaborate with technology providers, startups, and innovators in the FinTech space. By forming partnerships with these entities, companies can gain access to cutting-edge technologies and solutions that can drive their digital transformation efforts. Collaboration with external stakeholders can also help organizations identify emerging trends in digital finance and stay updated on best practices in the industry.

6. Ensure Scalability and Flexibility in Technology Adoption

As organizations adopt digital tools, it is crucial to ensure that these technologies are scalable and flexible enough to meet future needs. Cloud computing offers a scalable solution that allows companies to store and access financial data from anywhere in the world, providing the flexibility needed to support global financial operations. Moreover, adopting modular and adaptable digital platforms will enable organizations to integrate new technologies as they emerge, ensuring that their financial systems remain future-proof and capable of handling increased complexity.

By implementing these strategies, organizations can successfully navigate the challenges of digital transformation while maximizing the benefits of enhanced financial operations. Digital tools offer a pathway to greater efficiency, accuracy, and transparency in corporate finance, and those companies that embrace digital innovation will be well-positioned to thrive in an increasingly competitive global market.

REFERENCES

Accenture. (2021). *The future of finance: How digital transformation is reshaping corporate finance.* Retrieved from https://www.accenture.com

Braun, V., & Clarke, V. (2006). Using thematic analysis in psychology. *Qualitative Research in Psychology, 3*(2), 77–101. DOI: 10.1191/1478088706qp063oa

Das, S., & Mitra, A. (2024). *Advancing lightweight digital trust architectures in the internet of medical things: A multi-dimensional analysis.* In *Lightweight Digital Trust Architectures in the Internet of Medical Things (IoMT)*, 1-14. DOI: 10.4018/979-8-3693-2109-6.ch001

Deloitte. (2020). *Digital transformation in finance: The impact of AI, blockchain, and cloud computing on financial operations.* Deloitte Insights.

Ernst & Young. (2021). *Digital financial transformation: The role of AI and big data in financial decision-making.* Ernst & Young Global.

Field, A. (2013). *Discovering statistics using IBM SPSS statistics* (4th ed.). SAGE Publications.

Fowler, F. J. (2014). *Survey research methods* (5th ed.). SAGE Publications.

Kashyap, P. (2020). Digital transformation and financial reporting: The future of corporate finance. *Journal of Financial Management, 45*(2), 215–230.

Kothari, C. R. (2004). *Research methodology: Methods and techniques* (2nd ed.). New Age International.

Kshetri, N. (2021). Blockchain's roles in meeting key supply chain management objectives. *International Journal of Information Management, 39*, 80–89. DOI: 10.1016/j.ijinfomgt.2017.12.005

Mitra, A., & Jain, V. (2024). *Development and application of machine learning algorithms for sentiment analysis in digital manufacturing: A pathway for enhanced customer feedback.* In *Emerging Technologies in Digital Manufacturing and Smart Factories*, 26-38.

Mitra, A., & Sachdeva, P. (2023). Decoding the Twitter sentiment using artificial intelligence tools: A study on Tokyo Olympics 2020. *Lecture Notes in Networks and Systems*, *757*, 539–554. DOI: 10.1007/978-981-99-5166-6_37

PwC. (2020). *The role of digital technologies in reshaping corporate financial practices*. PwC Global Financial Report.

Rogers, E. M. (2003). *Diffusion of innovations* (5th ed.). Free Press.

Smith, J. A. (2015). *Qualitative psychology: A practical guide to research methods* (3rd ed.). SAGE Publications.

Vial, G. (2019). Understanding digital transformation: A review and a research agenda. *The Journal of Strategic Information Systems*, *28*(2), 118–144. DOI: 10.1016/j.jsis.2019.01.003

Section 2
Institutional and Regulatory Mechanisms for Risk Mitigation and Transparency in Corporate Finance

Chapter 4
Forensic Accounting: The Frontline Defence Against Corporate Frauds

Richa Diwakar
http://orcid.org/0000-0002-0439-9624
Amity University, Noida, India

Ritu Wadhwa
http://orcid.org/0000-0002-9712-5787
Amity Business School, Amity University, Noida, India

T. V. Raman
BIMTECH, India

Kavita Mangilal Joshi
http://orcid.org/0009-0000-9987-9323
Amity College of Commerce and Finance, Amity University, Noida, India

ABSTRACT

Forensic accounting is a crucial element in upholding the honesty of financial practices in the corporate sphere. This investigates convergence of forensic accounting and corporate finance examining the risks presented by corporate fraud. The growing intricacy of financial transactions has

DOI: 10.4018/979-8-3693-8247-9.ch004

created a fertile environment for fraudulent activities on global scale. Forensic accountants, armed with a combination of investigative skills and accounting knowledge are skilled at uncovering inconsistencies. The discussion spotlights significant cases where forensic accounting played a crucial role in revealing fraud. At the heart of the section are the methods employed by forensic accountants, including data analysis, examination of financial statements, digital forensics, and more. Additionally, the organizational role of forensic accountants within corporations is examined alongside the international aspect of forensic accounting. Lastly, the future direction of forensic accounting is considered, advancing technologies and methodologies will shape its role.

1. INTRODUCTION

1.1. Overview of the Chapter

This chapter explores the critical role of forensic accounting in detecting, investigating, and preventing corporate fraud within an increasingly complex financial landscape. It begins by defining forensic accounting as integrating accounting, auditing, and investigative skills, primarily focused on fraud detection. The evolution of forensic accounting is traced in response to high-profile corporate scandals and globalization, highlighting the urgent need for robust practices (Awolowo, 2019). Various methodologies, including data mining and digital forensics, are essential for forensic accountants to analyze vast amounts of financial data and provide credible evidence in legal contexts.

The chapter also addresses the international dimension of forensic accounting, noting the significant variations in practices and regulatory frameworks across jurisdictions. It contrasts stringent U.S. regulations, such as the Sarbanes-Oxley Act, with developing economies like India and China, where forensic accounting is rapidly evolving. The importance of international cooperation and compliance with global standards from organizations like the International Federation of Accountants (IFAC) and the Financial Action Task Force (FATF) is emphasized(De Bellis, 2013). Emerging technologies—such as blockchain, big data analytics, and artificial intelligence (AI)—are reshaping forensic accounting by enhancing fraud detection and prevention capabilities(Hossain, 2023). The chapter concludes with a look toward the future, advocating for a proactive approach to fraud prevention, which incorporates predictive analytics and emphasizes the expanded role of forensic accountants in corporate risk management, compliance, and governance. The chapter underscores organisations' need to strengthen their forensic accounting practices to safeguard against fraud, promote transparency, and foster an ethical corporate culture in the global financial environment.

1.2. Importance of Forensic Accounting in Corporate Finance

1.2.1. Fraud Detection and Prevention

Forensic accounting plays a pivotal role in identifying and preventing fraudulent organisational activities. It essentially identifies financial discrepancies and irregularities within a company's records. (Nigrini, 2020) Forensic accountants employ data analytics, trend analysis, and behavioural analysis to scrutinize financial transactions and identify anomalies that may indicate fraudulent behaviour. By implementing proactive measures, organizations can deter potential fraudsters and protect their assets. Scrutinizing financial transactions, accounting records, and financial statements helps forensic accountants detect warning signs of fraudulent activity, such as financial statement manipulation, embezzlement, or improper asset valuation. (Roszkowska, 2021) Detecting fraud early prevents significant financial losses, reputational damage, and legal consequences, reinforcing trust in financial reporting.

1.2.2. Litigation Support

Forensic accountants provide invaluable support in legal disputes involving financial matters by preparing detailed financial reports and analyses(Kranacher & Riley, 2019). Their expert testimony is critical in the legal discovery process particularly valuable in cases of shareholder disputes, bankruptcy, breach of contract, or insurance claims, where they quantify economic damages and trace illicit financial transactions. (Izedonmi & Ibadin, 2012) Forensic accountants analyse and compile complex financial data to be presented as compelling evidence during court proceedings. This allows them to serve as expert witnesses in court, where they can understandably explain complex financial issues to judges and juries. The crucial support offered by forensic accountants helps achieve favourable outcomes in litigation.

1.2.3. Corporate Governance

In today's corporate environment, effective governance requires robust internal controls, transparency in financial reporting and ethical management. Forensic accounting enhances corporate governance by promoting transparency and accountability within organizations(Alzoubi, 2023). Forensic accountants help design and evaluate governance frameworks that minimize fraud risks, ensure adherence to corporate policies, and safeguard stakeholders' interests. By conducting risk assessments and forensic audits, they identify governance weaknesses that could lead to fraud and provide recommendations to improve oversight mechanisms. By fostering this culture of accountability, organizations can mitigate risks associated with fraud and misconduct.

1.2.4. Mergers and Acquisitions

Forensic accounting is pivotal in mergers and acquisitions (M&A). By conducting forensic due diligence during mergers and acquisitions forensic accountants scrutinize the accuracy of financial statements, identify hidden financial risks or potential fraud within the target company, and uncover any financial manipulation that could affect the deal's value(Gulapalli et al., 2017). Their ability to analyse financial statements critically ensures that both parties in an M&A transaction have a clear, accurate understanding of the financial position, reducing the risk of post-transaction disputes, ultimately protecting shareholder interests.

1.2.5. Regulatory Compliance

Forensic accountants play a key role in ensuring organisations adhere to the local and international regulatory frameworks(Alhusban et al., 2020). They navigate the complex regulatory frameworks of modern businesses by ensuring implementation of internal controls that align with the regulations. They ensure that the corporations comply with anti-money laundering regulations, tax laws, the Sarbanes-Oxley Act, etc. By conducting compliance audit, forensic accountants work proactively to identify irregularities and ensure accurate reporting, which reduces the risk of non-compliance penalties and reputational damage.

1.2.6. Shareholder Assurance

Forensic accounting provides an additional layer of protection to shareholders by ensuring that financial information is accurate and free of manipulation(John Nwoye Ugochukwu, 2021). The assurance regarding reliability of financial statements directly impacts investment decisions by boosting shareholder confidence and fostering a trustworthy environment. Such trustworthiness provides for growth and market stability in the long run.

1.2.7. Ethical Practices

As discussed above, forensic accounting establishes a framework of accountability within an organisation which serves as a deterrence against fraudulent activities making forensic accountants the "guardian of ethical practices"(Roszkowska, 2021). Identifying unethical financial behaviour such as insider trading, bribery, financial misreporting, and other white-collar crimes by forensic accountants promotes a culture of integrity alongside maintaining public trust.

1.3. Purpose And Scope of the Chapter

The chapter investigates the ever-changing field of forensic accounting and its crucial function in uncovering, examining, and stopping corporate fraud in today's complex financial environment. Its goal is to offer a comprehension of how forensic accounting integrates various disciplines, such as accounting, auditing, and investigative methods, to effectively combat fraudulent activities. It commences by defining forensic accounting and tracing its development in response to major corporate scandals and the globalization of business. This historical background emphasizes the growing need for specialized financial oversight as companies operate across diverse jurisdictions. Subsequently, it explores the techniques utilized in forensic accounting, including data mining, digital forensics, and advanced analytics. These tools are essential for scrutinizing extensive financial data, identifying irregularities, and uncovering fraudulent practices. The sophistication of these methods enhances the effectiveness of forensic accountants in identifying fraud and assembling compelling evidence for legal proceedings. An international outlook is also presented, comparing established practices in developed economies like the United States with emerging approaches in countries such as India and China. The chapter emphasizes how differing regulatory frameworks and cultural attitudes towards fraud impact the efficiency of forensic accounting on a global scale. Considerable attention is placed on the transformative influence of emerging technologies, such as blockchain, big data analytics, and artificial intelligence (AI), which are transforming fraud detection and prevention strategies. These innovations enable a more proactive approach in identifying potential financial risks. Lastly, the chapter outlines future directions for forensic accounting, stressing its expanding role in corporate governance, risk management, and compliance. It advocates for a proactive approach to fraud prevention through predictive analytics and advanced tools to identify risks before they escalate. Ultimately, this chapter underscores the critical importance of robust forensic accounting practices in fostering transparency, accountability, and integrity in contemporary financial systems.

2. EVOLUTION OF FORENSIC ACCOUNTING

The field of forensic accounting has significantly evolved over the years as a specialized branch of accounting. Its origin can be traced from ancient financial systems, where primitive forms of bookkeeping were used to detect misappropriations of funds. Financial scandals of the 20th century highlighted the need for investigative financial practices. Later, the advancements in technology and increasing complexity of corporate fraud further pushed the role of forensic accountants.

2.1. Early Beginnings: Ancient and Medieval Accounting Practices

In ancient Mesopotamia, Egypt, and Greece, the government used early accounting methods to trade and manage taxes and state resources. These early systems were rudimentary but laid the groundwork for modern accounting practices.(Enofe et al., 2013) The Roman Empire made accounting more formal, particularly public finance. It employed auditors, called scribes, to audit financial transactions and detect any discrepancies in public accounts. Although forensic accounting as a distinct field did not exist, the principles of accountability and transparency in financial records were established during this period.

Auditing continued to develop in the medieval period, particularly in Europe, where merchants and traders adopted more systematic accounting practices. The double-entry system of bookkeeping, based on the work of the mathematician Luca Pacioli, emerged in the 15th century in Italy and provided a foundation for modern accounting by creating a more organized and reliable method for recording financial transactions(Orlandi, 2021). While fraud detection was not yet a central focus, establishing double-entry bookkeeping represented a crucial step toward the more investigative role that forensic accounting would eventually play(Karabayır, 2019).

2.2. The Industrial Revolution: Emergence of Modern Forensic Accounting

The 18th and 19th centuries witnessed significant economic growth, expansion of financial markets and the rise of large corporations due to the Industrial Revolution. This spurred the need for accurate financial reporting and fraud prevention. This period marked the formalization of forensic accounting practices as businesses began to recognise the importance of investigating financial irregularities(Umanhonlen et al., 2020). The role of accountants started to expand beyond bookkeeping. Accountants were increasingly called to investigate fraud, bankruptcy, and financial misconduct. The emergence of professional accounting bodies, such as the Institute of Chartered Accountants in England and Wales (ICAEW) in 1880, helped formalise the profession and establish ethical standards for accountants(Roy A Chandler, 2016). The late 19th century also saw the first use of the term 'forensic accounting', which refers to using accounting skills in legal proceedings. At this time, forensic accountants were primarily involved in bankruptcy investigations, where they analysed financial records to uncover fraudulent activity and mismanagement of funds. They also began to provide expert testimony in court, a role that would become a hallmark of forensic accounting.

2.3. The Early 20th Century: Expanding the Role of Forensic Accountants

Forensic accounting experienced significant growth during this time. The Great Depression of the 1930s exposed widespread corporate fraud and false financial reporting, leading to increased scrutiny of financial records. Forensic accountants were key in investigating these wrongdoings and assisting in legal proceedings (Karabayır, 2019). The stock market crash 1929 and the subsequent economic collapse demonstrated the need for greater financial oversight and transparency in corporate governance. During this period, the United States developed stricter financial regulations, such as the Securities Act of 1933 and the Securities Exchange Act of 1934, which required accurate financial reporting and accountability for publicly traded companies. Forensic accountants have helped ensure compliance and identify fraud and financial manipulation cases. Forensic accounting became more closely associated with law enforcement agencies during this time. Governments and regulatory agencies began hiring forensic accountants to investigate financial crimes such as embezzlement, tax evasion, and securities fraud (Özkul & Pamukçu, 2012). For example, the FBI established its first accounting department in the early 1900s and relied on forensic accountants to investigate white-collar crime

2.4. Post-World War II Era: Forensic Accounting in the Age of Regulation

The post-World War II period saw a significant increase in the regulatory framework governing corporate finance. The expansion of the global economy led to greater complexity in finance, and accountants were increasingly required to ensure compliance with regulations (Davies & Green, 2013). One of the most important developments of this period was the establishment of the US Securities and Exchange Commission (SEC) in 1934, which increased oversight of the financial markets. Accountants worked closely with the SEC to investigate insider trading, accounting fraud, and other financial crimes. Similar regulatory bodies were being established in UK and other countries to monitor corporate finance and ensure transparency during this period. This period also saw the expansion of forensic accounting into the field of tax investigations. Governments began to use forensic accounting to detect and investigate tax fraud and evasion, especially as tax codes became more complex (De Bellis, 2013). Forensic accounting has played a key role in high-profile tax evasion cases, including those involving organized crime syndicates and corrupt officials.

2.5. The Late 20th Century: Forensic Accounting in Corporate Scandals

The second half of the 20th century was marked by several high-profile corporate fraud scandals that brought forensic accounting into the spotlight. The collapse of companies such as Enron, WorldCom, and Arthur Andersen in the early 2000s revealed widespread financial fraud and the failure of traditional auditing methods to detect these crimes. These scandals highlighted the need for more robust forensic accounting techniques to prevent future corporate misconduct. In response to these corporate scandals, new regulations such as the Sarbanes-Oxley Act of 2002 were introduced to strengthen corporate governance and financial reporting standards (Ajayi-Nifise et al., 2024). Forensic accountants played a key role in enforcing these regulations by conducting detailed investigations into corporate fraud and financial mismanagement.

2.6. The Digital Age: Forensic Accounting in the 21st Century

The era of digitisation has fundamentally transformed the field of forensic accounting. Forensic accountants had to acquire new skills and tools to investigate digital frauds and cybercrimes(Andreea-Cristina Savu, 2021). D*igital forensics became* essential to forensic accounting investigations, as it recovered and analysed electronic data. In addition to digital forensics, forensic accountants now utilise advanced technologies such as data analytics, artificial intelligence (AI), and machine learning to detect and prevent fraud.

The modern global business landscape has expanded the role of forensic accounting. Forensic accountants are increasingly involved in cross-border investigations, requiring them to navigate complex legal and regulatory environments. They are also actively participating in anti-money laundering (AML) efforts, tracking the movement of illicit funds across international borders and ensuring adherence to global financial regulations.

3. CORPORATE FRAUDS: DEFINITION AND EMERGING THREATS

Corporate fraud encompasses a wide array of illicit actions carried out by individuals or entities to gain financially at the expense of others. In today's financial landscape, corporate fraud has become more intricate and challenging to uncover, owing to advancements in technology and the availability of increasingly complex financial tools (Amit Rohilla, 2024).

Companies with global operations, diverse revenue sources, and digital presence are particularly susceptible to fraudulent activities, especially those involving cybercrime and international transactions. The shift to digital platforms has enabled perpetrators to carry out fraud on a larger scale and with greater anonymity, making it much more difficult to detect, investigate, and prosecute. With the rapid rise of cryptocurrencies and blockchain technologies, fraudsters have found new ways to launder money or engage in illicit transactions without immediate detection by traditional financial oversight mechanisms. (Olatoye et al., 2024) Regulators struggle to keep pace with the expanding risk of fraud, necessitating the implementation of improved forensic accounting and risk management procedures.

Financial Statement frauds involve deliberate misrepresentation of financial information to create a misleading portrayal of a company's financial health (Etim, 2023). It manifests in several ways, including *inflating revenues* by recording fictitious sales or recognizing revenue prematurely, which gives the appearance of enhanced financial performance. Additionally, companies may understate their liabilities by hiding or minimizing their debt obligations, thereby presenting a more favourable financial position. Another common practice involves *improper asset valuations*, where companies overstate the worth of assets like inventory or real estate to strengthen their balance sheets (Bowers, 2023). Furthermore, *manipulating expenses*—such as deferring costs to future periods or capitalizing operating expenses—can create an illusion of greater profitability in the short term. Financial statement fraud poses significant risks as it misleads investors and distorts market perceptions, potentially leading to severe repercussions when the truth is revealed, as exemplified by notorious cases like Enron and WorldCom.

Asset misappropriation is another prevalent form of corporate fraud; it involves the theft or misuse of company resources by employees or insiders (Nakitende et al., 2024). This type of fraud can take various forms, such as the direct *theft of cash*, where individuals may falsify expense reports, make unauthorized withdrawals, or submit fraudulent invoices to steal funds. Additionally, it includes unauthorized use of company assets, where employees might use vehicles, equipment, or intellectual property for personal gain without permission. *Payroll fraud* occurs when individuals manipulate the payroll system to divert funds—this can involve creating fictitious employees or inflating labour hours. Although asset misappropriation may not be as complex as financial statement fraud, it can still result in substantial economic losses for businesses if it goes unchecked.

Corruption schemes entail the misuse of power or authority for personal benefit and are frequently more challenging to detect than other forms of fraud (Maulidi & Ansell, 2021). Conflicts of interest play a significant role in corruption, occurring when individuals engage in business dealings or relationships that prioritize their interests over those of the company. Additionally, bid rigging involves manipulating the bidding process to ensure that a specific party wins a contract, often in return for personal or financial incentives. The insidious nature of corruption often involves collusion among high-ranking executives, making it particularly difficult to identify and prosecute without external intervention. This secrecy can create an environment where unethical practices thrive, ultimately undermining organizational integrity and eroding stakeholder trust.

Corporate fraudsters increasingly employ cyber-based methods to execute their schemes in today's digital financial landscape. One prevalent form of *digital fraud* is *phishing attacks*, where cybercriminals impersonate legitimate organizations to trick employees into revealing sensitive financial information or approving fraudulent transactions. Another significant threat is *ransomware*, in which hackers gain unauthorized access to company systems and demand payment. The shift toward digital transactions, including *online banking and cryptocurrency* use, has broadened opportunities for fraud. Decentralized financial system advancements have presented fresh challenges for forensic accountants and regulators. Deceptive practices where fraudsters initiate *Initial Coin Offering* (ICO) to gather funds for projects that never materialize or are outright scams. Additionally, there are cryptocurrency-based Ponzi schemes, where fraudsters promise hefty returns but utilize funds from new investors to pay off earlier ones, essentially forming a classic Ponzi scheme. Moreover, cryptocurrencies' anonymity makes them an appealing option for money laundering, enabling criminals to transfer illicit funds across borders without detection.

Expanding businesses across international borders leads to increased complexity in detecting fraud. Fraudsters exploit differences in regulatory environments, cultural practices, and legal systems to carry out cross-border fraud, posing challenges for regulators and forensic accountants in their investigation and prosecution efforts (Trehan & Shah, 2024). This can involve *trade-based money laundering* tactics by manipulating international trade invoices to launder money, falsifying the price, quantity, or quality of goods. Companies engaging in *fraudulent transfer pricing schemes* to shift profits to low-tax jurisdictions and reduce their tax liabilities in countries with higher tax rates. Forensic accountants must hone specialized skills and develop tools to navigate this continuously evolving landscape.

4. HIGH-PROFILE CORPORATE SCANDALS: LESSONS AND FAILURES OF TRADITIONAL AUDITING

The three most infamous corporate frauds, Enron, WorldCom, and Lehman Brothers, shook the global financial world. The scandals exposed the shortcomings of traditional auditing and established the need for forensic accounting to uncover fraud and uphold corporate accountability.

4.1. Case Studies of Major Corporate Frauds

In 2001, the *Enron scandal* became one of history's most notorious instances of corporate fraud. Once a highly respected energy and commodities company, Enron utilized a complex network of off-balance-sheet Special Purpose Entities (SPEs) to conceal its growing debt and boost its reported earnings. Enron's executives, in collaboration with their auditing firm, Arthur Andersen, employed deceptive accounting tactics to deceive investors, analysts, and regulators into believing that the company was financially stable. Enron established SPEs to transfer debt off its balance sheet, presenting the company as more profitable and secure than it was. It falsified profits and manipulated its financial records by recording future energy contracts as current revenues. The company's leaders sold their stock for millions while publicly endorsing Enron as a solid investment. Enron's declaration of bankruptcy in December 2001 led to over $60 billion in shareholder losses. Numerous employees lost their jobs and retirement funds. Arthur Andersen, a prominent accounting firm among the "Big Five," was found guilty of obstructing justice and was eventually disbanded ((Bondarenko, 2024) (Palepu & Healy, 2003).

In 2002, *WorldCom*, the second-largest long-distance telecommunications company in the U.S., committed extensive accounting fraud to conceal decreasing revenues and uphold investors' confidence. WorldCom executives inflated the company's earnings by categorising operating expenses as capital expenditures, presenting lower costs and higher profits on their financial statements. WorldCom artificially increased its earnings and decreased its liabilities by misclassifying over $3.8 billion in regular operating expenses as capital expenditures. The company falsely reported billions in profits over several years to conceal its financial challenges. The fraud was exposed in 2002, leading to WorldCom's largest bankruptcy in U.S. history. Investors suffered an estimated loss of $180 billion, and thousands of employees were left unemployed. CEO Bernard Ebbers was sentenced to 25 years for masterminding the fraud (George, 2021) (Auburn University, n.d.).

Lehman Brothers, a worldwide financial services company, played a pivotal role in the 2008 financial crisis by utilising an accounting manoeuvre, Repo *105*. This manoeuvre allowed the company to temporarily eliminate up to $50 billion in debt from its balance sheet at the end of financial reporting periods, presenting the firm as less leveraged and more financially secure than it was. Ultimately, this strategy obscured the firm's risks in the housing market, leading to its downfall. The fraud occurred as Lehman Brothers engaged in Repo 105 transactions, selling assets to a third party committed to repurchasing them shortly after that. The firm characterized these sales as permanent, removing liabilities from its balance sheet to deceive investors about its financial standing. As the subprime mortgage crisis unravelled, Lehman's actual financial exposure became apparent, ultimately resulting in its collapse. The repercussions of Lehman Brothers' bankruptcy were significant, marking the largest in U.S. history with over $600 billion in assets. Its collapse induced widespread panic in the global financial markets, contributing to the 2008 financial crisis. This case underscored the breakdown in regulatory oversight and the intricacies of financial instruments that facilitated fraudulent reporting.

4.2. Why Traditional Audits Failed to Detect Frauds?

In these major scandals, the conventional audits did not uncover the fraudulent activities that led to the companies' collapses. There are several reasons why these audits were inadequate. Relying on Management's Representations was one of the major reasons for failure of traditional audits (Hutchinson et al., 2024). Auditors often heavily depend on a company's management's representations. In the cases of Enron, WorldCom, and Lehman Brothers, senior executives intentionally misled auditors by providing false information to conceal fraudulent activities (Kang, 2024). Traditional auditors typically focus on verifying that financial statements comply with accounting standards rather than investigating the intent behind transactions.

The *limited scope* of traditional audits aims to provide reasonable assurance that financial statements are free from material misstatement, but they are not infallible. Auditors carry out procedures based on materiality thresholds and often do not investigate smaller discrepancies that could lead to uncovering larger fraud schemes. In the case of WorldCom, (Patel, 2024) auditors overlooked the improper classification of billions in operating expenses because these entries were within acceptable limits when considered individually.

In some instances, clear conflicts of interest exist between the auditing firms and the corporations they were auditing. For example, Arthur Andersen had a dual role as auditor and consultant for Enron, creating a situation where the firm may have turned a blind eye to questionable accounting practices to maintain a lucrative business relationship(Buell, 2024).

Traditional auditing practices often lack the depth and tools to uncover complex fraud schemes. Auditors follow standard procedures, but forensic accountants use specialized techniques to trace transactions, identify fraud patterns, and analyze financial data in greater detail. (Henriques et al., 2024) The *lack of forensic tools* is one reason traditional audits failed to detect Enron's use of SPEs and WorldCom's capitalization of operating expenses.

In many cases, the fraud was deliberately designed to bypass standard audit procedures, as fraudsters engaged in *creative accounting*. For example, Enron's use of off-balance-sheet financing and Lehman Brothers' Repo 105 transactions were legal under certain accounting interpretations. Still, they were used in a misleading way to conceal financial problems. Traditional audits *failed to detect the intent* behind these schemes because they focused on compliance with accounting rules, not the ethics or purpose of the transactions.

4.3. Role of Forensic Accounting in Uncovering the Frauds

Forensic accounting is essential in uncovering corporate fraud that traditional audits cannot detect. Following these scandals, forensic accountants were tasked with investigating fraudulent activities and providing evidence for prosecution. Forensic accountants specialize in *tracking transactions to identify fraudulent activities* (Alsadah & Al-Sartawi, 2023). In the WorldCom case, forensic accountants discovered the improper capitalization of operating expenses by thoroughly examining financial records, transactions, and supporting documents. They connected these discrepancies to specific fraudulent activities that traditional audits had missed. Forensic accountants are also skilled at revealing *hidden liabilities* intentionally concealed from auditors. In the case of Enron, forensic accountants investigated the SPEs and uncovered how the company had used these entities to hide debt and inflate earnings. Through detailed financial analysis and the review of off-balance-sheet transactions, they were able to expose the true extent of Enron's fraud. Forensic accountants *utilize advanced analytical techniques*, such as ratio analysis and forensic analytics, to identify patterns of financial manipulation (Matar, 2023). In the Lehman Brothers case, forensic accountants analysed the firm's Repo 105 transactions and identified how they temporarily removed liabilities from the balance sheet. This thorough analysis helped regulators and the public comprehend the scope of the fraud and how it contributed to Lehman's downfall.

The most critical role that forensic accountant play is that the evidence gathered by them is often used in legal proceedings to prosecute corporate executives responsible for fraud. In the case of WorldCom, forensic accounting evidence played a crucial role in the conviction of CEO Bernard Ebbers. Similarly, forensic investigations into Enron and Lehman Brothers contributed to regulatory reforms and increased accountability in the corporate world.

5. FORENSIC ACCOUNTING TECHNIQUES AND TOOLS

Forensic accountants employ various specialized methods and instruments to identify, examine, and deter fraud in the corporate landscape. These instruments enable them to reveal concealed financial manipulations, track suspicious transactions, and offer crucial evidence in legal and regulatory issues. Here is a comprehensive explanation of some crucial forensic accounting methods. From data mining and digital forensics to using AI and traditional ratio analysis, these tools aid forensic accountants in identifying, investigating, and preventing fraud in an increasingly digital and global business environment.

5.1. Data Mining and Analysis of Financial Statements

Data mining in forensic accounting has become crucial, it enables forensic accountants to identify hidden patterns and trends within financial statements (Thomas, 2024), enhancing the effectiveness of traditional audits. Within forensic accounting, several key data mining techniques, such as cluster analysis, are commonly used, which groups data points based on similarities to identify unusual transactions or accounts deviating from established patterns. (Waleed Hilal et al., 2022) *Anomaly detection* focuses on identifying outliers significantly different from the norm, flagging irregular entries such as unusually high expenses or revenues for further investigation. *Predictive modelling* is also crucial in data mining for forensic accounting, allowing forensic accountants to build models based on historical financial data to forecast future trends(Nigrini, 2020). Any significant deviation from these expected patterns may indicate financial manipulation or fraud, raising red flags for further scrutiny. Data mining techniques in forensic accounting enhance the accuracy and efficiency of fraud detection, empowering professionals to make informed decisions based on solid evidence. As the volume and complexity of financial data continue to grow, the importance of data mining as a tool for uncovering fraud cannot be overstated, enabling forensic accountants to navigate through overwhelming amounts of information and pinpoint specific transactions relevant to their investigations. Data mining is essential to modern forensic accounting practices, allowing forensic accountants to identify potential fraud better and protect organisations from financial misconduct by leveraging advanced analytical techniques to extract meaningful insights from large datasets.

5.2. Digital Forensics and Cybersecurity Measures

As digital fraud continues to increase, the role of digital forensics in forensic accounting becomes increasingly significant. It allows forensic accountants to investigate cyberattacks, data breaches, and electronic fraud schemes. This specialised area of forensic science focuses on retrieving and examining digital evidence from electronic devices and systems. (Daraojimba et al., 2023) Within forensic accounting, digital forensics plays a critical role in tracking the movement of electronic funds, revealing fraudulent email communications, and recovering deleted or encrypted files that may contain crucial evidence of fraudulent activity.

Forensic accountants utilize various techniques in digital forensics to enhance their investigations. One significant method is *data recovery*, which involves retrieving deleted or altered files, emails, and financial records using advanced software tools. Another important technique is *network analysis*, where forensic accountants scrutinize network traffic and server logs to trace unauthorized fund transfers, monitor access to sensitive information, and identify malicious activities within corporate networks(Marcella, 2021). Forensic accountants analyse metadata, such as timestamps and authorship information, to gain insights into fraudulent activities. They employ strong cybersecurity measures to investigate fraud and shield organizations from financial misconduct effectively(Krishnan & Shashidhar, 2021). This includes using encryption technologies to safeguard critical financial information from unauthorized access.

5.3. Role of Artificial Intelligence (AI) and Machine Learning in Fraud Detection

Artificial intelligence (AI) and machine learning (ML) are revolutionizing forensic accounting by offering advanced tools for detecting and analysing fraud (Zayed et al., 2024). AI and ML enable forensic accountants to analyse vast amounts of financial data, significantly faster than traditional methods. AI algorithms are excellent at identifying subtle patterns that suggest fraudulent behaviour, such as irregularities in payment amounts, timing, or transaction locations. ML further enhances fraud detection capabilities by allowing models to improve over time as they are exposed to historical data. ML models are particularly effective at uncovering complex fraud schemes like layering, often used in money laundering, and round-tripping, which involves manipulating company transactions to create a false appearance of revenue. Anomaly detection algorithms are a strength of machine learning, as they can identify outliers in financial data that may indicate fraud. Unlike traditional rule-based systems that rely on predefined criteria, ML algorithms learn to recognize new fraud patterns as they emerge. Additionally, predictive analytics enables these models to predict future fraud risks based on past behaviours, allowing for proactive measures against potential fraud. By using real-time analysis and advanced pattern recognition techniques, these technologies provide a strong defence against fraudulent practices (Olufemi et al., 2024).

5.4. Forensic Accounting and Traditional Techniques

Forensic accountants use traditional ratios analysis and forensic analytics methods to uncover and examine fraud (Colleen Honigsberg, 2020). These tools are crucial for spotting financial inconsistencies and gaining deeper insights into a company's financial well-being. Ratio analysis involves comparing different financial ratios, such as profit margins and debt-to-equity ratios, with industry benchmarks or past performance. Significant deviations from these standards can indicate potential fraud, mismanagement, or financial manipulation. For example, an unusually high debt-to-equity ratio may suggest that a company is exaggerating its equity or downplaying its debt. (Verma & Singh, 2024) Forensic analytics combines data analysis with investigative techniques to reveal suspicious transactions, financial irregularities, or hidden patterns. One common method is *regression analysis*, which helps forensic accountants identify connections between variables (Rifani & Hasan, 2022). This technique can be especially useful in uncovering fraudulent activities such as revenue manipulation by linking revenue figures with sales volume or customer data. Another valuable statistical technique is *Benford's Law,* which predicts the frequency distribution of digits in naturally occurring datasets. Divergences from this expected distribution can point to potential fabrication of numbers in financial statements. Additionally, forensic accountants utilize various other tools to enhance their investigations. *Data visualization* tools enable them to visually represent financial data, making identifying trends and anomalies indicative of fraud easier. Furthermore, *text analytics* is employed to analyse text data from emails, contracts, and legal documents for keywords or patterns that may hint at fraudulent activity. By integrating ratios analysis and forensic analytics, forensic accountants are equipped with the tools to detect and investigate fraud effectively. Through the use of these methods, they can uncover financial irregularities and safeguard organizations from potential misconduct.

6. ORGANIZATIONAL ROLE OF FORENSIC ACCOUNTANTS

Forensic accountants play an increasingly crucial role within corporate structures, especially in corporate governance, finance teams, fraud detection, compliance, and risk management. Their responsibilities extend beyond post-fraud investigations to fraud prevention, regulatory compliance, and guidance on sound financial practices. Forensic accountants aid organizations in protecting their financial well-being and reputation, ensuring transparent and manipulation-free financial reporting and operations.

6.1. Integration Of Forensic Accountants in Corporate Governance and Finance Team

The role of forensic accountants extends beyond investigating financial crimes, they actively participate in shaping corporate governance policies and offering financial management advice. Forensic accountants assist organizations in establishing robust internal controls and governance frameworks to reduce fraud risk. They provide valuable guidance to boards of directors, audit committees, and senior management, fostering a culture of accountability, transparency, and ethical financial practices (Lupo, 2023). Their specialized knowledge ensures the accuracy of financial reporting processes and compliance with industry regulations while promoting ethical behaviour throughout the organization. Moreover, forensic accountants are instrumental in developing anti-fraud policies, whistleblower mechanisms, and ethical guidelines. They oversee financial transactions to identify potential fraud risks and contribute to internal audits and financial reviews, ensuring alignment with corporate governance principles and the integrity of financial statements. Forensic accountants enhance financial transparency and manage risks effectively. They engage in critical decision-making processes related to budgeting, investments, mergers, and acquisitions, providing insights into the financial implications of strategic decisions based on reliable data. Additionally, forensic accountants evaluate the effectiveness of internal controls to pinpoint vulnerabilities that could be exploited for fraudulent activities (Abubaker et al., 2022). They recommend improvements to financial procedures and controls to minimize opportunities for manipulation—their involvement in fraud detection, compliance, and risk management.

6.2. Role of Forensic Accountant in Fraud Detection, Compliance, and Risk Management

Forensic accountants are crucial in uncovering fraud, ensuring organizations adhere to legal and regulatory requirements, and managing financial risks(Aksoy & Uzay, 2021). Their in-depth knowledge of financial systems, regulations, and corporate finance is essential for upholding the honesty of financial operations. When spotting fraud, forensic accountants are responsible for pinpointing and examining fraudulent activities within companies. They utilize advanced methodologies such as data analytics, ratio analysis, and forensic software to scrutinize financial statements, track transactions, and identify irregularities. Corporate finance frequently scrutinises significant transactions, particularly those related to mergers, acquisitions, and large capital investments, where the risk of fraud is elevated (Polina et al., 2024). Forensic accountants undertake forensic audits in cases of suspected fraud to ascertain the extent of the misconduct. This involves analysing financial records, interviewing employees, and collecting evidence that can be used in internal investigations or legal proceedings. They also take a proactive approach to fraud detection by conducting risk assessments, monitoring for warning signs, and implementing automated systems that can identify unusual transactions or behaviours in real-time. A forensic accountant's role is ensuring compliance with industry regulations and corporate governance standards. This encompasses adhering to financial regulations such as the Sarbanes-Oxley Act (SOX) and International Financial Reporting Standards (IFRS), which oversee financial transparency and ethical practices (Efunniyi et al., 2024). Forensic accountants conduct compliance audits to verify that companies meet all relevant financial and legal requirements. These audits are vital for preventing financial misconduct and regulatory violations that could lead to fines or legal action. Moreover, forensic accountants evaluate vulnerabilities within an organization’s financial systems and propose measures to mitigate fraud risks. By identifying potential threats—such as insufficient internal controls or cybersecurity weaknesses—they assist organizations in protecting against future financial losses. In conclusion, forensic accountants have a multifaceted role in ensuring precise financial reporting and compliance while actively working to uncover and prevent fraud within organizations. Their expertise is invaluable in maintaining the integrity of financial operations and shielding companies from potential misconduct.

6.3. Collaboration With Legal Teams, Auditors, And Regulators

Forensic accountants are crucial in teaming up with legal professionals, auditors, and regulators to probe, identify, and prevent corporate fraud. Their diverse expertise allows them to connect finance, law, and compliance, ensuring effective handling of fraud at every stage. Forensic accountants closely work with legal teams to present financial evidence that holds up in court when it comes to fraud investigations or legal disputes(Chisty & Ahmmed, 2023). They play a key role in fraud investigations, providing insights into the financial aspects of cases, calculating damages, and preparing *expert testimony*. Forensic accountants compile detailed financial reports and analyses that legal teams utilize to construct their arguments. For example, in embezzlement cases, they track the flow of funds to support theft claims. Forensic accountants often act as expert witnesses in fraud cases, explaining intricate financial data and offering professional opinions on fraudulent activities and related financial losses. While auditors primarily focus on verifying the accuracy of financial statements, forensic accountants are dedicated to investigating and identifying instances of fraud. These roles complement each other, with forensic accountants frequently collaborating with auditors to address discrepancies or suspicious activities during routine audits. They aid external auditors by conducting thorough analyses when standard audits reveal irregularities. This investigative expertise is crucial in determining whether fraud has occurred and helps auditors grasp the financial implications of their findings. Forensic accountants also collaborate with internal auditors to strengthen fraud prevention measures within organizations. By sharing insights and data, they enhance auditors' capabilities to detect fraud at an early stage. (Ramolobe et al., 2023) *Regulatory bodies* such as the Securities and Exchange Commission (SEC), the Financial Industry Regulatory Authority (FINRA), or national tax authorities often enlist forensic accountants' help in investigations related to corporate fraud or regulatory violations. Their proficiency in tracing complex financial transactions, analysing data, and uncovering fraudulent schemes makes them valuable partners for regulators enforcing financial laws. In collaboration with regulatory agencies, forensic accountants investigate various forms of financial misconduct, including insider trading, market manipulation, and accounting fraud. They analyse corporate financial records and trace illicit transactions while aiding in prosecuting regulatory violations. Additionally, forensic accountants help companies prepare for *regulatory inspections* and maintain compliance with industry standards. This proactive approach enables organizations to avoid penalties while ensuring good standing with regulators. In summary, forensic accountants are essential collaborators in the fight against corporate fraud, providing critical expertise across various sectors to ensure accountability and compliance.

7. INTERNATIONAL DIMENSION OF FORENSIC ACCOUNTING

Forensic accounting has gained prominence globally as businesses expand across borders and financial crimes become increasingly sophisticated. This international dimension is characterized by varying practices, regulatory frameworks, and challenges those forensic accountants face in different jurisdictions.

7.1. Forensic Accounting in Different Global Jurisdictions

Forensic accounting practices vary significantly across countries due to differences in legal systems, cultural attitudes towards fraud, and regulatory environments. In the *United States*, for instance, the Sarbanes-Oxley Act of 2002 established stringent regulations to improve corporate governance and accountability following scandals like Enron (Solomon, 2020). Forensic accountants in the U.S. are often involved in compliance audits and fraud investigations, utilizing advanced techniques such as data analytics and digital forensics. In contrast, countries like *India* are rapidly developing their forensic accounting capabilities. The Indian government has recognized the importance of forensic accounting in combating financial fraud, particularly within its banking sector (Gangwani, 2020). Recent studies highlight the growing use of forensic accounting techniques to detect fraudulent activities in Indian banks, reflecting a shift towards more rigorous financial oversight. *China* is another country where forensic accounting is gaining traction. With its burgeoning economy and increasing instances of corporate fraud, China has invested heavily in forensic accounting education and practice (Ellili et al., 2024). A recent analysis indicated that China leads in research output related to data analytics in forensic accounting, emphasizing its commitment to enhancing fraud detection capabilities. *South Africa* also presents a unique case where forensic accounting plays a crucial role in corporate governance (Rehman & Hashim, 2021). The country's history of corruption scandals has led to increased scrutiny of financial practices, prompting organizations to adopt forensic accounting measures to ensure transparency and accountability.

7.2. Regulatory Frameworks and International Standards

The International Federation of Accountants (IFAC) is instrumental in standardizing forensic accounting practices globally, ensuring uniform standards of accuracy, transparency, and reliability in forensic investigations across different jurisdictions. Forensic accountants frequently conduct cross-border investigations into financial crimes like money laundering, tax evasion, and fraud involving multinational corporations, highlighting the necessity of global consistency in practices for credible and admissible findings in courts worldwide. (Shbeilat & Alqatamin, 2022) International bodies such as the *Financial Action Task Force (FATF)* influence how forensic accountants approach specific financial crimes by setting global standards to combat money laundering and terrorist financing. These standards are adopted by member countries, necessitating that forensic accountants align their investigative techniques with FATF's requirements when operating within these jurisdictions. Compliance with FATF's guidelines promotes increased cooperation between nations in identifying, investigating, and prosecuting financial crimes, facilitating more effective collaboration among forensic accountants on cases involving cross-border transactions. Global cooperation is crucial in today's interconnected financial environment as financial crimes often span multiple countries, currencies, and regulations. By adhering to international standards established by organizations like IFAC and FATF, forensic accountants not only uphold the accuracy and integrity of their investigations but also contribute to a unified effort in combating financial crime on a global scale. This commitment fosters international trust and enables more coordinated investigations across jurisdictions.

7.3. Cross-Border Corporate Frauds and Challenges for Forensic Accountants

Corporate fraud that crosses national borders presents unique challenges for forensic accountants, primarily due to differing legal systems, data privacy regulations, and financial reporting standards. For instance, European regulations like the General Data Protection Regulation (GDPR) can hinder investigations requiring vital information access. To combat cross-border fraud effectively, forensic accountants must collaborate closely with international regulatory bodies, governmental agencies, and law enforcement organizations (Florea & Florea, 2023). Such cooperation is essential for tracking fraudulent activities that span multiple jurisdictions.

Recent high-profile cases of corporate fraud have highlighted the necessity of this collaboration. Investigating multinational corporations often requires coordination among national agencies to compile evidence from diverse legal frameworks. Additionally, advancements in technology are aiding these collaborative efforts. For example, blockchain technology provides transparent transaction records that can be accessed internationally, significantly improving the ability to trace fraudulent activities. Furthermore, big data analytics empowers forensic accountants to analyse extensive datasets from various jurisdictions concurrently, enhancing their capacity to identify patterns indicative of fraud. The international dimension of forensic accounting involves a complex interaction of jurisdictional differences, evolving regulatory environments, and the essential need for cross-border cooperation. As globalization continues to shape corporate operations, forensic accountants must adapt their methodologies to effectively tackle the challenges posed by international fraud while utilizing emerging technologies to strengthen their investigative capabilities.

8. EMERGING TECHNOLOGIES SHAPING THE FUTURE OF FORENSIC ACCOUNTING AND CORPORATE FINANCE

Emerging technologies such as blockchain, big data, and artificial intelligence (AI) are significantly influencing the future of forensic accounting in corporate finance. These advancements are reshaping the landscape of financial investigations and enhancing the capabilities of forensic accountants in detecting, preventing, and managing fraud and financial misconduct.

Blockchain technology is revolutionizing the way transactions are recorded and verified. It provides a decentralized, secure, transparent, and immutable ledger that can be accessed by authorized parties (Tanwar, 2022). This characteristic makes it increasingly difficult for fraudsters to manipulate financial data. For example, companies like *Everledge*r use blockchain to track the provenance of high-value assets like diamonds. In corporate finance, blockchain can be applied to create transparent audit trails for transactions, making it easier for forensic accountants to identify discrepancies or fraudulent activities. Additionally, organizations like *IBM and Microsoft* have developed blockchain solutions tailored for supply chain management and financial transactions. These solutions enhance transparency and accountability, allowing forensic accountants to perform more thorough investigations with reliable data.

The explosion of *big data* presents both challenges and opportunities for forensic accountants. With vast amounts of financial data generated daily, traditional analysis methods may fall short in identifying fraudulent patterns. Big data analytics tools enable forensic accountants to quickly and efficiently analyse large datasets. *Deloitte* has integrated big data analytics into its forensic accounting practices (Chien, 2020). This capability allows them to detect suspicious activities in real time rather than relying solely on historical audits. Moreover, big data analytics can help forensic accountants identify trends over time. For example, if a company experiences sudden expense spikes or unusual revenue recognition patterns across different departments, these insights can trigger further investigation into potentially fraudulent activities.

Artificial Intelligence transforms fraud detection by offering sophisticated tools to recognise complex patterns indicative of fraudulent behaviour. Machine learning algorithms can analyse historical data to identify trends and predict future fraudulent activities. *KPMG* has developed AI-driven tools that enhance its fraud detection capabilities. These tools analyse real-time transaction data to flag suspicious activities based on learned patterns from previous fraud cases (Antwi et al., 2024). AI can also automate routine tasks such as data entry and preliminary analysis, allowing forensic accountants to focus on more complex investigative work. This increased efficiency speeds up the investigation process and reduces the likelihood of human error.

8.1. Anticipated Developments in Forensic Methodologies

As technology advances, future developments in forensic accounting methodologies will likely emphasize proactive fraud prevention strategies. Forensic accountants will increasingly leverage real-time data analytics and predictive modelling to identify risks before they escalate into significant issues.

For instance, *predictive analytics* can help organizations forecast potential fraud risks based on historical behaviour patterns (Javaid, 2024). By analysing past incidents of fraud within an organization or industry, forensic accountants can develop models that highlight areas of vulnerability. This proactive approach enables businesses to implement preventive measures before fraudulent activities occur.

Integrating advanced technologies such as *quantum computing* could further enhance the capabilities of forensic accounting. Quantum computing has the potential to process vast amounts of data at unprecedented speeds, allowing for more complex analyses that could uncover hidden patterns indicative of fraud.

Additionally, *enhanced encryption techniques* will be crucial in securing sensitive financial information during investigations. As cyber threats evolve, ensuring the confidentiality and integrity of economic data will be paramount for forensic accountants.

8.2. Role of Forensic Accountants in the Future Financial Landscape

As corporate fraud becomes more sophisticated and pervasive, the role of forensic accountants will expand beyond traditional fraud detection into broader areas such as corporate risk management, compliance, and governance (Lupo, 2023). Their expertise in analysing complex financial data and uncovering hidden risks will be indispensable in navigating an increasingly intricate global economic landscape. For example, after high-profile scandals like *Wirecard*, regulatory scrutiny has intensified across industries. Forensic accountants will ensure compliance with evolving regulations such as the Sarbanes-Oxley Act (SOX) and International Financial Reporting Standards (IFRS) (Bassey et al., 2020). Their ability to provide insights into financial integrity will help organizations mitigate risks associated with financial misconduct. Furthermore, as companies face increasing pressure from stakeholders for transparency and ethical conduct, forensic accountants will play a key role in fostering a culture of accountability within organizations. They will assist in developing robust internal controls and governance frameworks that minimize the risk of fraud while ensuring compliance with industry standards.

The future of forensic accounting is poised for transformation by adopting emerging technologies and advanced methodologies. As these tools become integral to their practice, forensic accountants will play a critical role in safeguarding corporate finance against fraud while promoting transparency and accountability within organizations.

9. CONCLUSION

In today's increasingly complex financial landscape, forensic accounting has emerged as an indispensable tool in the fight against corporate fraud. This chapter has provided an in-depth analysis of how forensic accounting plays a vital role in detecting, investigating, and preventing financial misconduct, highlighting its evolution and importance in modern corporate governance. As businesses continue to grow in size and complexity and operate across diverse regulatory environments, the role of forensic accountants has expanded beyond traditional fraud detection. Today, forensic accounting also encompasses broader areas of risk management, compliance, and corporate governance, making it a critical element in the financial health and ethical conduct of organizations.

The evolution of forensic accounting can be traced to a growing recognition of the need for specialized expertise in addressing financial fraud, particularly in the wake of major corporate scandals that have shaken public trust in businesses. Scandals such as Enron and WorldCom in the United States exposed significant gaps in corporate governance and the oversight of financial reporting, leading to reforms such as the Sarbanes-Oxley Act (SOX), which imposed stricter regulatory standards on financial practices. Forensic accounting, with its blend of accounting, auditing, and investigative skills, has thus become a frontline defence against corporate fraud.

This chapter has explored the key methodologies and techniques that forensic accountants employ, including data mining, digital forensics, and advanced analytics. These tools have proven invaluable in the ability to sift through vast amounts of financial data, identify irregularities, and provide concrete evidence in legal investigations. Forensic accountants no longer rely solely on traditional methods of auditing but increasingly use cutting-edge technologies to stay ahead of evolving fraud schemes.

The global aspect of forensic accounting has also been a significant focus in this chapter. Corporate fraud often transcends national borders, particularly as companies expand their operations across various jurisdictions. This presents unique challenges for forensic accountants who must navigate different regulatory frameworks and legal systems. For example, the rigorous standards imposed by the Sarbanes-Oxley Act in the United States contrast with the developing practices in countries such as India and China, where the need for stronger financial oversight is becoming increasingly recognized. Cultural attitudes toward fraud, as well as varying levels of regulatory enforcement, can significantly influence the effectiveness of forensic accounting practices in different regions.

This chapter has emphasized the importance of international collaboration and the adherence to global standards set by organizations such as the International Federation of Accountants (IFAC) and the Financial Action Task Force (FATF). These bodies help establish a foundation for standardizing forensic accounting practices, making it easier to conduct cross-border investigations and hold fraudsters accountable, regardless of jurisdiction. In an era of increasing globalization, the need for forensic accountants to work together across borders and align with international best practices is more critical than ever.

One of the most transformative factors shaping the future of forensic accounting is the adoption of emerging technologies. Blockchain, big data analytics, and artificial intelligence (AI) are revolutionizing how forensic accountants detect and prevent fraud. Blockchain, for instance, offers a decentralized and immutable ledger that enhances the transparency and reliability of financial transactions. Its potential to prevent tampering with financial records is particularly valuable in environments where trust in financial reporting is paramount. Meanwhile, big data analytics enables forensic accountants to process large datasets efficiently, allowing for the real-time detection of unusual patterns and behaviors that may indicate fraud. AI, through machine learning algorithms, adds another layer of sophistication, enabling forensic accountants to identify complex behavioral patterns that could go unnoticed with traditional methods.

The integration of these technologies is reshaping the landscape of forensic accounting, allowing professionals to adopt a more proactive approach to fraud prevention. Rather than merely reacting to fraud after it has occurred, forensic accountants are increasingly using predictive analytics and data-driven insights to identify potential risks before they escalate into serious issues. This shift toward proactive fraud prevention is critical as financial crimes grow more sophisticated, often exploiting technological vulnerabilities.

As forensic accounting practices continue to evolve, it is essential for organizations to strengthen their defenses against financial misconduct by investing in several key areas. First and foremost, organizations must prioritize the adoption of advanced technologies. By investing in tools like big data analytics, AI, and blockchain, companies can enhance their ability to detect fraudulent activities early and reduce the risk of financial losses. These technologies not only improve the efficiency of forensic investigations but also offer valuable insights that can help organizations identify trends and vulnerabilities in their financial systems.

Continuous training and professional development for forensic accountants is another crucial area of investment. Financial fraud schemes are constantly evolving, and it is imperative that forensic accountants remain up to date with the latest trends, techniques, and technologies. Organizations should establish ongoing learning programs that equip their forensic teams with the skills and knowledge necessary to address emerging fraud risks effectively. This investment in human capital ensures that forensic practices remain relevant and effective in a rapidly changing financial landscape.

Moreover, the establishment of robust internal controls is vital for reducing the risk of fraud within organizations. Forensic accountants should play an active role in designing and implementing these controls to ensure that they meet industry standards and best practices. Regular evaluations and updates of internal controls are necessary to address new vulnerabilities that may arise as businesses grow and evolve. By involving forensic accountants in the development of internal control systems, organizations can create a stronger framework for fraud prevention.

Promoting a culture of transparency and accountability is also key to preventing corporate fraud. Organizations must foster an environment where ethical conduct is valued and encouraged at all levels. Regular reporting on financial practices, fraud prevention measures, and compliance efforts can help build stakeholder trust and demonstrate a commitment to integrity. Whistleblower programs and open communication channels are effective initiatives that empower employees to report suspicious activities without fear of retaliation, further strengthening the organization's defenses against fraud.

International cooperation remains a cornerstone of effective forensic accounting in today's globalized economy. Organizations must work closely with international bodies such as the IFAC and FATF to align their practices with global standards. This collaboration not only facilitates cross-border investigations but also helps organizations stay ahead of the evolving tactics employed by fraudsters in different regions. By promoting international cooperation, forensic accountants can pool their expertise and resources to combat fraud on a global scale.

In conclusion, forensic accounting is set to undergo significant transformation as emerging technologies and advanced methodologies reshape the field. Organizations that invest in these technologies, prioritize continuous training, and strengthen their internal controls will be better equipped to detect and prevent financial misconduct. The future of forensic accounting lies in a proactive, data-driven approach that not only responds to fraud but anticipates and mitigates risks before they materialize. By embracing these advancements and fostering a culture of accountability, organizations can protect their financial integrity, build stakeholder trust, and navigate the evolving challenges of corporate governance in an increasingly complex global marketplace

REFERENCES

Abubaker, Z., Barzinji, Q., Wan, S., Wan sallha, Y., Sofian, M., Rosbi, B., Fairuz, M., Md Salleh, M. F., Abdullah, A., & Barzinji, Z. (2022). *International Journal of Economics, Commerce and Management United Kingdom Licensed under Creative Common THE EFFECT OF FORENSIC ACCOUNTING ON FRAUD PREVENTION, THE MODERATING ROLE INTERNAL CONTROL EFFECTIVENESS.*

Ajayi-Nifise, A. O., Olubusola, O., Falaiye, T., Mhlongo, N. Z., & Daraojimba, A. I. (2024). A REVIEW OF U.S. FINANCIAL REPORTING SCANDALS AND THEIR ECONOMIC REPERCUSSIONS: INVESTIGATING THEIR BROADER IMPACT AND PREVENTATIVE MEASURES. *Finance & Accounting Research Journal*, *6*(2), 2. Advance online publication. DOI: 10.51594/farj.v6i2.787

Aksoy, T., & Uzay, S. (2021). Relationship Between Fraud Auditing and Forensic Accounting. In Aksoy, T., & Hacioglu, U. (Eds.), *Auditing Ecosystem and Strategic Accounting in the Digital Era: Global Approaches and New Opportunities* (pp. 127–146). Springer International Publishing., DOI: 10.1007/978-3-030-72628-7_6

Alhusban, A., Alhusban, A., Haloush, H., Alshurafat, H., Al-Msiedeen, J., Abdel, A., Massadeh, A., & Alhmoud, R. (2020). THE REGULATORY STRUCTURE AND GOVERNANCE OF FORENSIC ACCOUNTANCY IN THE EMERGING MARKET: CHALLENGES AND OPPORTUNITIES. *Journal of Governance and Regulation (Print)*, *9*(4), 149–161. DOI: 10.22495/jgrv9i4art13

Alsadah, N., & Al-Sartawi, A. (2023). Forensic Accounting and Cybersecurity: A Literature Review Paper. In Hannoon, A., & Mahmood, A. (Eds.), *Artificial Intelligence, Internet of Things, and Society 5.0* (pp. 235–244). Springer Nature Switzerland., DOI: 10.1007/978-3-031-43300-9_20

Alzoubi, A. B. (2023). Maximizing internal control effectiveness: The synergy between forensic accounting and corporate governance. *Journal of Financial Reporting and Accounting, ahead-of-print*(ahead-of-print). DOI: 10.1108/JFRA-03-2023-0140

Antwi, B. O., Adelakun, B. O., Fatogun, D. T., & Olaiya, O. P.Bernard Owusu AntwiBeatrice Oyinkansola AdelakunDamilola Temitayo FatogunOmolara Patricia Olaiya. (2024). Enhancing audit accuracy: The role of AI in detecting financial anomalies and fraud. *Finance & Accounting Research Journal*, *6*(6), 6. Advance online publication. DOI: 10.51594/farj.v6i6.1235

Auburn University. (n.d.). *Center for Ethical Organizational Cultures*. Retrieved from https://harbert.auburn.edu/binaries/documents/center-for-ethical-organizational-cultures/cases/worldcom.pdf

Awolowo, I. (2019). *Financial Statement Fraud: The Need for a Paradigm Shift to Forensic Accounting - ProQuest*. https://www.proquest.com/openview/5543881754fa01cc976e6fae09fb2d8c/1?pq-origsite=gscholar&cbl=51922&diss=y

Bassey, B., Efiong, E., Efiong, J., & Inyang, W., Ashishie, Uklala, P., Ahaneku, R., Nnamdi, R., Igboke, & Patrick, S. (2020). Recent Relevant Legislations for the Regulation of Audit and Accounting Practices in Nigeria. *Test Engineering and Management*, *83*, 27257–27265.

Bondarenko, P. (2024, July 9). Retrieved from Encyclopedia Britannica: https://www.britannica.com/event/Enron-scandal/Downfall-and-bankruptcy

Bowers, S. L. (2023). *Accounting and Corporate Finance For Lawyers*. Aspen Publishing.

Buell, S. W. (2024). *The Limits of Individual Prosecutions in Deterring Corporate Fraud* (SSRN Scholarly Paper 4733141). https://papers.ssrn.com/abstract=4733141

Chien, H.-Y. (2020). Use of Business Analytics in Accounting Firms—Taking Deloitte as an Example. *E3S Web of Conferences, 218*, 03004. DOI: 10.1051/e3sconf/202021803004

Chisty, N., & Ahmmed, S. (2023). The Silent Detectives: Forensic Accountants and Their Battle against Financial Crime. *Asian Accounting and Auditing Advancement*, *14*, 21–30.

Daraojimba, R. E., Farayola, O. A., Olatoye, F. O., Mhlongo, N., & Oke, T. T. (2023). FORENSIC ACCOUNTING IN THE DIGITAL AGE: A U.S. PERSPECTIVE: SCRUTINIZING METHODS AND CHALLENGES IN DIGITAL FINANCIAL FRAUD PREVENTION. *Finance & Accounting Research Journal*, *5*(11), 11. Advance online publication. DOI: 10.51594/farj.v5i11.614

Davies, H., & Green, D. (2013). *Global Financial Regulation: The Essential Guide (Now with a Revised Introduction)*. John Wiley & Sons.

De Bellis, M. (2013). Global Financial Standards and Networks: The Global Administrative Law Perspective. *Revista de Derecho Público*, 1–28. DOI: 10.15425/redepub.30.2013.02

Efunniyi, A., Obiki-Osafiele, Agu, Adeniran, P., & Abhulimen, A. (2024). *1597-1616 4 Nigeria Inter-bank Settlement System Plc (NIBSS) 5 Zenith General Insurance Company Limited, Nigeria 6 International Association of Computer Analysts and Researchers*. DOI: 10.51594/farj.v6i8.1509

Ellili, N., Nobanee, H., Haddad, A., Alodat, A. Y., & AlShalloudi, M. (2024). Emerging trends in forensic accounting research: Bridging research gaps and prioritizing new frontiers. *Journal of Economic Criminology*, *4*, 100065. DOI: 10.1016/j.jeconc.2024.100065

Enofe, A. O., Okpako, P. O., & Atube, E. N. (2013). The Impact of Forensic Accounting on Fraud Detection. *European Journal of Business and Management*.

Etim, U. (2023). Accounting Ratios and False Financial Statements Detection. *Evidence from Nigerian Quoted Companies.*, *3*, 61–75.

Florea, R., & Florea, R. (2023, July 1). *Forensic Accounting—Key Tool in Detecting and Preventing Fraud and Financial Crimes. | EBSCOhost*. https://openurl.ebsco.com/contentitem/gcd:174676915?sid=ebsco:plink:crawler&id=ebsco:gcd:174676915

Gangwani, M. (2020). Suitability of forensic accounting in uncovering bank frauds in India: An opinion survey. *Journal of Financial Crime*, *28*(1), 284–299. DOI: 10.1108/JFC-07-2020-0126

George, B. (2021). *Fraudulent Accounting and the Downfall of WorldCom.* University of Carolina.

Gulapalli, E. K., Morand, C. L., & Wolski, G. E. (2017). Merger and Acquisition Transaction Disputes. In *Litigation Services Handbook* (pp. 1–35). John Wiley & Sons, Ltd., DOI: 10.1002/9781119363194.ch24

Henriques, J., Caldeira, F., Cruz, T., & Simões, P. (2024). A Survey on Forensics and Compliance Auditing for Critical Infrastructure Protection. *IEEE Access, 12*, 2409–2444. IEEE Access. DOI: 10.1109/ACCESS.2023.3348552

Honigsberg, C. (2020). *Forensic Accounting | Annual Reviews.* https://www.annualreviews.org/content/journals/10.1146/annurev-lawsocsci-020320-022159

Hossain, M. Z. (2023). *Emerging Trends in Forensic Accounting: Data Analytics, Cyber Forensic Accounting, Cryptocurrencies, and Blockchain Technology for Fraud Investigation and Prevention* (SSRN Scholarly Paper 4450488). DOI: 10.2139/ssrn.4450488

Hutchinson, B., Dekker, S., & Rae, A. (2024). How audits fail according to accident investigations: A counterfactual logic analysis. *Process Safety Progress*, *43*(3), 441–454. DOI: 10.1002/prs.12579

Izedonmi, F., & Ibadin, P. O. (2012). Forensic Accounting and Financial Crimes: Adopting the Inference, Relevance and Logic Solution Approach. *African Research Review*, *6*(4), 4. Advance online publication. DOI: 10.4314/afrrev.v6i4.9

Javaid, H. A. (2024). Improving Fraud Detection and Risk Assessment in Financial Service using Predictive Analytics and Data Mining. *Integrated Journal of Science and Technology, 1*(8). https://ijstindex.com/index.php/ijst/article/view/63

Kang, G. (Grace). (2024, April 1). *We Learn from History: Earnings Management and Business Scandals in the Early of 2000s. | EBSCOhost.* DOI: 10.31966/jabminternational.v31i1.945

Karabayır, M. (2019). *Forensic Accounting: Development and Practices Around the World* (pp. 47–62).

Kranacher, M.-J., & Riley, R. (2019). *Forensic Accounting and Fraud Examination*. John Wiley & Sons.

Krishnan, S., & Shashidhar, N. (2021). *Interplay of Digital Forensics in eDiscovery*.

Lupo, M. F. (2023). *The Importance and Evolution of Forensic Accounting* [Doctoral Thesis, Universita degli studi di Salerno]. http://elea.unisa.it/xmlui/handle/10556/7266

Marcella, A. J. (2021). *Cyber Forensics: Examining Emerging and Hybrid Technologies*. CRC Press. DOI: 10.1201/9781003057888

Matar, D. O. (2023). The role of forensic accounting strategies in reducing financial and administrative corruption cases. *American Academic & Scholarly Research Journal, 14*(3), Article 3. https://aasrc.org/aasrj/index.php/aasrj/article/view/2198

Maulidi, A., & Ansell, J. (2021). Tackling practical issues in fraud control: A practice-based study. *Journal of Financial Crime, 28*(2), 493–512. DOI: 10.1108/JFC-07-2020-0150

Nakitende, M. G., Rafay, A., & Waseem, M. (2024). Frauds in Business Organizations: A Comprehensive Overview. In *Research Anthology on Business Law, Policy, and Social Responsibility* (pp. 848–865). IGI Global. DOI: 10.4018/979-8-3693-2045-7.ch045

Nigrini, M. J. (2020). *Forensic Analytics: Methods and Techniques for Forensic Accounting Investigations*. John Wiley & Sons.

Olatoye, A. O., Ojeyinka, A. G., Adenuga, O., Olusola, T. A., & Egho, E. (2024). MANAGER USAGE OF FORENSIC ACCOUNTING AND FRAUD DETECTION IN LAGOS STATE. *SAPIENTIA FOUNDATION JOURNAL OF EDUCATION, SCIENCES AND GENDER STUDIES, 6*(1), Article 1. http://www.sfjesgs.com/index.php/SFJESGS/article/view/505

Olufemi, B., Bello, O., Olufemi, K., & Author, C. (2024). *Artificial intelligence in fraud prevention: Exploring techniques and applications challenges and opportunities. 5*, 1505–1520. DOI: 10.51594/csitrj.v5i6.1252

Orlandi, A. (2021). The emergence of double-entry bookkeeping in Tuscan firms of the thirteenth and fourteenth centuries. *Accounting History*, *26*(4), 534–551. DOI: 10.1177/10323732211032298

Özkul, F. U., & Pamukçu, A. (2012). Fraud Detection and Forensic Accounting. In Çaliyurt, K., & Idowu, S. O. (Eds.), *Emerging Fraud: Fraud Cases from Emerging Economies* (pp. 19–41). Springer., DOI: 10.1007/978-3-642-20826-3_2

Palepu, K., & Healy, P. (2003). The Fall of Enron. *The Journal of Economic Perspectives*, •••, 3–26.

Patel, N. (2024). Auditor Independence: Moving toward Harmonization or Simplication? *Southern California Law Review*, *97*, 495.

Polina, S., Taukebay, S., & Gaukhar, S. (2024). *Window Dressing and Misleading of Investors Based on Lehman Brothers Case*. Analysis From Different Perspectives.

Ramolobe, K., Pillay, S., & Ngcamu, B. (2023). *Towards an Inclusive Society: Promoting Disability Inclusion in Local Government Municipalities*.

Rehman, A., & Hashim, F. (2021). Can forensic accounting impact sustainable corporate governance? *Corporate Governance (Bradford)*, *21*(1), 212–227. DOI: 10.1108/CG-06-2020-0269

Rifani, R. A., & Hasan, H. (2022). Disclosure of Fraud Through Forensic Accounting, Audit Investigation and Auditor Professionalism. *Jurnal Economic Resource*, *5*(2), 2. Advance online publication. DOI: 10.57178/jer.v5i2.364

Rohilla, A. (2024). Strengthening Financial Resilience: A Holistic Approach to Combatting Fraud. *Indian Journal of Economics and Finance*, *4*(1), 20–23. DOI: 10.54105/ijef.A2566.04010524

Roszkowska, P. (2021). Fintech in financial reporting and audit for fraud prevention and safeguarding equity investments. *Journal of Accounting & Organizational Change*, *17*(2), 164–196. DOI: 10.1108/JAOC-09-2019-0098

Roy, A. Chandler. (2016). *Questions of ethics and etiquette in the Society of Accountants in Edinburgh, 1853–1951—Roy A Chandler, 2017*. https://journals.sagepub.com/doi/abs/10.1177/1032373216675912

Savu, A.-C., & Bolcu, L. D. (2021). Implementation of judicial accounting expertise in the digital context. *Revista de Studii Financiare*, *6*(11), 109–121. DOI: 10.55654/JFS.2021.6.11.08

Shbeilat, M., & Alqatamin, R. (2022). Challenges and forward-looking roles of forensic accounting in combating money laundering: Evidence from the developing market. *Journal of Governance and Regulation*, *11*(3), 103–120. DOI: 10.22495/jgrv11i3art10

Solomon, J. (2020). *Corporate Governance and Accountability*. John Wiley & Sons.

Tanwar, S. (2022). Introduction to Blockchain Technology. In Tanwar, S. (Ed.), *Blockchain Technology: From Theory to Practice* (pp. 1–41). Springer Nature., DOI: 10.1007/978-981-19-1488-1_1

Thomas, N. S. (2024). *The Applications of Data Mining Techniques in Detecting Occupational Fraud: A Qualitative Review of Forensic Accounting Practices*. https://esource.dbs.ie/items/caa8d886-fb6e-4bc6-b4e3-5c7d455e7134

Trehan, M. A., & Shah, P. (2024). An Impact Of Forensic Accounting Training On Strengthening Banking Fraud Controls. *Educational Administration: Theory and Practice*, *30*(1), 1. Advance online publication. DOI: 10.53555/kuey.v30i1.5494

Ugochukwu, J. N. (2021). EFFECTIVE DEPLOY OF DIGITAL FORENSIC TECHNIQUES AND THE SUSTENANCE OF MATERIAL MISSTATEMENT-FREE FINANCIAL REPORTING IN NIGERIA. [JARE]. *Journal of Academic Research in Economics*, *13*(3), 442–470.

Umanhonlen, F. O., P, O. J., & Osikhenaogiedu, K. (2020). Combating economic and financial crimes in nigeria: The role of the forensic accountant. *Journal of Management and Science*, *10*(4), 4. Advance online publication. DOI: 10.26524/jms.10.7

Verma, A., & Singh, V. (2024). International Journal of Research Publication and Reviews THE USE OF DATA ANALYTICS IN FORENSIC ACCOUNTING: A REVIEW OF CURRENT TRENDS AND TECHNIQUES. *International Journal of Research Publication and Reviews*, *5*, 4197–4203.

Waleed Hilal, S. Gadsden, A., & Yawney, J. (2022). *Financial Fraud: A Review of Anomaly Detection Techniques and Recent Advances—ScienceDirect*. https://www.sciencedirect.com/science/article/pii/S0957417421017164

Zayed, L. M. M., Nour, M. I., Al Attar, K., Almubaideen, H., & Abdelaziz, G. A. M. (2024). Role of Artificial Intelligence (AI) in Accounting Information Systems in Detecting Fraud. In Musleh Al-Sartawi, A. M. A., & Nour, A. I. (Eds.), *Artificial Intelligence and Economic Sustainability in the Era of Industrial Revolution 5.0* (pp. 397–409). Springer Nature Switzerland., DOI: 10.1007/978-3-031-56586-1_30

Chapter 5
Competition Law and Corporate Finance in India: Evaluating a Decade of Leniency Program Impacts and Challenges

Ankit Srivastava
http://orcid.org/0000-0002-1330-6717
Rajiv Gandhi National University of Law, India

Anwesha Ghosh
http://orcid.org/0000-0003-4167-2121
Amity Law School, Amity University, Mumbai, India

Divyansha Kumar
http://orcid.org/0000-0002-6720-2753
Chitkara University, Punjab, India

ABSTRACT

The purpose of this chapter is to provide an in-depth analysis of the leniency program under the Competition Act of 2002 in India, focusing on its evolution, effectiveness, and impact over the past decade. This chapter

DOI: 10.4018/979-8-3693-8247-9.ch005

seeks to critically evaluate how well the leniency program has achieved its objectives, compare its effectiveness with global practices, and propose recommendations for its improvement. In doing so, the chapter will examine the intersection of competition law and corporate finance. In doing so, the chapter will examine the intersection of competition law and corporate finance, shedding light on how competition policies influence corporate strategies and market dynamics in India.

INTRODUCTION

Cartel is an umbrella term used to describe anti-competitive agreements such as price-fixing, output restricting, and bid-rigging, among others (UNCTAD, 1959). Over time, the punishment, as well as the conviction rate imposed on cartel conspirators, has been drastically increased worldwide. Nevertheless, this menace is time and again obliterated from the scrutiny of anti-trust watchdogs, especially in India. Having imposed huge penalties on enterprises in a number of cases with a view to creating deterrence, the Competition Commission of India (CCI/ Commission) is yet to bust a number of cartels that are already in existence, especially in the digital era (Prasad, 2021). When confronted by the CCI, the conspirators have no choice but to face severe penalties. This becomes the main aspect of deterrence and the main reason for the introduction of the leniency program (Tiptur & Tripathi, 2021). With fear of imposition of heavy penalty by the Commission, enterprises having indulged in such cartel tend to voluntarily confess their wrongdoings before the Commission under the leniency program, through which the conspirators or the co-conspirators plead for complete or partial immunity. Leniency is a lenient mechanism conferring the grant of immunity, either partially or wholly, to the alleged offender/s who has/have been involved in carrying out a cartel by breaking a code of silence among cartel conspirator/s and ultimately uncovering the same (OECD, 2001). The rationale for breaking the silence is premised on the infamous 'Prisoner's Dilemma Theory'. Ulrich Blum argues that adhering to an unenforceable agreement that could do nothing to protect any of the parties, can certainly induce one of the parties to confess the wrongdoings and to get mitigated punishment in return (Blum et al., 2008). Miller (2009), through his study, has showcased that "leniency enhances deterrence and detection capabilities." The application of leniency programs is not uniform across jurisdictions. With its introduction in the United States, other countries in the mid- 2000s started using this as a tool to curb the cartel menace and have shown a subsequent increase in the conviction rate (Bhattacharjee & De, 2021). By following developed jurisdictions, India took a remarkable step and introduced a leniency program with the enactment of the Competition Act of 2002; nonetheless, unlike several countable other jurisdictions, India does not impose a criminal sanction upon the cartel infringer, which becomes the obvious reason for low conviction rate and fewer leniency applications. Acceptance of leniency application in pre-investigation itself does not increase the leniency applications automatically (Conference on Research on Economic Theory and Econometrics, 2009). Thereby, it encourages conspirators to confess about their co-conspirators by disclosing 'insider evidence' that could implicate them for contravention (Bhat, 2019).

By promoting compliance, lowering financial risks, and improving market integrity, the leniency program established by the Competition Act of 2002 is essential to the development of corporate finance. The initiative assists companies in drastically reducing heavy financial penalties by providing incentives for enterprises engaged in anti-competitive conduct, such as cartels, to voluntarily self-report and cooperate with the CCI. Companies may protect their cash reserves, prevent expensive proceedings, and continue making a profit owing to this decrease in fines. In terms of finances, it reduces the possibility of significant fines that might upset the company's balance sheet, encouraging improved financial standing and long-term expansion (Corradi & Nowag, 2023). Additionally, by encouraging businesses to have strong internal compliance procedures, the leniency program promotes openness and sound corporate governance. In addition to preventing anti-competitive behaviour, good governance procedures enhance a company's financial management and creditworthiness, increasing their value among creditors and investors. By encouraging fairness and openness in the market, which are critical for attracting money and investment, the program also bolsters investor trust. A more equal playing field for companies results in more effective resource allocation and increased operational efficiency as markets grow fairer and more competitive. Overall, through lowering legal uncertainties, promoting ethical conduct, and strengthening investor confidence, the leniency program promotes sustainable financial growth and, in the process, improves the climate for corporate financing. A company's financial management and creditworthiness are enhanced by effective governance methods, which also deters anti-competitive behaviour and increases the company's appeal to creditors and investors. In addition, the program boosts investor trust by encouraging market fairness and openness, both of which are necessary to attract money and investment (Kaur, and Tanwar, 2024). Companies benefit from equal playing fields created by more competitive and equitable markets, which promotes effective resource allocation and increased operational efficiency. Ultimately, the leniency program contributes to a healthier corporate finance environment by reducing legal risks, promoting ethical practices, and reinforcing investor trust, thereby supporting sustainable financial growth in ever-evolving markets (Ghoset. al.2024).

The researcher compares the Indian leniency program with comparable frameworks in developed competition law jurisdictions and offers a brief overview of the program in this study. The study reveals how, by reducing the financial risks connected to anti-competitive behaviour, leniency programs in developed nations have helped maintain fair competition while safeguarding the financial viability of companies. In the subsequent portion, the researcher concentrates on improving India's existing leniency regime through concrete recommendations, with a specific focus on corporate finance.

RESEARCH OBJECTIVE AND QUESTIONS

This research paper aims to evaluate the present leniency regime in India and to fill the lacune existing in the present regime. For that, the research paper is premised on the following questions:

1. What is the current trend of adjudicating marker systems in leniency applications? In answering the question, it is argued that the current trend of adjudicating disputes can be made stronger, plausibly by the

introduction of an additional explicit marker system as is prevalent in Japan, which gives relief to the second and subsequent applicant for their cooperation in terms of additional variable reduction, to say the least.

2. Whether the penalty upon enterprises is effectively levied by the Commission? In answering the question, emphasis is placed on the secondary data where it is concluded that though the Commission is imposing penalty effectively when it comes to levying, it suffers from mitigation, as in several cases concerning leniency, orders were challenged in an appeal, the time frame of which has denuded the intensity of the imposed penalty.
3. What is the stance of the Commission in granting leniency to the applicants and if it is showing progressiveness? In answering it, the stance of the Commission in granting and adjudicating leniency applications in its initial years has been studied. For ascertaining progressiveness, the recent orders, especially the ones given considering mitigating circumstances have been analyzed.
4. Whether the repeat cartel offenders should be provided with a reduction in penalty? The researcher answers the question negatively. However, the grant of immunity must be made under exceptional circumstances to the repeat applicant as well.
5. Is the proposed amendment to the existing leniency regime fruitful? In answering the question, the researcher comparatively analyses the proposed leniency 'plus' amendment with the existing regime in the United States. The researcher argues that without inviting the concept of penalty 'plus' into the Indian competition law regime, the proposed amendment can prove to be detrimental.
6. How do enhanced leniency measures, such as the 'leniency plus' system, impact corporate financial stability and investor confidence in India? The researcher explores whether adopting these provisions could reduce financial penalties, encourage self-reporting, and strengthen corporate governance, ultimately fostering greater investor confidence and a fairer business environment.

A BRIEF OVERVIEW OF LENIENCY PROGRAM IN INDIA AND AROUND THE WORLD

With the dawn of the Monopolistic and Restrictive Trade Practices Act, 1969 (MRTP Act) due to its weak enforcement, the Competition Act, 2002 (Act) emerged with the establishment of a novel anti-trust watchdog- the CCI which since its inception has had naive leniency program in the Act. The understanding of leniency program in India requires a vivid understanding of cartels. Having defined under Section 2(c) of the Act, cartels are agreements executed between enterprises not to compete on *"price, product (including goods and services) or customers" (Competition Commission of India, 2024)*. Horizontal agreements including cartels are presumed to be void for having an Appreciable Adverse Effect on Competition (AAEC), while vertical agreement runs contrary and are adjudged on the 'rule of reason' approach (Competition Commission of India, 2024).

A. Leniency Program in India

Forming cartels is in itself an egregious competition law offence that can effectively be countered by leniency programs (Mehta & Pati, 2016). Initially, implemented by the U.S., leniency programs are bearing fruits in bursting cartels. Likewise, certain amendments to the existing U.S. regime gave a pace with cartel cases increasing at a rate of 60 cases per year (Mehta & Pati, 2016). Since then, it has filled the void of deterrence up to a certain extent; that is, it has acted as a catalyst for the detection of cartels and for an offer of 'cease and desist' to the Commission.

By acting as a whistle-blower program that is premised on the fact that either blow the whistle or face the music (Dugar et al., 2020), the applicant seeking leniency as defined under Section 46 of the Act, must satisfy the Commission with mandate enshrined under the provision. For one, there must be full, true and vital disclosure of material fact; two, the disclosure must be made before the investigation report has been received under Section 26; three, the seeker must cooperate with the Commission till the competition of the proceedings; four, the seeker must not give false evidence, not-so vital disclosure and must comply with the conditions as was imposed by the Commission while disposing of the leniency application. The ambit for *'adjudicating leniency applications* was further strengthened by the amendment of 2007, which scholars believe showcases a *'rush effect'*. The leniency applications are being adjudged pursuant to the Competition Commission of India (Lesser Penalty) Regulations, 2009 (Lesser Penalty Regulation/Reg.). Reg. 3(1) imposes certain conditions upon the applicant seeking benefit under Section 46 while Reg. 3(1A) mandates the applicant to declare the names of individuals who have been involved in the cartel on its behalf. As a deterrence, pursuant to Reg. 3(3), the Commission can impose any other conditions or restrictions on its discretion.

Further, vide Competition Commission of India (Lesser Penalty) Amendment Regulations, 2017, a marker system was introduced and allowed penalty reduction of up to or equal to 100 percent to the first application who makes a vital disclosure (The Competition Commission of India (Lesser Penalty) Regulations, 2009, Reg. 4(a)) concerning cartel, either before the Commission has formed a prima facie opinion (The Competition Commission of India (Lesser Penalty) Regulations, 2009, Reg. 4(b)) or when the Director General (DG) is partaking investigation and does not have sufficient evidence (The Competition Commission of India (Lesser Penalty) Regulations, 2009, Reg. 4(c)(i)); a penalty reduction of up to or equal to fifty percent of the full penalty leviable to the second applicant (The Competition Commission of India (Lesser Penalty) Regulations, 2009, Reg. 4(c)(ii)) and; a reduction of up to or equal to thirty percent of the full penalty leviable to the third or subsequent applicants. The marker system has not only increased transparency but has also eliminated uncertainty (Dugar et al., 2020). As per the order (In Re: Cartelization in Respect of Tenders floated by Indian Railways for supply of Brushless DC Fans, 2014), it is not necessarily that the first-in applicant shall get 100% deduction, rather it shall be subject to strong evidence coupled with making such disclosure even before the investigation has been initiated. While the procedure for grant of lesser penalty is governed by Reg. 5 wherein the application containing material information relating to the existence of cartel can be made either orally or through e-mail or fax (The Competition Commission of India (Lesser Penalty) Regulations, 2009, Reg. 5(1)) which shall be put up by the designated authority (DA) before the Commission for its consideration. After marking the priority status of the applicant, the Commission requires the application to be submitted in a written form within fifteen days (The Competition Commission of India (Lesser Penalty) Regulations, 2009, Reg. 5(2)) or else the applicant may forfeit its claim for priority status and also of lesser penalty (The Competition Commission of India (Lesser Penalty) Regulations, 2009, Reg. 5(4)). Following the marker system, subsequent applicants shall move up in order of priority status when the benefit of priority status of the preceding applicant gets forfeited (The Competition Commission of India (Lesser Penalty) Regulations, 2009, Reg. 5(8)). Pursuant to the non-obstante clause under Reg. 6, the DG or Commission, shall treat the identity and information furnished under Reg. 5 as confidential with a rider. Thus, filling leniency application in the first place does not confer sure-shot leniency rather merely confers a 'conditional benefit', it mainly depends on the smoking gun evidence by the applicant.

To tackle the ever-changing nature of the market and the coming of the new-age markets, the Competition (Amendment) Act, 2023, has been passed. The Commission has further made amendments to the law by introducing the draft Lesser Penalty Regulations (LPR), 2023 (Competition Commission of India, 2023). Once it gets notified it shall replace the LPR, 2009. The amended regulation shall operationalise the leniency plus provision introduced by the Competition (Amendment) Act, 2013.

The purpose of the leniency plus facility is to incentivize an existing cartel's leniency applicant (also known as a "Existing Applicant") to divulge information regarding a second cartel that the CCI is unaware of (Cyril Amarchand Mangaldas, 2023). The leniency plus applicant shall get the additional 30% penalty reduction in the first cartel and shall be eligible for up to or equal to 100% penalty reduction in the newly disclosed cartel (Competition Commission of India, 2023). The only cartels recognized by the LPR 2009 administration were "horizontal" ones, or cartels between rivals. The LPR 2023 will grant participants in hub and spoke cartels access to the benefits of leniency and leniency plus facilities (Khan, 2023).

B. Comparative analysis of Leniency Program around the developed jurisdictions

The competition market varies from country to country because of different sets of per-capita income and varying policies (Borrell et al., 2013), a true copy of another's competition law regime may not fit ours (Mehta, 2003). This becomes the reason to constructively analyze regimes across developed jurisdictions and implement only those aspects that adhere to the Indian regime.

1. United States

Under the US framework, the leniency programme is worked through two pivotal agencies, the Anti- Trust Division (AD) and the Department of Justice (DOJ). The AD is situated at the fulcrum of the whole leniency process as it is an agency that grants amnesty to corporations and individual players. With the passing of the Sherman Act, the US has shown a remarkable increase in leniency application. Primarily, two policies- the corporate leniency policy and the Individual leniency policy- govern the leniency program. While there is no explicit difference between the offences that are civil or criminal in nature, (Australian Competition and Consumer Commission, 2020) the US's anti-trust policy showcases bid-rigging, market or customer allocation, and agreement to fix prices as per se violation of the Sherman Act. Because of this reason, the DOJ is empowered to impose criminal as well as civil sanctions. The Corporate Leniency Policy stipulates two types of kinds of leniency categories: Type A and Type B (U.S. Department of Justice, 1993). These two categories are premised on the lines of pre- dawn raids and post- dawn raids period. Simply put, the type of leniency that a corporation or an individual can be accorded with depends on their promptness to inform the AD of a cartel. The defining factors is the beginning of the investigation. Accordingly, Type A and Type B leniencies are conferred considering before and after investigation scenarios, respectively.

In order to draw benefit out of the Type A leniency, a corporation must satisfy the conditions laid down by the AD such as comprehensive cooperation, cessation of involvement in the cartel, the disclosure of cartel information without compromising the genuineness of the information, no coercion to others involved in the cartel. Type B leniency ensure that the corporate must comply with condition that it should be the first cartel chiseler to join the investigation, when it does the join the investigation it is needed to adduce evidence where the AD is bereft of any to bring the conspirators to the books, cessation of cartel activity with an assurance to compensate injured parties.

The AD has introduced Individual Leniency (Buretta & Terzaken, 2022, p. 324) as well to encourage the individual associated with the corporate entity to report violations. Individual Leniency also springs into action subsequent to a corporation's disclosure of cartelization. The cardinal principle that runs through the entire fabric of individual leniency is the degree of cooperation offered to the AD. The clarion is clear- NO COOPERATION, NO AMNESTY. Under the individual leniency scheme, the AD is inclined to see individuals of the corporation- directors, employees, and officers- cooperate extensively without concealing or distorting the factual matrix of market manipulation. If the individual, conceals or distorts facts, the AD marks him as a 'carve outs' and attaches a high degree of culpability to such acts (Buretta & Terzaken, 2022, p. 329). That apart, Individuals (directors, employees and officers) are legally shielded from the oppressiveness of the corporation in cases where they report anti-trust violations by the Criminal Anti-Trust Anti- Retaliation Act (CAARA) enacted for this special purpose (Department of Justice, 2023). Therefore, the whistleblower regime in the US is undergirded by the CAARA legislation, a vital legal instrument absent in most jurisdictions.

The marker system of the AD is conspicuously a stringent one. Though the threshold to acquire a conditional maker that is rendered by the AD or the Director of Criminal Enforcement (DCE) for thirty days (with the possibility of extension) is relatively low and is solidified by providing information on the nature of cartel conduct, evidentiary support and cooperation by the applicant, leapfrogging is completely dispensed with and is only permissible under very narrow and limited circumstances (Buretta & Terzaken, 2022, p. 327). This results in a leniency process that is infused with an apparent and carefully crafted rigidity as the AD provides only one leniency marker per case.

One of the tangible benefits that the US jurisdiction has offered the world from its anti-trust enforcement mechanism is the methodic contrivance of the Leniency Plus and the Penalty Plus framework. This framework has exhibited to be a decisive cog in the wheel of leniency administration and has been successful in thwarting inchoate cartelists from furthering their anti-competitive goals. Leniency Plus simply postulates the idea that an applicant who is a participant in more than one cartel and wishes to seek reduction in penalty for the cartel under investigation, is required to disclose the operations and involvement in all the others cartels. However, for any litany of logical reasons, the perjurer- applicant shall face the wrath of exemplary penalties. The Penalty Plus, an obverse to the Leniency Plus, caters the AD with the perfect legal instrument to chastise the perjurer-applicant with exponentially enhanced penalties (as high as 80%) (Buretta & Terzaken, 2022, p. 325). Therefore, the combination of Leniency Plus and Penalty Plus makes it incumbent on the corporation (or individuals) to proactively divulge to the AD of any similar and simultaneous wrong-doings when under cartel investigation.

To accentuate this point, the *Bridgstone* (U.S. v. Bridgestone Corporation, 2011) case serves as a classic example. Bridgestone, a Japanese company in the business of manufacturing marine hose, was found to have been engaged in an international cartel by the AD. The company pleaded guilty and provided cooperation in return for amnesty. However, it later came to the knowledge of the AD that the same company had concealed information about its cartel activities in the anti-vibration rubber products in the automobile manufacturing sector and had flouted the norms of the Leniency program. Resultantly, criminal charges were brought against the conspirators (Buretta & Terzaken, 2022, p. 325).

Without any surmises, the Leniency programme has, undoubtedly, yielded positive results that have ameliorated competitiveness in the market. For instance, the Air Cargo case offers an astute insight into this statement. The airlines industry that saw a slew of changes in the 1990s through privatization of national airlines, resisted the change to its archaic practice of coordinating prices even after slipping from the grip of governments and landing in the hands of the private players. The collusion (price coordination) was premised fundamentally on an understanding/ arrangement concocted with the intent to regulate carrier chargers by responding to fuel price hike though the introduction of equal, coordinated rise in freight surcharges. Thereby, adopting this approach, the air carriers were able to eliminate the possibility to competition by fixing prices and denying any chance of lower freight charges to the customers which would be a outcome of the usual course of the market. The collusion went unnoticed for a long while until Lufthansa broke the news of its cooperation with the anti-trust watchdogs. This evidently cause a rippling effect world over and major players cracking in the face of crisis.

In the context of the USA, the AD and the DOJ were clueless with regard to the existence of cartel in the air freight carrier industry. In most of the jurisdiction, including the USA, Lufthansa was granted amnesty. For its plausible and arduous cooperation over three years, Lufthansa and its employees were also exempted from any criminal prosecution along with an upper limited on treble damages. The success of such cases is a clear affirmation of the Leniency policy adopted in various jurisdiction that has single- handedly enabled competitive watchdogs to obviate market manipulation. In this particular case, the US Leniency Programme conspicuous played a crucial role to provide the cartel chiseler with a persuasive and efficient legal framework to adequately report instances of cartelization.

2. Australia

Having recognized four categories of cartels, the Australian Competition and Consumer Commission (ACCC) imposes both criminal and civil sanctions on cartelists. Australia's leniency regime is remarkably similar to the US's regime in so far as amnesty 'plus' and marker system is concerned. Though first-in applicant is entitled to a complete immunity, the private enforcement for the damage, by the suffering company, can be levied. Further, a derivative immunity can also be claimed by the corporation up until cooperation with ACCC is in place. Further, owing to COVID-19, ACCC has allowed statutory protection for cartel conduct[1], provided it has formed an opinion "public benefit from the conduct outweighs any public detriment"[2].

At this point, it is of essence to comprehensively consider the leniency process in Australia. The process of leniency kickstarts with an application by a cartelist to the competitive authority (ACCC) highlighting the existence of a cartel. Cooperation agreement is the first step taken by the ACCC to ensure that the cartel chiseler is brought on record. The contents of this agreement indicate the requisite procedure to be followed thereafter. This includes admission of guilt, declaration of bona fide statements with respect to infringements, cessation of involvement in the cartel, extension of cooperation, maintaining confidentiality, among other things. A conditional immunity and a marker is then granted after the corporation has duly acknowledged the Cooperation Agreement. Apparently, the marker is only available for the first leniency applicant, an identical trait of the US jurisdiction.

Further, the ACCC conducts its investigation and collects evidences and information in connection with the allegations levelled. After the completion of the investigation, the applicant is preferred to produce a certificate signifying its cooperation with the ACCC. Subsequently, the process enters the "Proofer Stage" where the applicant is advance evidences/information about the functioning of the cartel for the purpose of satisfying the conditions enumerated in the Cooperation Agreement in a detailed fashion. On successfully meeting the criteria set out by the ACCC the first applicant is offered complete immunity for penalties.

It is worth noting that only the first applicant can be accorded any immunity, there is no bracket system in place. Moreover, the corporate entities are entitled to exact derivative immunities for directors and employee who exercise a controlling interest in it subject to the conditions of individual immunity. However, immunities granted by the ACCC do limit the enforcement of private action against violators. The ACCC has, as well, adopted a Leniency Plus model which proposed that it can advise the Court to consider extra reduction in penalties. The Courts are the final arbiters in competitive matters in Australia.

On the point of criminal prosecution, the ACCC has no jurisdiction whatsoever in the criminal sanctions against the cartelists. It the Commonwealth Director of Public Prosecution (CDPP) that has discretion to prosecute. Recently, the ACCC achieved a rare feat by successfully completing a criminal prosecution in the case of Nippon Yusen Kabushiki Kaisha (NYK) (Australian Competition and Consumer Commission, 2023). In this case, the NYK entered into an arrangement/understanding with other shipping companies to distort the supply of automobiles in

Australia and plead guilty of cartelization and extended full cooperation to the ACCC in its investigation. Ultimately, the CDPP, despite cooperation in investigation for anti- competitive activity, chose to arraign NYK. In the overall analysis, it can be observed that the Australian regime suffers from a weakened leniency framework because despite of the cooperation proffered by applicants only civil immunity is assured. Whereas, the avenues for criminal prosecution and private actions are always open which eventually will deter most applicants to bring forth existence of cartels and many cartels may go undetected for years. This milieu effectively defeats and frustrate the cardinal objectives of a leniency programme as it was found principle of immunity from penalties and punishments to crack the cartels from within. Therefore, in Australia, the cartel chiseler lose money through private action and is incarcerated by the CDPP. For the proper fixation of this predicament, the ACCC shall be the final authority on initiating prosecution.

3. Japan

Japan's antitrust watchdog 'Japan Fair Trade Commission' (JFTC) that adjudicates antitrust violations, provides immunity from administrative surcharges against any cartel infringement through leniency. Mori & Tomotsune, 2021 suggest that JFTC has had a narrow discretion which, through an amendment to the Japanese Leniency Program, has been broadened. Firstly, because the cap for providing surcharge reduction to a maximum of five companies is detached; Second, because, other than the first applicant, the order of application is determined by the degree of co-operation during the investigation. The first-in applicant is entitled to full-immunity, second to 20%, from third to fifth- 10%, thereafter each subsequent applicant to 5%. Further, an additional variable reduction of up to 40% is granted according to the degree of cooperation. Where the cooperation is shown after a dawn raid, this 40% cap gets reduced to 20%. JFTC also allows applicants to make oral submissions in order to mitigate the risk of discovery. According to the Antimonopoly Act, the JFTC has the discretion to impose criminal sanctions on the second and subsequent applicants and to provide such immunity to the first-in applicant until it cooperates with the JFTC.

The JFTC, over the years, has devised a methodic approach towards the more coherent Leniency Programme. Its stringent underpinnings are evident from an absence of the Leniency Plus regime, indicating a single-minded approach to a particular case of distortion in market competitiveness. The leniency process that the JFTC has adopted can be explained through the "Before and After Dawn Raid" approaches.

Any applicant who prefers to avail the benefits of the leniency program in an efficient manner has to maneuver other cartel members by applying before the dawn raid. This route demands the submission of Form 1 shedding light on the relevant product and duration of infringement. This leads to all the applicant submitting Form 1 being eligible for a marker indicating their leniency status. Further, in order to strengthen the leniency status, the applicant is required to submit a Form 2 detailing the working of the cartel and naming its members along with certain evidences within a stipulate time- period by the JFTC. At this stage, the First Applicant may require to produce any additional documentation under Form 4 to reap the harvest of full immunity for administrative surcharge. By this method, only those applicants qualify for full immunity who apply for amnesty 'before the dawn raids.' Interestingly, in the post dawn raid scenario, there is a leniency application marathon as every enterprise/individual involved in the cartel attempts to make the first move to eliminate any obstacle in the path of considerable reduction in surcharge. As a first move, the applicants are initiated to tender cartel information under a prescribed Form 3 (similar to Form 2) within 20 working days. Subsequently, for sealing the leniency status, applicants have to facilitate a Form 4 within 10 working days. Meanwhile, it is incumbent upon the 'after dawn raids' applicant to apprise the JFTC about the epiphany of the assiduous assistance offered by them about the existence of a cartel.

The Japanese leniency structure seems to be on a progressive road with the recent developments of class action (on limited grounds) including reforms in discovery policy and scrapping of the JTFC quasi- court hearing. However, rigidity in considering relevant markets in granting of amnesty, and the conspicuous absence of the Leniency Plus regime calls for a more innovative overhauling of the present system in place that would yield more better and effective results.

4. European Union

European Union's leniency regime is similar to India's leniency regime as far as a civil penalty and proposed leniency plus is concerned. To seek total immunity on penalty, the first applicant has to submit information to the Commission, which could enable it to find an infringement of Article 101 of the Treaty on the Functioning of the European Union (TFEU) and to carry out necessary inspection. The subsequent applicants seeking immunity have to provide 'significant added value' to the evidence that is already in the hands of the Commission. For that, the Commission shall look upon such evidence that "is contemporaneous; is directly relevant to the facts in question; does not require corroboration from other sources" After successful leniency applicants, a reduction of 30% to 50% is given to the first successful applicant, 20% to 30% to the second successful applicant, and up to 20% to the subsequent successful applicants.

The Leniency process under the Commission commences with a Leniency Notice (Official Journal of the European Union, 2006) that evinces conditions that are needed to be promptly followed in an obsequious manner by an undertaking desiring immunity under law for cartel activities. Conditional immunities are granted to undertakings until the investigation and the final order of the Commission is declared. During this period, the Commission reviews the behavioral compliance of the undertaking and the genuineness of the relevant material averred by the leniency applicant, which could be appreciated in the investigation. Behavioral compliance, among other things, includes cooperation at every stage of the investigation, non- concealment and supply of true evidence/ information, and the cessation of involvement in cartel activities. By the marker system, the Commission scrutinizes the relevancy of the material placed before it by a leniency applicant to burst an ongoing cartel, and to secure a place in the queue to avail the benefits of leniency offered. The EU leniency framework has also brought into existence a "favorable treatment" tag for those undertaking who cannot be accommodated in the immunity programme but have afforded the Commission with substantial information in its cartel probe that was essential into order to avoid distortion of market.

In order to fully appreciate the practical application of the EU laws, the Raw Tobacco Italy case (European Commission, 2006) is an apt example. In this case, three companies, namely, Deltafina, Dimon and Transcatab were engaged in the business of tobacco as "processors" (entities who buy tobacco from original producers/farmers and act as intermediaries between final tobacco product manufacturers) in cross country operations across the EU. These companies were were legally permitted by the local law to form a cultivation contract with producers to ensure and grade the quality of tobacco. However, they were found to have infringed the local laws by fixing and coordinating tobacco prices and production quotas. All the three companies, were found to have negotiated an agreement and/or concerted practice that enabled them to regulate trading conditions for the purchase of tobacco. Subsequently, these companies entered into a plea of leniency from the Commission against the exchange of substantial information relating to the cartel (Official Journal of the European Union, 2006, p. L353/48). Following the law, the Commission issued Leniency Notices. Dimon and Transcatab were conferred broadly, for their substantial information, a generous reduction in fine, whereas, the condiditonal immunity conferred to Deltafine was forfeited after the apparent violation of the confidentiality clause in the Leniency Notice (Official Journal of the European Union, 2006, p. L353/49).

The anonymity/confidentiality of the complainant is also found to be carrying great weight, a corresponding scenario in the Indian laws. In *Salzgitter v. Commission (2004)*, it was rightly underscored by the Court that the evidence submitted by a whistleblower willing to stay secluded and anonymous shall be accorded to with probative value. Interestingly, the Court meant that anonymity of the whistle bowler cannot be countenanced as a ground for disregarding the evidences tendered by him. Further, the robustness of the EU regime is signified by the jurisdiction exercisable by the EU Court in matters where the Commission has failed to effectively deal with the issues particularly that of competition. For instance, the disproportionate time taken by the Commission to decide a matter can brought into question or any other act that dampens competition in the market (Whish & Bailey, 2012).

JUDICIAL PRONOUNCEMENTS CONCERNING LENIENCY: A PROGRESSIVE APPROACH OF CCI

Scholars have unequivocally pointed out that cartelization is the worst crime against competition. Though a source of monopoly, argues Milton, cartels are mostly unstable and short-lived unless the government has a notoriety for lackluster law enforcement (Friedman, 2002). However, the transplantation of this experience to the Indian regime is earmarked by peculiarity. Certainly, the progressive trajectory of the Commission merits the demand for candor. The vestiges of the leniency programme that is modelled to expose and obliterate the menace of cartelization are clearly detectable by the dearth of applications received by the Commission in its initial days. The initial dilettante disposition of the Commission is patently attributable to this phenomenon, or maybe, the vice- versa as the Commission could only scrutinize four applications (Singh et al., 2018) in a period of two year since the filing of the first ever leniency application.

At this juncture, we shall endeavor to analyze the important leniency application matters decided by the Commission to gauge the degree of reforms and efficiency in this particular field. Commission's first leniency order that came in the matter *Indian Railways* evinces that the essential bedrock of the leniency programme is the distinctive significance of the information revealed. In this case, M/s Pyramid Electronic, after a report filed by the Central Bureau (CBI) chronicling bid- rigging in tenders, came forward to extend its cooperation to the CCI in return of amnesty. Later, in the opinion of the CCI, M/s Pyramid Electronic can be accorded completely immunity but a reduction in penalties considering its cooperation in the investigation, and valuable information brought forth in the process because it sprang into action only after the report of the CBI, alluding to the post- dawn raids instance.

The 2007 Amendment and 2009 Lesser Penalty Regulations that solidified the beginning of a new leniency era met with a bottleneck situation in *Nagrik Chetna Manch (Nagrik Chetna Manch v. Fortified Securities Solutions, 2015)*, where the Commission was circumscribed by the prescribed limitation on the number of applicants that can be conferred reduction in penalty. Further, only 'enterprises', and not 'individuals' could fit the legal criterion to avail the benefits of the leniency provision prior to 2017. This position of law was transformed by the introduction of the 2017 Amendment, according to which the Commission could henceforth grant leniency in penalty and immunity to indefinite number of enterprises and individuals who divulge vital cartel information. Indeed, a profoundly wide ambit of authority by this amendment is at the disposal of the Commission.

However, with the fledging leniency programme, the Commission that ventured into the uncharted territory of competition enforcement, inadvertently, stumbled upon few conflicting conclusions. In the *Zinc Carbon Dry Cell Batteries (In Re: Cartelisation, 2016 & 2017)* fiasco, Panasonic being the cartel chiseler was accorded a 100% reduction in penalty for the disclosure of sensitive and vital information. Soon after, the leniency bandwagon was joined by Eveready and Nippo, who settled for 30% and 20% decrease in penalties, respectively, even though no substantial information was provided by them. That apart, the Commission averred that Eveready and Nippo failed to shed light on essential facts on strategic time (Sandeepan & Fatima, 2021). Interestingly, this decision of the Commission highlights its, obvious, conundrum- ridden and contradictory decision- making process. It is hard to reckon the ambit of the elements that can be discerned as constituting strategic time. The foremost question that looms before the applicant is that what is a strategic time other than an explicit expression of ambiguity by the Commission. This reasoning, if at all considered as one, goes against the very grain of *Nagrik Chetna Manch (Nagrik Chetna Manch v. Fortified Securities Solutions, 2015)* dictum, where the Commission refused to invoke the leniency provision to applicants who significantly cooperate in disclosing vital and relevant information (Deo & Verma, 2023).

Identically, in the anti- vibration rubber product cartel case (aforementioned as the Bridgestone case), the Commission decided to turn a blind eye to the internationally operative cartel ratiocinating that because no actual sales have taken place in the said sector, and only evidences of efforts to coordinate price through communication are available, it cannot be determined as market manipulation. Further, in case where a leniency applicant sort amnesty by disclosing the existence of cartel, the Commission took the view that '*ends of justice would be met if the parties cease such cartel behavior and desist from indulging in it in future*'.

Despite the sporadic sprucing of the anti-trust enforcement mechanism, the approach of the Commission has been fairly styled as 'consistently inconsistent'. This apparent, stinging portrayal of the grim picture of the endeavors of the Commission encapsulates the meretricious way of functioning and is suggestive of the nemesis of the leniency programme underway.

Apart from the direct concerns of leniency, the Commission that is a body of experts incorporated with the foremost task of administrating and maintaining effective competition in the market exercises wide ranging authority vested in it while deciding leniency application and granting immunities. Such authority is not only amenable to the principles of natural justice but also the constitutionally pervading doctrine of Proportionality. The Doctrine of Proportionality seeks to embrace decisions that are judiciously balanced. The primary objective of this doctrine, opines Barak, is to safeguard individuals from the overwhelming power the State by investigating any decision- making by it on four pillars of proportionality, namely, proper purpose, rationale connection, necessity and balancing.

Often the detractors have argued that the order of CCI must clearly explicate the ratio for grating penalty reduction to one applicant and depriving such reduction to the other applicant (Singh et al., 2018). Time and again there have been discrepancies for strictly adhering to the marker system. On one hand, the Commission enjoys wide discretion in allowing full immunity on the basis of vital disclosure *(Nagrik Chetna Manch v. Fortified Securities Solutions, 2015)*, on the other hand, the Commission strictly scrutinizes the significant added value to second and subsequent applicants. In the backdrop of CCI being not consistent in its approach of following marker system, critics argue for having- stage at which the information is provided by the applicant and the intensity of use of information, to remain consistent in its approach. In one case *(In Re: Cartelisation, 2016 & 2017)*, the Commission granted a 30% reduction in punishment to the applicant who has applied for leniency after CCI's raid, even the same does not come within 'significant added value'. While in another case (In Re: Cartelisation by Broadcasting Service Providers, 2013), the applicant, even after being second and disclosing prior to the initiation of the raid, was granted only a 30% reduction in penalty.

Consequentially, strict adherence to the Doctrine of Proportionality is vital and paramount for the Commission for a successful rate of cartel bursts. This doctrine perspicaciously assesses, first, the reasonableness of the purpose of any act or decision, second, rational connections tend to gauge the justification between means and ends, thirds, necessity looks into the adoption of the choice of discretion among available alternative methods appropriate for the purpose sought to achieve and forth, balancing, the heart and soul of proportionality, measure the harms to rights against the benefits gained out limiting rights. In other words, this doctrine is antithetical to the disproportionate use of statutory, legislation or discretionary authority without reasonable cause hurting individual rights. Therefore, the Commission while entertaining leniency application of few and rejecting other has to act in accordance with the dictum of Proportionality.

Now, focusing on the recent orders rendered by the Commission, it can be undisputedly contended that the Commission has shown progressiveness in comprehensively dealing with the leniency cases. It can be exemplified by the case of In *Re: Alleged anti-competitive conduct in Beer Market in India (Competition Commission of India, 2017)*, where the Commission has provided a 100% reduction to OP-2 who provided vital disclosure that led to the formation of prima facie view by the Commission. Likewise, in *Anti-competitive conduct in the Paper Manufacturing Industry v. Banwari Paper Mills Limited and Ors. (Competition Commission of India, 2016)* the Commission gave full immunity to OP-21, who filed for leniency after the Commission had formed prima facie opinion but before DG has submitted its report to the Commission, and has given vital information. The order clearly enlists the statements of OP-21 under Para 193, 194 and 195 thereby, leaving no coin unturned in granting them immunity with reasonableness.

While it has been argued (Chand & Bala, 2023) that letting go the penalty on cartels during the crisis could plausibly distort the market, especially where the parties does not even qualify itself within the actual meaning of crisis, as can be ascertained from the orders rendered in *Auto-bearing Case* and *CBB Case (In Re: Cartelisation in industrial and automotive bearings, 2017)*. Nevertheless, the orders (In Re: Chief Materials Manager, 2016) passed by the Commission in the past couple of years, especially during the time of COVID-19 concerning the Micro, Small and Enterprises, showcases its strong commitment to invite more and more leniency applications for bettering the competitiveness by busting the cartels that could have been un-fetchable in the first place.

WAYS FORWARD FOR A BETTER LENIENCY REGIME

a. The Penalty has to be Levied Effectively

While there has been a study by Ezrachi and Kindl (2011), which evidences deterrence by the criminalization of cartels, the researcher opines that it cannot be implemented in India, for one- CCI is a regulatory body; for two- cartels are premised on the principle of preponderance on probabilities rather on, proving beyond reasonable doubt. Therefore, emphasis has to be laid on making the existing punishment effective. Looking at exorbitant profits that a firm and an individual makes, imposing ten percent average penalty of the last three years could not prove to be a reasonable impediment, it can easily be recovered from ninety percent of the remaining average profit of the last three preceding years since it is a collective exercise. Moreover, individual liability has to be ascertained more prudently, as the study by Somsekhar & Tripathi, 2021 (Tiptur & Tripathi, 2021) suggests that CCI has not imposed individual penalty in several of the non-cartel cases but has imposed the same in cases concerning leniency applications. It further suggests that from total of 44 cartel orders, 34 have been appealed. Therefore, the time that is taken for adjudicating a dispute and consequently imposing a penalty, on average being three years, nevertheless, the majority of the matters go for an appeal, thereby resulting in a huge time lag. This denudes the intensity of the penalty thus imposed and consequently the impact of leniency which is granted. For that, the compound interest principle may prove to be fruitful, provided the claim is made on the genuineness of the party. The researcher further suggests levying additional penalty on aggravating circumstances when the consumer harm proposed to be caused by cartelization, could not have been reasonably assessed at the time of promulgating the order, nevertheless, on mitigating circumstances, the Commission must remain lenient.

b. Significant Added Value Must Include Cooperation by Parties Within Itself

Significant added value (SAV) as explicated under the Regulation, 2009 must be made more explicit. It leaves huge discretion on the Commission to treat the significance of added value by the second and subsequent applicants. Depending upon the stage of the investigation, the leniency applicant may not prudently ascertain the ambit of 'significant' added value, and consequently pull such an applicant towards penalty without leniency. To counter this discrepancy, the Commission must make available the evidence (non-confidential) which is already in their possession, to the stakeholders' especially the contravening individuals, who can ascertain if the evidence which the Commission possess comes under the 'significant' category. In general, 'significant added value' must be such so as to reinforce the ability of the Commission to prove the infringement (Mayock & Meirsch, 2023). Even if the applicant does not significantly add value, the Commission must grant certain immunity to the applicant for upkeeping their positive gesture and applying 'leniency' within its true meaning. An additional cap for the same in line with that of Japan (40% additional reduction in penalty for the second and subsequent applicant for cooperating) can be made available. It could reduce unpredictability and, in any case, would grant certain immunity in the penalty, which could attract leniency applications.

c. Exclusion of Total Immunity in Exceptional Circumstances

Enterprises have achieved remarkable heights in innovating and forming cartels, 'Mystery Shopping Agencies' (In Re: Alleged anti-competitive conduct by Maruti Suzuki India Limited, 2019) being one of them, without getting caught by the anti-trust watchdog, pre-supposes that in exceptional circumstances where there is huge consumer-centric loss have occurred due to illegal activities, the Commission must not grant full immunity to the first applicant (Chen & Rey, 2013). While there is a study that showcases the effectiveness of leniency program by restricting the grant of immunity to the second and subsequent applicant, the researcher does not affirm with the study, because there are certain aspects of cartels that could not be known solely to the first applicant like the exact way in which cartel was carried out by each colluder (Chen & Rey, 2013).

Another exceptional circumstance could be where the offender repeats the collusive practice. There is evidence where the parties were found to be repeat offenders in violating fair competition in India, however, as far as the repeat offender in the case of cartel especially where leniency has already been granted is concerned, there is none (Bhattacharjea & De, 2021). Thus, the researcher argues that immunity to the applicant with respect to another subsequent leniency application must not be granted. Provided where after the first leniency, the applicant informs the Commission before the Commission has formed a prima facie opinion and before the investigation has commenced, the Commission can grant such an applicant immunity. Disallowing such leniency application could prove to be less impactful because the exact contours of carrying out a cartel are known to the cartelist.

d. Leniency Plus: Extra Carrot but no Sticks- A Call for Penalty Plus

The Competition (Amendment) Act, 2023 introduced clause 3 in Section 46 of the Competition Act, 2002. Having been inspired by the U.S. anti-trust law, India, by the said clause is set to introduce leniency plus (LP) and LPR 2023. In theoretical parlance, LP pertains to giving an additional relief against penalty to the applicant who discloses the existence of another cartel in an unrelated market, provided, the disclosure enables the Commission to form a prima facie opinion under Section 26(1) of the Act. The author here argues that there is a hidden minus in leniency plus, which could do more harm than good to the Indian competition regime. While adopting LP for a better competition law regime, the legislature seems to have missed the critical aspects of the U.S. competition law regime such as criminal sanctions[3] and penalty plus[4]. Non-adherence with full complexities of leniency may call for pro-collusive effects, which could deteriorate the existing regime and thereby become a potential tool serving cartelists but consumers (Martyniszyn, 2015). Amnesty plus, what the U.S. calls it, gives leverage to a conglomerate firm to induce a cartel in one market and partake in excessive gains from another market (Dijkstra & Schoonbeek, 2009). This could possibly stabilize the cartel so formed, which might not even have existed had there been no leniency plus.

To adhere to leniency 'plus', more deterrence has to be legislated in the existing regime. For that, credible threat of sanctions with sufficient scale will probably eliminate the intent of engagement and consequently its application. Calling for criminal liability is far-fetched especially in India, thus, the proposition for making the existing penalty regime more deterrent through penalty 'plus' is the need of the hour. Indian competition law regime is quite similar to that of the European Union, which too does not have criminal sanction for cartels, ergo it would be plausible to impose a penalty *"equal the expected gains from the violation multiplied by the inverse of the probability of a fine being effectively imposed"* (Wils, 2013). On other terms, the proposed amendment, on a plain reading, is set to pre-define the percentage of immunity that shall be granted to the LP applicant. That said, the U.S. does not propose any pre-defined immunity rather it adjudicate such applications on a case-to-case basis (Martyniszyn, 2015). While in India, as it seems from the proposed amendment, there is no positive obligation upon the applicant to disclose the contravention for claiming the benefit of LP, the U.S. does have a compulsory positive obligation to report the contravention taking place in the other market, else to face the interplay of the penalty 'plus'. Indian regime is weak on this ground as well, thus the translation of U.S. LP in India is improbable.

The concept of Leniency Plus, popularly known as Amnesty Plus traces its genesis to the US competition law. In United States, both undertakings and individuals are allowed to take the benefit of the Amnesty plus Leniency. In United States, the instrument is implemented as a mandatory part of Leniency program (Martyniszyn, 2015). In the program, the instrument is implemented along with the instruments of omnibus questions and penalty plus. During investigation, when an informant is subpoenaed, the informant is sworn testimony under perjury and compelled to provide all the information related to illegal activities in the sphere of competition law, failing to provide accurate information or concealing information is punishable up to 5 years along with fine. No fixed marker is provided to calculate the penalty to be imposed on the informant for disclosing the information rather the penalty is determined according to the facts of the case. In US, by providing information about the cartel, the informant can secure immunity from the criminal prosecution and substantial reduction in the quantum of fine.

As per the Office of Fair Trading, UK, the instrument of Leniency Plus is optional rather than compulsory. The reason for it being an optional is that there is no sanction or penalty being imposed for not disclosing the information about the informant's involvement in another cartel. There are no criminal actions that can be taken against the undertakings involved in cartel rather only fines can be imposed.

In the European Union, the instrument of leniency plus has not been formally introduced. The concept has been enforced by the Union under the instrument of Leniency Notice introduced in 2006. As per this, the first informant shall be granted immunity from the fines, and subsequent informants will be granted a reduction in the fines provided the information provided by them is in addition to the information possessed by the Commission and helps in the detection of cartels. Thus, in the absence of any criminal or monetary sanctions, the Leniency Plus is optional under EU Competition Law.

In Canada, the concept of Leniency Plus is known by the name of Immunity Plus (Competition Bureau Canada, 2023). Under this instrument, if the informant discloses any information that leads to the detection of any other offence as defined under the Competition Act, the informant shall be granted immunity from the prosecution for the other offence and Immunity Plus Credit will be granted to the informant according the relevance of the information provided by the informant (Competition Bureau Canada, 2023). In Canada, the penalty is calculated on the basis of the following formula-

Final Penalty = Base Fine -+ (Net effect of Aggravating or Mitigating Factor) – Leniency Cooperative Credit (Competition Bureau Canada, 2023).

The Informant is bound to disclose "any and all" information related to agreements prohibited by the Competition Act (Competition Bureau Canada, 2023). The failure to reveal information related to these agreements will result in increased penalty and revocation of Immunity granted (Martyniszyn, 2015). The concept of Omnibus Question is also in Canada and failure of the informant or witness to disclose it will make him/her liable for prosecution under section 64 *(Government of Canada, 1985, s. 64(1))* of the Competition Act on criminal charge of obstruction and for causing perjury or obstruction under Criminal Code. Thus, we can say that Immunity Plus in Canada is compulsory, as non-disclosure of information will make liable under criminal sanctions and penalty.

It is evident from the above discussion that not all the jurisdictions have penalty plus. The question we are concerned here with is which approach India should adopt to achieve the aim with which Leniency Plus is being introduced, i.e., disclosure of other existing cartels.

The authors believe that leniency plus without penalty plus will remain an ineffective tool. Firstly, it needs to be noted that criminal sanctions are not imposed for antitrust violations in India. Due to the absence of deterrence, persons will not be motivated to disclose their participation in other cartels in other markets. This is even so when the economic benefit gained by participation in the cartel outweighs the penalty that will be imposed on the discovery of the cartel by CCI. In such a scenario, the company has nothing at stake if it does not disclose another cartel. At most, the company will only get an additional benefit if it chooses to disclose the other cartel in another market.

The author is of the view that India should adopt the instrument of Leniency Plus along with the instrument of Penalty Plus based on the US model. There must, however, be no criminal charges that can be framed against the informant for not disclosing the information. The imposition of penalty for not disclosing information to the authorities will serve as a deterrence for the informant to not to withhold the information.

Moreover, the quantum of the fine should not be fixed and pre-defined. Rather, it shall be calculated on the facts of each case. If the firm's expected profit is more than the gain from disclosing the information, it will not disclose the information (Wils, 2013). Deciding the quantum of the fine on a case-to-case basis will ensure that the participating cartels will not be able to calculate its expected profit from not disclosing the information in comparison to the gains that the firm will make by disclosing the information (Lefouili & Roux, 2012).

LENIENCY PLUS: BOOSTING CORPORATE FINANCE AND INVESTOR CONFIDENCE IN INDIA

The 'Leniency Plus' approach has the potential to profoundly alter the corporate finance landscape by influencing the way companies manage risk and make strategic financial decisions (Infobank, 1994). Companies involved in multiple cartels have the chance to lower their fines by declaring their involvement in unrelated cartels through enhanced leniency measures. This framework profoundly transforms the way in which corporations appraise the financial risks associated with anti-competitive conduct. In the past, fines and penalties related to involvement in cartels have been seen as irregular but significant financial risks that could negatively impact a company's balance sheet. However, by encouraging early collaboration with regulatory bodies, "Leniency Plus" would enable companies to more effectively anticipate and avoid these risks. As a result, companies would probably incorporate compliance strategies into their long-term financial planning, viewing compliance as an investment that is required to maintain financial stability. This change may encourage businesses to take a more proactive approach to risk management, viewing the expense of internal compliance and supervision initiatives as a means of protecting themselves from future fines and harm to their name.

The "Leniency Plus" method's impact on capital allocation is a crucial aspect that it shares with corporate finance. Companies may reallocate some of their cash to improve internal compliance frameworks, monitoring systems, and employee training programs targeted at identifying and preventing cartel participation if they place a greater emphasis on compliance. The long-term advantages would be significant, even though there would be an immediate rise in operating costs. Companies would reduce the risk of unforeseen financial liabilities by discouraging cartel behaviour and utilising leniency mechanisms when violations do arise. In the end, this would lead to a stronger, more competitive financial position (Xede, Dak-Adzaklo, Ofosu, & Adza, 2023). The money saved may then be used towards strategic initiatives like R&D, mergers, acquisitions, and market expansion. In this way, the "Leniency Plus" system would promote improved financial governance and the reallocation of resources to profitable, growth-oriented projects, in addition to decreasing fines and improving corporate financial health.

Furthermore, the "Leniency Plus" approach may affect a company's perception in the financial markets more broadly, especially with regard to investor confidence and creditworthiness. Companies are likely to gain more credibility with investors and credit rating agencies if they actively participate in leniency programs and show a commitment to regulatory compliance (Corradi & Nowag, 2023). A business that has a strong compliance record is less likely to be subject to significant financial penalties or the unpredictability that comes with regulatory investigations. Higher credit ratings may result from this consistency, which would facilitate and lower the cost of the company's capital raising efforts in the debt or stock markets. As a result, the company would be better equipped to finance growth plans, buy out rivals, and enter new markets while still retaining a strong financial position. Additionally, a larger pool of investors who are increasingly concerned with corporate governance and ethical business conduct would probably be drawn in by the greater openness and adherence to fair business practices recommended by "Leniency Plus." This enhanced investor confidence would result in a more favourable financial environment, in which companies are better equipped to grow sustainably without the imminent threat of regulatory penalties or reputational damage.

In a nutshell the "Leniency Plus" system is more than just a tool for lowering fines; it signifies a more significant change in the way businesses handle financial management, compliance, and corporate governance. Improved leniency provisions enable businesses to incorporate compliance into their financial strategy, lower financial risks, and draw in additional investment by creating a more open and competitive business climate (Corradi & Nowag, 2023). In the end, this improves the corporate finance environment in India and establishes a positive feedback loop whereby improved financial results from good governance encourage continued adherence to regulatory requirements. The introduction of 'Leniency Plus' could be a critical step in aligning corporate financial health with ethical business practices, thereby promoting long-term growth and stability across industries, as India continues to refine its competition law regime.

CONCLUSION

This study has meticulously identified many shortcomings in the proposed legislative framework that could potentially impede the development of a strong competitive regime in India, resulting in a weakened and inefficient Leniency Plus regime. These shortcomings make it more difficult for the Commission to effectively promote a market environment that is favourable to competition, especially with regard to the leniency program. Given the Commission's obligation to eliminate any obstructions to equal competition, it is imperative that it take proactive measures to resolve the identified deficiencies.

According to the critical analysis that has been presented, there are numerous suggestions that should be implemented. As a first step in the fight against cartelisation, the Commission and the Legislature ought to forego imposing criminal penalties. Secondly, Penalty Plus, in the form of compound interest with penalties relevant to each case, particularly in cases of non-disclosure, needs to be incorporated into the current Leniency Plus framework. With this modification, penalties wouldn't be predetermined and non-disclosures would receive the appropriate punishments. Third, depending on the degree of cooperation and disclosure, applicants should be granted higher benefits, up to and including full immunity, in order to incentivise more cartel disclosure. Fourth, there should be no forgiveness, and habitual offenders should be subject to more severe penalties. Finally, there is an urgent need to harmonise the Act with applicable regulations to ensure that enforcement is clear and consistent.

In addition, the Commission has to take a more comprehensive stance given the increasing overlap of corporate finance and competition law, especially in regards to maintaining market integrity and preventing anti-competitive actions that cause financial market distortions. Enhancing the leniency regime will guarantee that market participants function within an open and competitive environment, which will directly contribute to the development of fairness in corporate finance. In order to promote economic stability and corporate governance, the Indian competition regime can be elevated to a more progressive and elevated trajectory by adopting a global perspective and operating domestically.

REFERENCES

Australian Competition and Consumer Commission. (2020, September 3). Supermarkets authorised to continue cooperating on COVID-19 response. https://www.accc.gov.au/media-release/supermarkets-authorised-to-continue-cooperating-on-covid-19-response

Australian Competition and Consumer Commission. (2023). NYK convicted of criminal cartel conduct and fined $25 million. https://www.accc.gov.au/media-release/nyk-convicted-of-criminal-cartel-conduct-and-fined-25-million

Bhat, S. (2019, May 29). Regulating cartels: Challenges for competition law. CEERA. https://ceerapub.nls.ac.in/regulating-cartels-challenges-for-competition-law/

Bhattacharjea, A., & De, O. (2021, March). India's cartel penalty practices, optimal restitution and deterrence. Institute of Economic Growth. https://iegindia.org/upload/profile_publication/doc-010421_162610WP424fc.pdf

Blum, U., Steinat, N., & Veltins, M. (2008). On the rationale of leniency programs: A game-theoretical analysis. *European Journal of Law and Economics*, *25*(3), 209–229. DOI: 10.1007/s10657-008-9046-x

Borrell, J.-R., Jiménez González, J. L., & García Coto, E. (2013). Evaluating antitrust leniency programs. *Journal of Competition Law & Economics*, *10*(1), 107–136. DOI: 10.1093/joclec/nht017

Buretta, J., & Terzaken, J. (Eds.). (2022). *The cartels and leniency review* (10th ed.). Law Business Research., https://thelawreviews.co.uk/edition/the-cartels-and-leniency-review-edition-10/

Chand, A., & Bala, S. (2023). Title of the article. International Bar Association. https://www.ibanet.org/article/43fb2d60-ac81-4baa-8e35-3d2da5a1762f

Chen, Z., & Rey, P. (2013). On the design of leniency programs. *The Journal of Law & Economics*, *56*(4), 917–943. DOI: 10.1086/674011

Competition Bureau Canada. (2023). *Immunity and leniency programs under the Competition Act*. Government of Canada. https://ised-isde.canada.ca/site/competition-bureau-canada/en/how-we-foster-competition/education-and-outreach/immunity-and-leniency-programs-under-competition-act

Competition Commission of India. (2016). Suo Motu Case No. 05 of 2016.

Competition Commission of India. (2017). Suo Motu Case No. 06 of 2017

Competition Commission of India. (2023). Draft lesser penalty regulations. https://cci.gov.in/images/stakeholderstopicsconsultations/en/draft-lesser-penalty-regulations1697431514.pdf

Competition Commission of India. (2024). Advocacy booklets. https://www.cci.gov.in/advocacy/publications/advocacy-booklets

Conference on Research on Economic Theory and Econometrics. (2009, June 17). Conference on Research on Economic Theory and Econometrics. https://www2.aueb.gr/conferences/Crete2009/Tinos_program_updated17June.pdf

Corradi, M., & Nowag, J. (Eds.). (2023). *Title of the book*. Cambridge University Press., DOI: 10.1017/9781108899956

Cyril Amarchand Mangaldas. (2023, October). Draft lesser penalty regulations: Key takeaways. https://www.cyrilshroff.com/wp-content/uploads/2023/10/CLIENT-ALERT-Draft-Lesser-Penalty-Regulations-Key-Takeaways.pdf

Deo, S. P., & Verma, T. (2023). Leniency and competition law: A closer look. Lexology. https://www.lexology.com/library/detail.aspx?g=aa815dea-0368-431f-a825-bfa6f1adf63f

Department of Justice. (2023). Justice Department applauds passage of the Criminal Antitrust Anti-Retaliation Act. https://www.justice.gov/opa/pr/justice-department-applauds-passage-criminal-antitrust-anti-retaliation-act

Dijkstra, P., & Schoonbeek, L. (2009). Amnesty plus and multimarket collusion. Academia.edu. https://www.academia.edu/846411/Amnesty_Plus_and_Multimarket_Collusion

Dugar, S. M.. (2020). *Guide to competition law* (8th ed.).

European Commission. (2006). Case COMP/C.38.281/B.2, Raw Tobacco Italy, 2006/901/EC. https://eur-lex.europa.eu/legal-content/EN/TXT/PDF/?uri=CELEX:32006D0901

Ezrachi, A., & Kindl, J. (2011). Criminalization of cartel activity – A desirable goal for India's competition regime? *NLSI Review*, *23*(1), 9–28.

Friedman, M. (2002). *Capitalism and freedom*. University of Chicago Press. DOI: 10.7208/chicago/9780226264189.001.0001

Government of Canada. (1985). *Canadian Competition Act* (RSC 1985, c 19). Section 64(1).

In Re: Alleged anti-competitive conduct by Maruti Suzuki India Limited (MSIL) in implementing discount control policy vis-a-vis dealers, Suo Moto Case No. 01 of 2019.

In Re: Cartelisation by Broadcasting Service Providers by Rigging the Bids Submitted in Response to the Tenders Floated by Sports Broadcasters, Case No. 02 of 2013.

In Re: Cartelisation in industrial and automotive bearings, Suo Motu Case No. 05 of 2017.

In Re: Cartelisation in respect of Zinc Carbon Dry Cell Batteries Market in India, Suo Moto Case No. 02 of 2016 & Case Nos. 02 & 03 of 2017.

In Re: Cartelization in Respect of Tenders floated by Indian Railways for supply of Brushless DC Fans, Suo Moto Case No. 03 of 2014, at 7.11.

In Re: Chief Materials Manager, South Eastern Railway, Reference Case No. 03 of 2016.

Infobank. (1994). Banking law, capital market, corporate finance/mergers and acquisitions, competition - EC, competition - UK, employment, environmental law, financial services, information technology, and more. *Business Law Review, 15*(10), 262–284. DOI: 10.54648/BULA1994077

Kaur, R., & Tanwar, A. (2024), "Role of Green Investment on Economic Aspects of Sustainable Development", Taneja, S., Kumar, P., Reepu, Balusamy, B., Sood, K. and Grima, S. (Ed.) *Sustainability Development through Green Economics (Contemporary Studies in Economic and Financial Analysis, Vol. 114)*, Emerald Publishing Limited, Leeds, pp. 91-106. DOI: 10.1108/S1569-375920240000114006

Khan, A. (2023, October 3). Competition Commission of India publishes the draft lesser penalty regulations. Mondaq. https://www.mondaq.com/india/cartels-monopolies/1380552/competition-commission-of-india-publishes-the-draft-lesser-penalty-regulations

Lefouili, Y., & Roux, C. (2012). Leniency programs for multimarket firms: The effect of amnesty plus on cartel formation. *International Journal of Industrial Organization*, *30*(6), 624–634. DOI: 10.1016/j.ijindorg.2012.04.004

Martyniszyn, M. (2015). Leniency (amnesty) plus: A building block or a Trojan horse? *Journal of Antitrust Enforcement*, *3*(3), 391–409. DOI: 10.1093/jaenfo/jnv005

Mayock, C., & Meirsch, G. (2023). Leniency. European Commission. https://competition-policy.ec.europa.eu/cartels/leniency_en

Mehta, P. S. (2003). Competition policy in developing countries: An Asia-Pacific perspective. Asia Pacific Economic Cooperation Bulletin, 79(2002/03), 1–25.

Mehta, U. S., & Pati, S. (2016, January). Designing effective leniency programme for India: Need of the hour. CUTS International. https://cuts-ccier.org/wp-content/uploads/2019/01/Designing_Effective_Leniency_Programme_for_India-Need_of_the_Hour.pdf

Miller, N. H. (2009). Strategic leniency and cartel enforcement. *The American Economic Review*, *99*(3), 750–768. DOI: 10.1257/aer.99.3.750

Nagrik Chetna Manch v. Fortified Securities Solutions, Case No. 5 of 2015.

Official Journal of the European Union. (2006). Notice on leniency in cartel cases, OJ C 298/17, L353/48.

Official Journal of the European Union. (2006). Notice on leniency in cartel cases, OJ C 298/17, L353/49.

Official Journal of the European Union. (2006). Notice on leniency in cartel cases, OJ C 298/17.

Prasad, G. C. (2021, March 26). Probing cartels a challenge in digital age, says CCI chief. Mint. https://www.livemint.com/market/mark-to-market/probing-cartels-a-challenge-in-digital-age-cci-11616756956947.html

Salzgitter v. Commission, Case T-308/00, ECLI:EU:T:2004:199 (General Court of the European Union, 2004).

Sandeepan, N., & Fatima, M. (2021, May 5). Leniency regime in India: The CCI's consistently inconsistent approach. The Times of India, 1.

Singh, N., Nair, V., & Oberoi, P. (2018, August 13). Evolving leniency regime under the Indian competition law. Oxford Law Faculty. https://www.law.ox.ac.uk/business-law-blog/blog/2018/08/evolving-leniency-regime-under-indian-competition-law

The Competition Commission of India (Lesser Penalty) Regulations. 2009, Reg. 4(a) (India).

The Competition Commission of India (Lesser Penalty) Regulations. 2009, Reg. 4(b) (India).

The Competition Commission of India (Lesser Penalty) Regulations. 2009, Reg. 4(c)(i) (India).

The Competition Commission of India (Lesser Penalty) Regulations. 2009, Reg. 5(1) (India).

The Competition Commission of India (Lesser Penalty) Regulations. 2009, Reg. 5(2) (India).

The Competition Commission of India (Lesser Penalty) Regulations. 2009, Reg. 5(4) (India).

The Competition Commission of India (Lesser Penalty) Regulations. 2009, Reg. 5(8) (India).

The Competition Commission of India (Lesser Penalty) Regulations. 2009, Reg. 4(c)(ii) (India).

Tiptur, S., & Tripathi, P. (2021, December). Cartel leniency program in India: Why no race here? National Law School of India University. https://nls.ac.in/resources/cartel-leniency-program-in-india-why-no-race-here/

UNCTAD. (1959, November 25). U.N. UNCTAD.

U.S. Department of Justice. (1993). Corporate leniency policy.

U.S. v. Bridgestone Corporation, No. 4:11CR00651-001 (S.D. Tex. Oct. 07, 2011). https://www.justice.gov/atr/case-document/file/489816/download

Whish, R., & Bailey, D. (2012). *Competition law* (7th ed.).

Wils, W. P. J. (2013). Antitrust compliance programmes and optimal antitrust enforcement. *Journal of Antitrust Enforcement*, *1*(1), 52–76. DOI: 10.1093/jaenfo/jns006

Xede, J., Dak-Adzaklo, C. S. P., Ofosu, E., & Adza, S. W. D. (2023). Competition laws, external financing and investment. *Journal of International Financial Markets, Institutions and Money*, *82*, 101700. DOI: 10.1016/j.intfin.2022.101700

Section 3

Financial Planning, Capital Allocation, and Institutional Frameworks in Dynamic and Resource-Constrained Economic Environments

Chapter 6

Best Practices for Financial Planning and Analysis in the Context of COVID-19

Jitin K. Gambhir
http://orcid.org/0009-0006-6525-6172
KR Mangalam University, India

ABSTRACT

The global COVID-19 pandemic has had a profound impact on economies and businesses worldwide, disrupting financial markets, supply chains, and consumer behavior. In this unprecedented crisis, organizations have faced numerous challenges in effectively planning and analyzing their financial performance. This abstract explores the practices that have emerged in financial planning and analysis (FP & A) to navigate the uncertainties brought about by the pandemic. The COVID-19 pandemic has highlighted the critical importance of agile and adaptable financial planning processes. Traditional static forecasting models have proven inadequate in capturing the rapidly evolving landscape. Instead, organizations have embraced dynamic scenario planning, incorporating various potential outcomes and their corresponding financial implications. By considering multiple scenarios and assessing the associated risks and opportunities, businesses can make more informed decision

DOI: 10.4018/979-8-3693-8247-9.ch006

INTRODUCTION

The outbreak of the COVID-19 pandemic has caused unprecedented disruptions to global economies and businesses, forcing organizations to reassess their financial planning and analysis (FP & A) practices. The rapidly changing landscape, volatile markets, and shifting consumer behavior have created immense challenges for financial professionals in accurately forecasting and strategizing in this uncertain environment. As a result, new practices and approaches have emerged to enhance FP & A processes and enable organizations to navigate the complexities brought about by the pandemic. This introduction sets the stage for understanding the importance of effective financial planning and analysis during the COVID-19 crisis. It highlights the need for agility, real-time data analysis, collaboration, and risk management in the context of FP & A. By adopting these practices, businesses can make informed decisions, adjust their financial strategies, and safeguard their financial health amidst the ongoing uncertainties. The subsequent sections of this paper will delve deeper into the specific practices that have gained prominence in financial planning and analysis during the COVID-19 pandemic. It will explore dynamic scenario planning, real-time data analysis, collaboration and communication, and risk management as essential components of an effective FP & A framework. These practices offer insights into how organizations can navigate the challenges posed by the pandemic and position themselves for resilience and success in an evolving business landscape. (Alonso et al., 2020)

FINANCIAL PLANNING MEANING

Financial planning refers to the process of evaluating an individual's or organization's current financial situation, setting goals, and creating a comprehensive plan to achieve those goals. It involves analyzing income, expenses, assets, and liabilities to develop strategies for budgeting, saving, investing, and managing debt. The goal of financial planning is to ensure financial stability, security, and growth by making informed decisions about spending, saving, and investing, particularly during periods of economic uncertainty such as the COVID-19 pandemic (Shaharuddin et al., 2021). It considers various factors such as income levels, expenses, risk tolerance, time horizon, and financial objectives to create a roadmap for individuals or organizations to achieve their financial aspirations and navigate economic challenges effectively.

NEED OF THE STUDY

Because of the Covid-19 pandemic, there is a greater demand for financial planning and analysis (FP & A). The global health crisis has upended economies around the world, offering previously unheard-of challenges for businesses across a wide range of industries. Organizations must assess and adjust their financial practices in order to properly manage the ongoing crisis. The Covid-19 pandemic has had a significant impact on the financial climate, affecting supply networks, revenue streams, and consumer demand (Singh et al., 2020). As a result, businesses have suffered significant declines in revenue, rising expenses, and cash flow issues. Competent FP & A becomes critical in such scenarios for firms to assess their current financial state, identify potential risks and opportunities, and make sound decisions to ensure their survival and longevity. Through careful financial planning and analysis, businesses can gain a comprehensive understanding of their financial health, liquidity, and solvency. This includes conducting scenario planning and sensitivity analysis to assess the potential impacts of different recovery scenarios and develop appropriate contingency plans. FP & A also enables organizations to optimize their resource allocation, identify cost-saving opportunities, and manage working capital efficiently. It provides them with the necessary tools to assess risks, seize opportunities, and make informed decisions to navigate the challenges posed by the ongoing crisis successfully. By adopting robust FP & A practices, organizations can increase their resilience, enhance their financial performance, and position themselves for long-term success in a post-pandemic world. (Verma & Gustafsson, 2020).

PRE-COVID-19 FINANCIAL PLANNING

Before the COVID-19 pandemic, financial planning was conducted in a relatively stable economic environment, where individuals, families, and organizations focused on setting and achieving their financial goals based on predictable conditions. Pre-COVID financial planning involved several key elements. To make the most of their money, individuals and families first created budgets. They examined their costs, including housing, transportation, food, utilities, and leisure, and modified their spending appropriately to ensure that their income met their necessities while leaving room for savings and investments. Savings and investments were significant components of financial planning prior to COVID. People attempted to save for emergencies, plan for retirement, and invest in stocks, bonds, mutual funds, or real estate. They considered their level of comfort with risk, time horizon, and long-term financial objectives when making investment decisions. Prior to COVID, access to credit was also a consideration in financial planning. The use of credit cards, loans, and mortgages as payment for goods and services is common in the United States. They maintained high credit scores and paid their bills on time to obtain favorable terms and interest rates. Long-term financial goals were an important aspect of financial planning prior to COVID. People desired to quickly achieve significant goals such as purchasing a home, paying for college, starting a business, or retiring. They engaged in financial planning, sought guidance from financial professionals, and implemented methods to ensure they stayed on pace to meet their objectives.

LITERATURE REVIEW

Mohin, P. V., & Chinni, N. (2022)

This study investigates how the COVID-19 pandemic influenced personal financial planning among persons in various occupations. The pandemic's extensive disruptions in economies and financial markets have had a severe influence on individuals' financial well-being and planning strategies. The phrase "soap" refers to a product or service description.

The study looks at how the pandemic affected people's income, expenses, savings, and investing strategies, as well as how they felt about their financial security and capacity to prepare for the future. Healthcare workers may have more work to perform and more financial security during the pandemic because their jobs are so crucial. People who work in the service industry, on the other hand, may lose their jobs, earn less money, and experience greater financial uncertainty.

Bimal Bhatt. (2011)

Financial management is critical to the success and longevity of all organizations. The fact that it is the subject of a recent study emphasizes the importance of this topic. The study examines the most significant aspects of financial management, including budgeting, financial planning and forecasting, risk management, capital structure, and investment analysis. It demonstrates how critical it is to effectively manage financial resources to achieve organizational goals, maximize profits, and minimize financial hazards. Financial management is necessary to make strategic decisions. It's important to remember that you can't beat a good thing when it comes to your health. The study also examines the use of financial models and tools for evaluating investment opportunities, estimating returns on investment, and making prudent resource allocation decisions. Better financial management leads to improved financial performance, increased cash flow, and increased shareholder value. It also highlights the importance of financial management in making sure regulatory obligations are satisfied and financial reporting is transparent.

Parimala Kanthi and Ashok Kumar (2015)

This study in Coimbatore City investigates individual investors' investment preferences and practices. To properly guide and address the demands of individual investors, financial institutions, lawmakers, and investment advisors must understand how they make their investment decisions. The study employs a mixed-methods approach, including surveys and interviews, to gather information on individual investors' investment preferences, risk tolerance, time horizon, and behavior in Coimbatore

City. The study explores a variety of characteristics related to investment decisions, including financial literacy, income, age, and occupation. The study's findings provide insight into the investment preferences of individual investors in Coimbatore City. The most common investment options, including stocks, mutual funds, real estate, and fixed deposits, are outlined, and the logic for each is analyzed. The study also investigates investors' level of risk appetite and explores the role of risk horizon in affecting investment decisions.

PROBLEM STATEMENT

The COVID-19 pandemic has presented unprecedented challenges for businesses, making financial planning and analysis (FP & A) more critical than ever. The problem lies in the need to adapt traditional financial planning and analysis practices to the unique circumstances and uncertainties brought about by the pandemic. The outbreak of COVID-19 has disrupted global economies, leading to revenue declines, supply chain disruptions, and increased costs for businesses across sectors (Villacé-Molinero et al., 2021). As a result, organizations face the urgent need to reassess their financial strategies, allocate resources efficiently, and make informed decisions to ensure their survival and sustainability. The problem statement refers to the lack of a comprehensive framework for FP & A that considers the consequences of COVID-19. Traditional financial planning and analysis approaches may be unable to account for how quickly the pandemic is changing and how uncertain it is, resulting in inaccurate estimates and poor judgements. The pandemic has introduced new variables and hazards that need to be considered in financial planning and analysis. These include things like changing client demand, new legislation, and government assistance programs for firms. Financial plans that aren't flexible or resilient enough to deal with recurring interruptions can be the result of failing to account for these variables. The pandemic has also demonstrated the need for scenario planning and sensitivity analysis in FP & A. Organizations need to be prepared to analyze and predict various recovery scenarios, accounting for how varying timescales, vaccination rates, and economic conditions may affect the result. Companies that lack excellent scenario planning may struggle to respond swiftly and proactively to changing events. (Sangeetha et al., 2022)

CORONAVIRUS (COVID-19) RISKS MAJOR SETBACKS FOR FINANCING FOR SUSTAINABLE DEVELOPMENT

The coronavirus (COVID-19) pandemic has posed significant risks and challenges to financing for sustainable development. The global health crisis has had far-reaching economic impacts, disrupting industries, supply chains, and financial markets worldwide. As a result, the progress made towards achieving the aims of the Sustainable Development aims (SDGs) is at risk. One of the most serious threats is that the pandemic will slow the economy. Many countries have experienced recessions and declines in economic activity, resulting in reduced government revenues and increased public debt. This has limited governments' capacity to dedicate sufficient resources to programs and projects for sustainable development. The pandemic has also caused significant damage to the private sector. Reduced revenues, disrupted operations, and increased borrowing costs are just a few of the financial issues that businesses in a variety of industries have encountered. This has resulted in less funding being allocated to sustainable projects and a change in priorities towards short-term financial stability. The pandemic has caused increased risk perceptions among investors and lenders. This has resulted in a decline in foreign direct investment and a tightening of credit, particularly in emerging and developing economies. As a result, funding for sustainable development projects such as green energy, infrastructure, and social welfare schemes has become more difficult to get. As a result of the pandemic, public resources have been shifted to address urgent health and humanitarian needs. This has diverted attention and funds away from sustainable development priorities. This has created a potential setback in achieving the SDGs, including poverty eradication, quality education, climate action, and gender equality. To mitigate these setbacks, it is crucial to prioritize and integrate sustainable development into post-pandemic recovery plans. Governments, international organizations, and the private sector need to collaborate and mobilize resources towards sustainable projects and initiatives. This includes adopting innovative financing mechanisms, promoting public-private partnerships, and strengthening international cooperation for sustainable development.

RESULTS

The financial impact of COVID-19 has varied across different country income categories, with each category experiencing unique challenges and implications. Here is an overview of the general trends observed:

Figure 1. Financial Impact of COVID-19, by Country Income Category

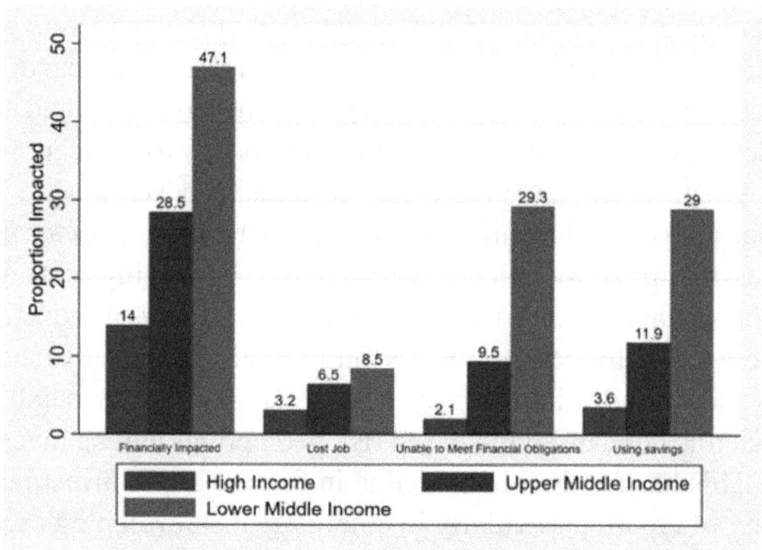

High-Income Countries: High-income countries have generally been better equipped to handle the financial impact of the pandemic. These countries typically have robust healthcare systems, fiscal resources, and access to capital markets. While they have still faced economic contractions and fiscal strains, many high-income countries have implemented significant stimulus packages to support businesses, protect jobs, and provide social safety nets. However, the recovery has been uneven, with some sectors and industries still facing challenges.

Upper-Middle-Income Countries: Upper-middle-income countries have experienced a diverse range of financial impacts. Some countries in this category, particularly those heavily reliant on sectors like tourism or commodities, have been hit hard. They have faced significant declines in revenue, increased borrowing costs, and limited fiscal capacity to implement large-scale stimulus measures. Other countries in this category with more diversified economies and stronger healthcare systems have fared relatively better.

Lower-Middle-Income Countries: Lower-middle-income countries have faced significant financial challenges due to the pandemic. These countries often have limited fiscal resources, weak healthcare systems, and high levels of informality. They have experienced disruptions in sectors such as tourism, remittances, and export-oriented industries, leading to reduced revenue and increased debt burdens. Many of these countries have relied on international assistance and emergency financing from multilateral institutions to mitigate the economic impact.

It is important to note that the financial impact within each country income category can vary significantly depending on factors such as the size of the country, the structure of the economy, and the effectiveness of policy responses. The ongoing vaccination campaigns and efforts to build resilience will play a crucial role in shaping the financial recovery across all income categories.

Figure 2. Scatterplot of Social Progress Index versus Proportion Whose Finances Were Adversely Impacted

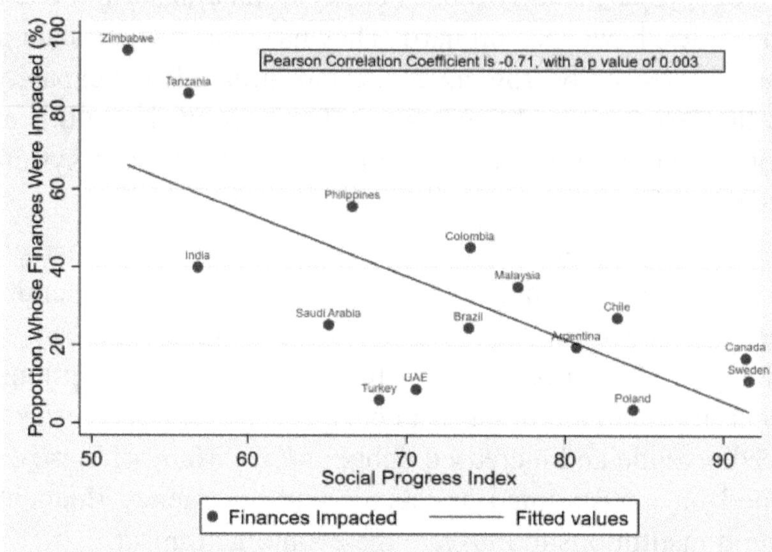

A scatterplot comparing these two variables would help visualize the relationship between the SPI and the financial impact of COVID-19 across different regions or countries. The x-axis would represent the SPI, which measures a region's overall happiness and quality of life while taking several social and environmental aspects into account. The proportion of people or households reporting adverse financial impacts because of the pandemic would be represented on the y-axis. We might see different trends in a scatterplot like this. In countries or regions with higher SPI scores, there may be a positive association between social advancement and social resilience during the pandemic, as indicated by a reduced proportion of persons reporting adverse financial impacts. This could be due to improved social safety nets, efficient health-care systems, and more diverse economies. The proportion of people reporting adverse financial impacts may be larger in countries or regions with lower SPI scores, indicating a possible inverse relationship. These areas may struggle to provide adequate assistance, have inferior health-care systems, or rely heavily on sectors affected by the epidemic.

CONCLUSION

The COVID-19 pandemic has underscored the crucial importance of financial planning and analysis (FP & A) in navigating the challenges and uncertainties brought about by the crisis (Ngoc et al., 2020). Traditional financial planning approaches have proven insufficient in addressing the rapidly evolving landscape, making it imperative to adapt FP & A practices to the unique context of COVID-19. The conclusion drawn is that organizations need to adopt a comprehensive and adaptive framework for FP & A that incorporates the specific variables and risks associated with the pandemic. To provide precise and timely insights, real-time data, advanced modelling approaches, and scenario analysis are used. Businesses may better forecast and plan for many ways the economy could improve by employing scenario planning. This ensures that their financial plans are adaptable to changes in the economy. This strategy allows people to make quick decisions and adjust their plans as the circumstance changes. Finally, it is underlined that firms must employ technology and data analytics to strengthen their FP & A capabilities. Because of the availability of real-time financial data and cutting-edge analytical tools, organizations may obtain deeper insights into their financial health, identify risks and opportunities, and make sound decisions in a turbulent environment. The COVID-19 epidemic has demonstrated the importance of FP & A in assisting organizations in dealing with the financial challenges that the crisis entails. In the face of persistent uncertainty, businesses may strengthen their financial stability and position themselves for long-term success by taking a rigorous and flexible approach, leveraging technology and data analytics, and embracing scenario planning.

REFERENCES

Alonso, A. D., Kok, S. K., Bressan, A., O'Shea, M., Sakellarios, N., Koresis, A., & Santoni, L. J. (2020). COVID-19, aftermath, impacts, and hospitality firms: An international perspective. *International Journal of Hospitality Management, 91*, 102654. DOI: 10.1016/j.ijhm.2020.102654 PMID: 32863526

Bhatt, B. (2011). Financial Management Importance. (From) http://www.blognbuzz.com/financial-management-importance.html. Retrieved 12 April 2012

Kanthi, K. & Kumar, K. (2015). "A Study on Investment preferences and behavior of individual investors in Coimbatore City", Bonfring International Journal Industrial engineering and Management Science, Vol 5 (4), pp 170-174

Mohin, P. V., & Chinni, N. (2022). Impact of Covid-19 on Personal Financial Planning: An empirical study of different professions. *Central European Management Journal, 30*(4), 1509–1521.

Ngoc, N. M., Tien, N. H., & Anh, D. B. H. (2020). Opportunities and challenges for real estate brokers in post Covid-19 period. *Journal of Science and Technology, 170*(10), 203–208.

Sangeetha, M., Hoti, A., Bansal, R., Hasan, M. F., Gajjar, K., & Srivastava, K. (2022). Facilitating artificial intelligence supply chain analytics through finance management during the pandemic crises. *Materials Today: Proceedings, 56*, 2092–2095. DOI: 10.1016/j.matpr.2021.11.418

Shaharuddin, N. S., Zain, Z. M., & Ahmad, S. F. S. (2021). Financial planning determinants among working adults during Covid 19 pandemic. *International Journal of Academic Research in Accounting Finance and Management Sciences, 11*(1), 285–304. DOI: 10.6007/IJARAFMS/v11-i1/8998

Singh, I., Singh, J., & Baruah, A. (2020). Income and Employment Changes Under COVID-19 Lockdown: A Study of Urban Punjab. *Millennial Asia, 11*(3), 391–412. DOI: 10.1177/0976399620957630

Verma, S., & Gustafsson, A. (2020). Investigating the emerging COVID-19 research trends in the field of business and management: A bibliometric analysis approach. *Journal of Business Research, 118*, 253–261. DOI: 10.1016/j.jbusres.2020.06.057 PMID: 32834211

Villacé-Molinero, T., Fernández-Muñoz, J. J., Orea-Giner, A., & Fuentes-Moraleda, L. (2021). Understanding the new post-COVID-19 risk scenario: Outlooks and challenges for a new era of tourism. *Tourism Management, 86*, 104324. DOI: 10.1016/j.tourman.2021.104324 PMID: 36540617

Chapter 7
Navigating the Corporate Finance–Time Value of Money Nexus by Resilience of Capital Rationing in Ethiopia

Shashi Kant
http://orcid.org/0000-0003-4722-5736
St. Joseph University in Tanzania, Tanzania

Tafese Niguse
http://orcid.org/0009-0008-6536-6392
Bule Hora University, Ethiopia

Mohit Verma
http://orcid.org/0009-0005-3036-3894
O.P. Jindal Global University, India

ABSTRACT

Enhancing asset results requires knowledge of how financial activities affect decision-making, especially given the resource restrictions that

DOI: 10.4018/979-8-3693-8247-9.ch007

these firms frequently confront. Information was collected from 359 Small scale corporate firms using a quantifiable investigation method. The information were then analyzed using a variety of statistical approaches, such as Kaiser-Meyer-Olkin (KMO) analysis, exploratory factor analysis (EFA), and structural equation modeling (SEM) with AMOS software. The results manifest that sound finances of a corporate procedure have a substantial positive effect on rationing of capital and improve comprehension and implementation of the money value according to time. The link among finances of a corporate and the money value according to time was manifest to be mediated by rationing of capital, proposes that corporates that are dealing with capital limits can nevertheless depict the importance of future cash flows. The outcomes imply that indirect effects is more noteworthy in influencing asset choices.

INTRODUCTION

A vital notion in investment is the time-based worth of money (TVM), which states the knowledge that a quantity of money is worth more right now than it will be later on because of its potential for growth. This idea is essential for worldwide corporate management of finance as well as for individual investing choices. Understanding how finances of corporate activities influence TVM is crucial for optimizing asset returns and guaranteeing sustainable development as firms deal with more volatile marketplace circumstances. The consequences of finances of corporate strategies on TVM in the context of Ethiopia, where economic growth is quickly changing, merit careful examination, especially in light of the peculiar difficulties encountered by local industries (Cheong & Hoang 2021). The idea of time worth of money has its roots in early financial theories that placed a strong emphasis on asset possibilities and interest rates. This idea has been incorporated throughout time into a number of financial models and procedures, influenceing how choices are made in both personal and business finance. The capacity of a company to maximize the money worth according to time is directly influenceed by efficient finances of a corporate management, which assimilates capital budgeting and asset evaluation, according to empirical investigation. Investigation has indicated that companies using a strategic capital allocation approach typically have advanced financial sustainability as a outcome of realizing the long-term potential of their assets (Li et al., 2023).

Nevertheless, in developing economies such as Ethiopia, realizing the benefits of TVM is sometimes hindered by practical problems. The practice of restricting capital expenditures due to financial limitations is known as rationing of capital, and it may have a big influence on asset choices and, in turn, the efficient management of TVM. Ethiopian corporates usually have trouble obtaining finance, which makes them prioritize some initiatives over others and may outcome in less-than-ideal asset choices. These difficulties impede development and make it more difficult to comprehend how money worth according to time and finances of a corporate procedures interact (Brealey et al., 2023). Regarding the mediating function of rationing of capital in the link among finances of a corporate and the money worth according to time in the Ethiopian setting, despite the body of literature already in existence, there are still a number of noteworthy investigation gaps. The influence of rationing of capital on asset choices and the overall financial sustainability of developing-nation corporates has not received much attention in investigation. By examining the interactions among finances of a corporate, TVM, and rationing of capital, this chapter seeks to close these gaps and provide practitioners and academics with guidance on how to deal with the challenges associated with making financial choices in Ethiopia.

This investigation's primary investigation question is: *"How does rationing of capital mediate the link among finances of a corporate and money worth according to time in Ethiopian firms?"* By answering this query, the investigation objectives to provide light on the activities by which finances of corporate policies influence financial sustainability, giving decision-makers in government and industry more information with which to work. The outcomes will deepen our understanding of Ethiopia's financial environment and, in the end, help practitioners and future scholars nurture efficient plans for managing assets and allocating reactions.

Investigation objectives are as follows:

1. Evaluate how Ethiopian enterprises' time worth of money is influenceed by corporate finance procedures.
2. Examine capital rationing observes in the context of project prioritizing according to projected returns.
3. Analyze how mediation functions in conversations about investment strategies and capital rationing.
4. Assess the influence of corporate finance techniques on Ethiopian financial decision-making.

BACKGROUND OF INVESTIGATION

As Ethiopia's economy grows, firms looking to optimize returns on their assets will manifest it more and more noteworthy to comprehend and implement TVM (Birhane et al., 2024). Though TVM has a well-established theoretical foundation, there are several obstacles to its practical deployment in Ethiopia, especially because of capital restriction (Dirman, 2020). The struggles of Ethiopian medium along with small sized corporates (Small scale corporate firms) to obtain financing are one noteworthy case investigation. For example, because of their high interest rates and strict lending requirements, many Small scale corporate firms are unable to get sufficient operating capital from banks or other financial institutions. As a outcome, these companies frequently turn to rationing of capital, giving noteworthy initiatives first priority while passing up potentially return on investmentable ventures. Due to this circumstance, reactions are misallocated, and these corporates are less able to take advantage of the money worth according to time. These Small scale corporate firms hinder their overall development and contribution to the economy by not investing in projects that have the potential to deliver large returns over time (Baker et al., 2021).

The lack of financial literacy among managers and business owners is another practical issue. Though many Ethiopian business owners may grasp TVM in theory, they often manifest it difficult to put it into reality (Nyoach et al., 2024). For instance, a investigation of many agricultural cooperatives in Ethiopia revealed that although cooperative leaders understood the benefit of making timely assets to boost output, they frequently made inaccurate estimates of the present assets' future worth. Due to this insufficiency, poor choices were made, such as postponing essential infrastructure or technology purchases that may have eventually augmented yields and return on investmentability (Graham, 2022). Moreover, the implementation of Total Quality Management (TVM) in Ethiopia is complicated by macroeconomic issues including devaluation and inflation. For example, real returns decrease in high inflation times, making it difficult for corporates to influence project the future worth of their assets. According to a case investigation looking at the Ethiopian construction industry, budgeting and project financing were noteworthy unclear due to varying inflation rates. The incapacity of construction industries to account for the money worth according to time in the face of economic volatility sometimes outcomes in instances where predicted return on investments did not materialize as anticipated.

STATEMENT OF PROBLEM

In an ideal world, corporates would use TVM principles to guide their asset choices and optimize their financial outcomes. But the truth is that a lot of Ethiopian companies have a hard time putting these ideas into practice because of major obstacles. Even while TVM is theoretically understood in financial literature, its actual use is still uneven and frequently erroneous (Brealey et al., 2023). The empirical literature has conflicting information about the association among corporate financial activities and TVM. While some investigation indicates that efficient capital allocation can augment financial sustainability by maximizing the money worth according to time, other investigation manifests that these advantages are undermined by things like rationing of capital and restricted financing options. This discrepancy indicates that further investigation is necessary to fully understand how these factors interact in the Ethiopian environment (Cheong & Hoang 2021). Also, the outcomes of current investigation are frequently equivocal, especially when it comes to the mediating function of rationing of capital in the connection among TVM and finances of a corporate (Jabo & Kant, 2023). This gap in the investigation is a reflection of a larger theoretical one about the ways in which rationing of capital influences financial outcomes and asset choices. There is a substantial gap in both theoretical and practical knowledge since, despite considerable investigation; few investigations' have combined the notion of rationing of capital with TVM in a coherent framework (Li et al., 2023).

There are still knowledge gaps, especially when it comes to the unique difficulties Ethiopian corporates have applying TVM concepts. Many studies concentrate on theoretical models, failing to sufficiently address the practical difficulties and intricacies faced by Ethiopian industries in the real world. Also, it is clear that there are context gaps because the majority of the work currently in publication focuses exclusively on developed economies, ignoring the distinct socioeconomic aspects that influence financial decision-making in developing nations (Dirman, 2020). The situation is made more difficult by practical issues since many Ethiopian corporates lack the financial literacy needed to properly implement TVM ideas. High rates of inflation, restricted capital availability, and a deficient financial system aggravate these problems and lead to poor asset choices (Guye et al., 2024). This circumstance emphasizes the critical necessity for focused investigation that tackles these particular obstacles and offers useful information to practitioners and decision-makers (Baker, 2021).

By examining the interactions among finances of a corporate, the money worth according to time, and rationing of capital in the Ethiopian setting, this investigation seeks to close these gaps. In order to give a thorough knowledge of the difficulties encountered by Ethiopian companies, this investigation looks at how rationing of capital mediates the link among finances of a corporate activities and TVM. The outcomes will provide a more sophisticated theoretical framework and useful suggestions for enhancing financial decision-making. Also, the knowledge collected from this investigation will help future scholars and decision-makers nurture plans that augment how TVM principles are applied, eventually leading to a stronger economic climate in Ethiopia.

THEORITICAL FOUNDATION

Capital Asset Pricing Model (CAPM): It depicts the connection among an asset's systemic risk and projected return. This model plays a key role in manifesting how venture capitalists assess possible assets over time by accounting for cash flow risk. The CAPM is pertinent to investigating how finances of a corporate procedures might maximize the application of time-based worth of money (TVM) since it emphasizes the consequence of both risk and time in asset choices (Khan & Shoaib, 2024).

Net Present Worth theory: NPV manifests the consequence of valuing future cash flows at present instead than future rates. This theory offers a quantitative approach to evaluating the worth of assets over time, which makes it closely related to TVM (Asefa et al., 2023). Corporates may optimize their financial sustainability by giving initiatives with positive net present worth (NPV) priority, manifesting the need of wise capital allocation. The idea, however, does not take into consideration the limitations imposed by rationing of capital, which might prevent a company from making assets in ventures that would otherwise provide return on investment able returns (Cheong & Hoang 2021).

The Agency Theory: It is pertinent as well since it discusses stakeholder conflicts of interest, especially those that arise among shareholders and management. According to agency theory, managers in the framework of finances of a corporate could decide to make assets that are not in the best interests of shareholders, especially in situations where capital is rationed. This may outcome in underfinancing of initiatives that successfully use the money worth according to time, which would influence the sustainability of the company as a whole (Brealey et al., 2023).

Behavioral Finance Theory: provide information on the psychological aspects of financial decision-making. According to this theory, emotional and cognitive biases might outcome in illogical asset choices, which could make the actual use of TVM in finances of a corporate even more challenging. Behavioral finance can help explain why corporates frequently struggle to adopt TVM concepts successfully, particularly in underdeveloped nations like Ethiopia where financial literacy may be low (Li et al., 2023).

DEFINITION AND ORIGIN OF CONCEPTS

Time worth of Money: It is a notion in finance which states that the earning ability of a quantity of money makes it worth different amounts today than it will in the future. Essentially, funds that are accessible today can be invested to produce returns or earn interest, increasing their worth relative to the same funds in the future. TVM is based on the fundamental idea that interest rates rise with time and that's why timing cash flows is noteworthy when making financial choices. This idea has its roots in the understanding of the worth of interest in transactions by ancient societies like the Greeks and Babylonians (Coles & Li2023).

Capital Budgeting: It is used to describe the process of organizing and assessing financial commitments to long-term projects or assets. In order to make wise financial choices, this procedure entails assessing prospective expenses and figuring out their anticipated returns over time. For corporates, capital budgeting is essential because it facilitates the efficient use of reactions to meet strategic objectives and optimize return on investmentability (Dirman, 2020).

Rationing of capital: It is an financial tactic used when a business restricts its capital expenditures because of financial restrictions like tight budgets or scarce financing. Corporates are forced by this method to prioritize some initiatives above others, which frequently outcomes in judgments that are made based more on subjective evaluations than on scientific information. When scholars started examining the influences of resource limitations on business asset choices in the middle of the 20th century, the idea of rationing of capital was born. The idea became well-known as corporates looked to manage financial constraints and maximize their capital allocation, especially in unstable economic times (Graham, 2022).

Net Present Worth: NPV is a technique castoff in investment budgeting to calculate a project's or asset's cost-influenceness. The modification among the contemporary worth of cash inflows and discharges over a certain time period is determined by net present worth, or NPV. A project is probably going to be return on investmentable if the projected earnings on asset (NPV) are optimistic, which manifests that the ventures predicted earnings surpass its expenses (Dereso et al., 2023)

EMPIRICAL LITERATURE REVIEW

Corporate Finances and Time Worth of Money

Several studies have demonstrated how well-thought-out finances of a corporate tactics may maximize TVM's implementation, improving organizational sustainability. For example, a investigation conducted in 2024 by Kant & Adula questioned CEOs of big firms and discovered that NPV calculations—a method used in capital budgeting—were crucial in assessing potential assets. According to their outcomes, companies that used thorough financial analysis tools were in a augmented position to optimize the money worth according to time, which produced superior financial outcomes (Li et al., 2023). Panigarhi et al. (2023) conducted a noteworthy investigation to examine the influence of structure of capital on asset choices made in developing countries. The authors found that corporates were augmented at applying TVM principles in their asset assessments when they had a well-structured capital framework. By giving priority to initiatives with positive net present worths (NPVs), these companies could efficiently utilize their reactions, leading to augmented return on investmentability. This investigation underlines the relevance of strong finances of corporate procedures in allowing the influence deployment of TVM, particularly in environments where financial limitations are prominent (Brealey et al., 2023).

Along with, actual information from a investigation by Durga et al. (2024) in the Nigerian manufacturing sector manifested that companies with a deeper grasp of TVM were those that actively used capital budgeting tools such payback period analyses and internal rate of return. According to the investigation, these companies were able to overcome rationing of capital difficulties more skillfully, which eventually outcomeed in advanced financial sustainability and more informed asset choices. This investigation emphasizes how crucial strategic capital management and financial literacy are to successfully implementing TVM (Adula et al.,

2023). However, other investigation has manifest noteworthy obstacles to TVM's successful application in finances of a corporate. For instance, a 2023 investigation by Guyo et al. discovered that corporates with inadequate working capital management frequently had trouble understanding the money worth according to time, which led to postponed expenditures and lost opportunities. The outcomes of this investigation indicate that in order to influence capitalize on the potential advantages of TVM, finances of corporate frameworks must incorporate complete working capital strategies (Baker, 2021). Also, investigation has manifest that behavioral aspects play a bigger part in financial decision-making. A 2023 investigation by Adula et al. looked at how firms' use of TVM principles might be influenceed by cognitive biases that cause departures from rational financial conduct. This draws attention to a crucial void where empirical investigation and behavioral finance converges, implying that psychological variables might impede the best use of finances of a corporate tool, especially when making asset choices (Dirman, 2020).

H1: Corporate Finances has a substantial association with Time-Worth of Money.

Finances of a Corporate and Rationing of Capital

External causes like high interest rates, restricted access to financing, or internal restrictions that limit capital expenditures are frequently the cause of this dilemma. Navigating these limitations requires influence finances of a corporate procedures, which help corporates, decide which initiatives to take on (Coles & Li, 2023). The way that corporates handle rationing of capital is strongly influenced by finances of corporate methodologies, such as capital budgeting and asset assessment tools. Corporates that use strong capital budgeting tools are augmented able to determine which projects are most likely to meet their strategic goals and maximize their limited capital eruptions. Investigation indicates that firms utilizing methodical capital budgeting procedures have an augmented probability of influence identifying and prioritizing assets that augment their overall financial outcomes (Mulyungi, 2021).

In addition, the influence of finances of a corporate on rationing of capital is more noticeable in settings with unstable economies or restricted access to markets (Li et al., 2023). For instance, studies manifest that since emerging economies lack developed financial markets and institutional backing, corporates there frequently suffer more severe capital limitations. Finances of corporate procedures that prioritize careful project review and risk assessment become crucial in these situations. Even in the face of capital restriction, corporates may more efficiently spend reactions by methodically evaluating possible assets, which augments project selection and financial outcomes (Ademosu, 2022). Also, corporate governance is a major factor in determining how rationing of capital policies are implemented. Transparent capital allocation decision-making activities may be facilitated by influence governance structures, guaranteeing that funds are allocated to initiatives that manifest the firm's long-term strategic objective. On the other hand, inadequate governance might lead to less than ideal asset choices, worsening the problems associated with rationing of capital. Studies have indicated that companies possessing robust governance protocols are superior at handling their capital limitations as they are in a augmented position to give priority to initiatives that promote long-term expansion (Baker, 2021).

H2: Corporate Finances has a substantial association with rationing of capital.

Rationing of Capital and Time Worth of Money

Corporates that experience rationing of capital are forced to prioritize some initiatives above others because they have limited financing for them. This restriction may cause corporates to make less-than-ideal asset choices that ignore TVM's possible advantages because they prioritize short-term return on investments over a thorough analysis of long-term cash flows (Brealey et al., 2023). A prominent consequence of capital restriction is the propensity of industries to underestimate their future cash flows. In a perfect world, companies evaluate the present worth of projected returns from different initiatives, enabling them to make well-informed choices that optimize their long-term financial outcomes. But under capital restriction, corporates frequently choose initiatives with shorter payback times, which might cloud their perception of the actual worth of assets. This narrow emphasis on short-term return on investments might outcome in lost possibilities for longer-term cash flow analysis and potentially more lucrative initiatives (Coles & Li, 2023). Moreover, the difficulties associated with the discount rate used in TVM computations may be made worse by rationing of capital. In order to take into consideration the perceived risks assimilated with asset choices, corporates with limited reactions may turn to advanced discount rates. This method has the potential to further reduce the current worth of future cash flows, giving the impression that some projects are not as desirable as they may be. As such, the distortion of TVM application outcomes in judgments that do not accurately represent asset possibilities (Dirman, 2020).

Also, capital restriction frequently compels corporates to make choices based on qualitative standards as opposed to quantitative investigation. The core tenets of TVM may be compromised by this move away from information-driven decision-making as subjective assessments might not fully take the time-based worth of future cash flows into account. Instead of carefully examining a project's NPV or internal rate of return, a manager may, for example, prioritize it based on instinct or past experience. This dependence on non-quantitative elements may outcome in less total returns and inefficient capital allocation (Ademosu, 2022). Likewise, a reactive rather than a proactive attitude to investing may outcome from capital restriction. Corporates might put off or give up on potentially return on investmentable ventures because they are waiting on circumstances in the market or for future financing that could never come through. This cautious approach may lead to a vicious cycle of under asset, in which the company's capacity to use the money worth according to time is further hampered by delayed assets. This might eventually hinder innovation and growth when corporates lose out on chances to produce long-term compound returns (Coles & Li, 2023).

H3: Rationing of capital has a substantial association with TVM.

Mediation of Rationing of Capital Among Finances of a Corporate and TVM

A noteworthy field of investigation that clarifies how budgetary restrictions influence asset choices and the estimation of future cash flows is the mediation influence of rationing of capital in the link among finances of a corporate and the time-based worth of money (TVM). Corporates are forced to prioritize some assets above others when faced with rationing of capital, which may have a big influence on how they use TVM principles in their financial decision-making (Mulyungi, 2021). Through its modification of finances of corporate procedures, rationing of capital serves as a mediator. For instance, when corporations participate in capital planning, they often employ methodologies like Net Present Worth (NPV) and Internal Rate of Return (IRR) to analyze possible assets. But when cash is scarce, the emphasis frequently moves from the most valuable long-term ventures to those that provide faster returns. This change may cause corporates to misapply TVM principles as they may underestimate future cash flows from initiatives that have the potential to provide large returns over a longer period of time (Markonah et al., 2020).

Also, the discount rates that corporates use to determine the current worth of future cash flows are influenceed by rationing of capital. Corporates may raise their discount rates in a capital-constrained environment in order to take perceived concerns like cash flow unpredictability and the opportunity cost of capital into account. This modification may reduce the current worth of future returns, which might distort the perceived worth of some assets. Thus, the link among finances of a corporate activities and the successful implementation of TVM is distorted by the mediation influence of rationing of capital (Dirman, 2020). Along with, rationing of capital can limit the information available for decision-making. When reactions are scarce, firms may not invest in comprehensive financial analyses or market investigation, leading to choices based more on intuition than on rigorous financial evaluation. This lack of thorough analysis can exacerbate the challenges of applying TVM influence, as firms miss critical insights that could inform more optimal asset choices. Thus, rationing of capital mediates the association by constraining the decision-making process and limiting the capacity for informed financial planning (Brealey et al., 2023).

H4: Mediation of rationing of capital manifest among finances of a corporate and TVM

CONCEPTUAL FRAMEWORK

Figure 1. Conceptual framework

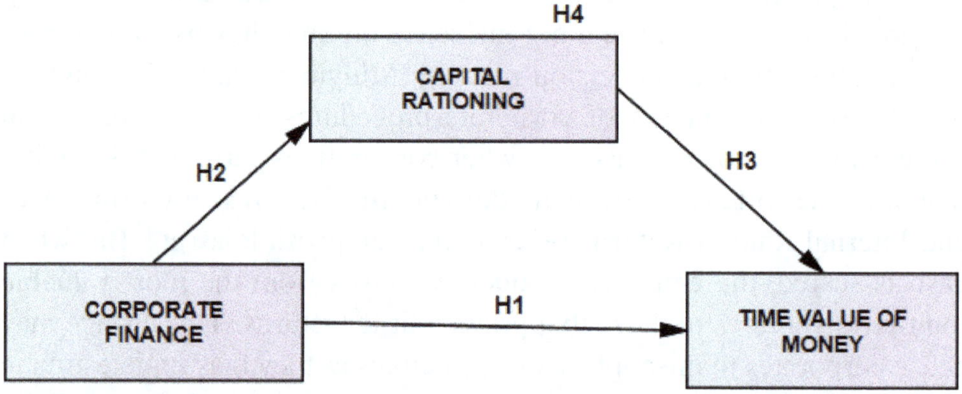

Source: Synthesis on Hypothesis

INVESTIGATION METHODOLOGY

The influence of finances of a corporate on the money worth according to time was examined in this investigation using a quantitative investigation methodology, with an emphasis on the mediating function of rationing of capital. A rigorous selection process was used to choose 359 participants from medium along with small sized firms (Small scale corporate firms) that are active in Ethiopia. The investigation focuses on a broad sample of 359 volunteers from small along with medium-sized companies in Ethiopia. These companies were chosen deliberately to financial managers and owners represent the changing environment of small-scale business operations in the nation. The demographic mix of the participants was fairly balanced, with around 55% reporting as male and 45% being female. Such gender distribution is critical for understanding viewpoints on business finance including capital rationing because it guarantees that ideas come from a diverse variety of experiences. The participants' ages varied from 25 to 60, with the majority lying among 30 and 45. This age group is noteworthy because it often assimilates people with extensive professional knowledge along with a deep grasp of corporate finance processes. Furthermore, respondents' educational backgrounds differed, with 40% holding bachelor's degrees, 35% holding master's degrees, and the other 25% holding certificates or other credentials. This educational variety enriches the data obtained by capturing various degrees of financial knowledge and management experience. A thorough and systematic process was used to select respondents, ensuring that the sample correctly reflected the target demographic of Ethiopia's medium along with small-sized businesses (SMEs). Initially, a thorough list of active enterprises was prepared, with an emphasis on those that fulfilled the Ethiopian government's standards of medium along with small size. A stratified sample strategy was used to guarantee that all sectors of this demography were well represented, especially production, services, as well as commerce. After creating the initial list, the 359 participants were chosen using a random sample method. This strategy reduced selection bias and permitted the inclusion of organizations from various geographical locations and industries, increasing the potential for generalization of the outcomes. Participants were recruited via a mix of phone interviews as well as direct outreach, outcomeing in a high response rate. Each chosen business was expected to appoint a representative, usually a financial manager and owner, whom was familiar with the company's financial procedures and issues. This technique not only guaranteed that the obtained data was relevant, but it also allowed for in-depth talks regarding the time relevance of monetary and financial rationing policies in Ethiopia.

It was determined that this sample size would be adequate to guarantee the generalizability of the outcomes and to offer a strong statistical analysis. Bartlett's test of sphericity and the Kaiser-Meyer-Olkin (KMO) score were computed to assess if the information were suitable for factor analysis. The information were deemed eligible for additional analysis when the KMO worth exceeded 0.6, indicating that the sample size was sufficient for the exploratory factor analysis (EFA) to be carried out. The money worth according to time, rationing of capital, and finances of a corporate constructions' underlying factor structures were determined by the use of the EFA. The measuring scales employed in the investigation were augmented with the aid of this analysis.

The scales' elements were taken from well-known works of literature and modified to make them appropriate for Ethiopia. The validity of the scale construction procedure was confirmed by the exploratory factor analysis, which identified unique components for every concept. Structural Equation Modeling (SEM) was used with AMOS software to examine the proposed correlations among the structures after the EFA. Through the simultaneous analysis of several connections made possible by SEM, a thorough knowledge of how rationing of capital, through the mediation of finances of a corporate, influences the money worth according to time was obtained. In order to make sure that the proposed model accurately reflected the information, the model fit was evaluated using a variety of indices, such as the Chi-square statistic, Comparative Fit Index (CFI), and Root Mean Square Error of Approximation (RMSEA). The process of developing the scale assimilates extensive validity and reliability testing. The measuring scales' internal consistency was evaluated using Cronbach's alpha coefficients, where worths greater than 0.7 denote respectable reliability. The EFA outcomes further manifested construct validity by manifesting that the items loaded correctly into the corresponding components.

DATA ANALYSIS

Table 1. KMO and Bartlett's Test

Sampling Adequacy by Kaiser-Meyer-Olkin Measure		**.849.998**
Sphericity by Bartlett's Test	Chi-Square estimate	1399.730
	Df	87
	p-worth	.002

Source: survey outcomes, 2024

The outcomes of Bartlett's Test of Sphericity and the Kaiser-Meyer-Olkin (KMO) measure of sample adequacy are manifest in Table 1, which are both essential for assessing whether or not information are suitable for factor analysis. With a KMO score of 0.850, a high degree of sampling adequacy is indicated. In general, KMO levels more than 0.6 are regarded as appropriate, while worths around 1.0 suggest exceptional fit for factor analysis. Because the sample size is sufficient and the variables are likely to have common components, the exploratory factor analysis (EFA) used in this investigation is justified, as manifest by the worth of 0.850. The information's suitability for factor analysis is further manifested by Bartlett's Test of Sphericity. With 87 degrees of freedom (df), the test yielded an estimated Chi-square score of 1399.730. This test's consequence level (Sig.) is 0.002, which is noteworthy less than the accepted cutoff of 0.05. This outcome manifests the notion that the information is appropriate for component analysis by indicating that there may be substantial correlations among the variables. The null hypothesis is essentially rejected, indicating that the correlation matrix is not an identity matrix and that it is permissible to move on with EFA because the variables are linked.

Table 2. Total Variance Elucidated

Component	Initial Eigenworths			Extraction Sums of Squared Loadings			Rotation Sums of Squared Loadings		
	Total	% of Variance	Cumulative %	Total	% of Variance	Cumulative %	Total	% of Variance	Cumulative %
1	4.43	31.236	31.236	4.43	31.236	31.236	3.00	20.452	20.452
2	1.38	9.787	42.022	1.38	9.787	42.022	2.16	15.491	36.942
3	1.23	9.087	50.101	1.37	9.087	50.101	1.98	14.168	50.101
4	.952	6.778	56.887						
5	.871	6.223	63.120						
6	.768	5.521	69.628						

Abstraction Process: Major Component Analysis.
Source: survey outcomes, 2024

Table 2 manifests the total variance explained. The original eigenworths manifest how much of the variation was explained by each component prior to extraction. With an eigenworth of 4.43, the first component explains 31.236% of the variation in the whole. This large proportion indicates that this component is noteworthy for comprehending the underlying structures since it captures a considerable amount of the variability in the information. Its consequence is confirmed by the cumulative percentage of 31.236% that follows the initial component. Interestingly, the eigen-worth of the fourth component, which is 0.952—just below 1.0—indicates that it might not be as noteworthy to keep in the analysis. A noteworthy portion of the structure of the information can be described by the first three components alone, as seen by the cumulative percentage of variation explained by these factors reaching 50.101%. The retention of the same components after extraction is confirmed by the extraction sums of squared loadings, which match the original eigenworths. The distribution of variation among the retained factors is further elucidated by the rotation sums of squared loadings, wherein the first three components account for 20.452%, 15.491%, and 14.168% of the variance, respectively.

Confirmatory Factor Analysis

Confirmatory principle component examination is a sort of statistics that is used to validate the principle component arrangement of a group of directed proxies. Studies can assess hypotheses using CFA based on the underlying frame job and correlatives among observable proxies. The investigation used CFA under table 3 to assess the hypothesis that there is a association among the proxies that are being guided and the latent ideas that manifest them.

Table 3. Co-variances

Covariance			Estimate	S.E.	C.R.	P	Hy.
Rationing of capital	<-->	Finances of a corporate	.238	.017	8.227	.00	**H2**
Rationing of capital	<-->	Money worth according to time	.300	.030	7.590	.00	**H3**
Finances of a corporate	<-->	Money worth according to time	.261	.32	7.826	.00	**H1**

Source: survey outcomes, 2024

Table 3 presents the covariance estimates. With a standard error (S.E.) of 0.017, the correlation among finances of a corporate and rationing of capital is predicted to be 0.238. The statistical notation (.00) indicates that the critical ratio (C.R.) of 8.227 is very noteworthy, indicating a strong positive link among these two constructs. This conclusion suggests that finances of corporate activities have a major influence on rationing of capital, which is consistent with hypothesis (H2) that corporates may traverse capital restrictions with the aid of competent management of finance. Similarly, 0.300 is presented as the covariance with a S.E. of 0.030 and a C.R. of 7.590 among rationing of capital and the money worth according to time. According to this strong and substantial association (.00), which is consistent with hypothesis H3, rationing of capital influences asset choices as well as how corporates see and use money worth according to time. This implies that capital limits may cause future cash flows to be worthd less than they would otherwise be which is consistent with the worries expressed in the literature about the influences of capital constraints.

Table 4. Validity Concern

	CR	AVE	MSV	MaxR(H)	CF	CR	TVM
CF	0.737	0.650	0.226	0.859	**0.663**		
CR	0.765	0.664	0.139	0.770	0.178	**0.672**	
TVM	0.784	0.610	0.267	0.790	0.376	0.186	**0.676**

Note: CF= Finances of a corporate; CR= Capital Rationing; TVM= Money worth according to time

Source: survey outcomes, 2024

Key validity metrics for constructs are compiled in Table 4. The CR is 0.784 for money worth according to time, 0.765 for rationing of capital, and 0.737 for finances of a corporate. Each of these numbers is advanced than the appropriate cutoff point of 0.7, indicating that the questions measure the relevant constructs accurately and yield dependable information for analysis. Convergent validity of the constructs is further manifested by the Average Variance Extracted (AVE) worths, which manifest that TVM is at 0.610, CR is at 0.664, and CF is at 0.650. Since all of these worths are advanced than the suggested cutoff point of 0.5, it may be concluded that the constructs account for a substantial percentage of the variance in the corresponding items. This outcome adds to the overall validity of the investigation by confirming that the measuring scales are useful in capturing the targeted ideas. Additional guarantee of dependability under various situations is provided by the Maximum dependability (MaxR(H)) worths, which have TVM at 0.790, CR at 0.770, and CF at 0.859. The statistics which all surpass the 0.7 criterion and manifest good dependability provide additional evidence for the constructs' robustness. Finally, there are positive correlations among the constructs as indicated by the correlation factors, which are 0.186 for CR and TVM, 0.178 for CF and TVM, and 0.376 for CF and TVM. The fact that these correlations manifest a association among the constructs but are not overly strong manifests the notion that each construct measures a different component of the investigation model.

MEDIATING ROLE EXAMINATION

Figure 2. Structural equation model

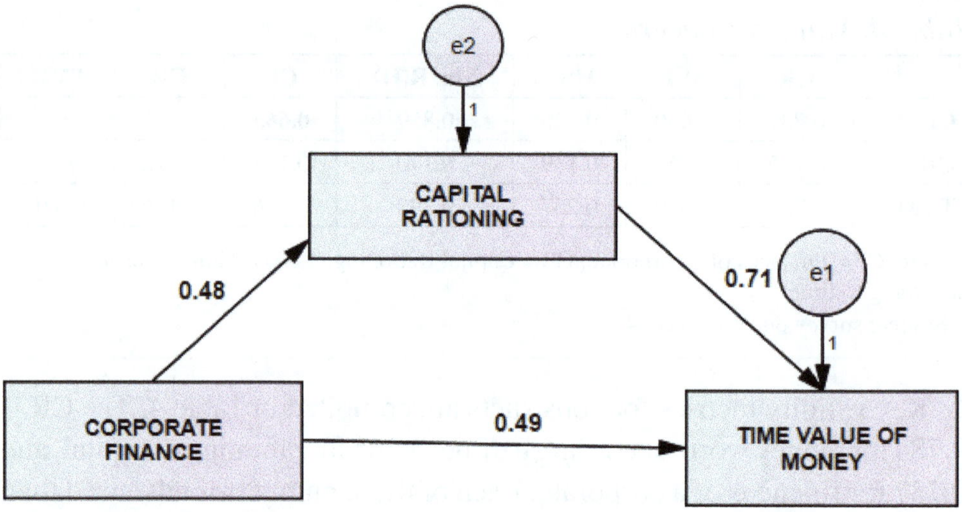

Source: AMOS output, 2024

Model Fit Indices

Table 5. indices for Model Fit

Sig.	Chi-Sq	RMR	Fitness Goodness	Fitness Confirmatory	TLI	RMSEA
0.002	1.961	.042	0.926	0.813	0.812	.032

Source: survey outcomes, 2024

The model fit indices, which are manifest in Table 5. The stated worth of the Chi-square statistic is 1.961. A better-quality fit is indicated by a lower Chi-square worth in relation to the degrees of freedom. Even though there appears to be some disparity, this number should be viewed in conjunction with other fit indices. The average residual among the observed and projected covariance matrices is measured as the Root Mean Square Residual (RMR), and it is recorded as 0.042. A good fit is often indicated by an RMR worth less than 0.05, which manifests that the model appropriately captures the information. The model has an excellent overall fit, as manifest by the reported Goodness of Fit Index (GFI) of 0.926. A GFI worth of 0.926 indicates that a noteworthy amount of the variance is explained by the model, and worth's above 0.90 are generally seen as indicative of a good fit. It states that the Comparative Fit Index (CFI) is 0.813. A outcome of 0.813 manifests a fair match, albeit it implies there is space for augment. CFI worth's above 0.90 are generally preferable. With advanced worth's denoting greater sustainability, this index compares the fit of the given model to a baseline model. Along with, the Tucker-Lewis Index (TLI) is reported to be 0.812. TLI worth's above 0.90 are preferable, much like the CFI, however a TLI of 0.812 still indicates a good match. This index provides a balance among fit and parsimony by taking into consideration the complexity of the model. Lastly, 0.032 is recorded for the RMSEA less than 0.05, while a fair fit is suggested by worth's among 0.05 and 0.08. An outstanding fit is manifest by an RMSEA of 0.032, which manifests the model's general adequacy.

Table 6. Regression Examination

Relative			Est.	S.E.	C.R.	P	Ass.
Rationing of capital	<---	Finances of a corporate	.870	.149	7.593	.00	H2
Money worth according to time	<---	Rationing of capital	.334	.137	2.859	.00	H3
Money worth according to time	<---	Finances of a corporate	.963	.198	7.964	.00	H1

Source: survey outcomes, 2024

The outcomes of the regression analysis are displayed in Table 6, which also manifests the connections among money worth according to time (TVM), rationing of capital (CR), and finances of a corporate (CF). With a S.E. of 0.149, the regression coefficient for rationing of capital as a dependent variable influenceed by finances of a corporate is 0.870. Since the C.R. worth is 7.593, it is noteworthy at the (.00) level. This robust coefficient validates hypothesis H2, indicating that finances of a corporate noteworthy influences rationing of capital in a favorable way. It suggests that efficient management of finance tools greatly augment a company's capacity to deal with capital limits, allowing for the making of augmented asset choices. Next, a coefficient of 0.334 with a S.E. of 0.137 illustrates the link among rationing of capital and the money worth according to time. This association has a C.R. of 2.859, which is also noteworthy (.00). This outcome confirms hypothesis H3, manifesting that rationing of capital has a beneficial influence on how the money worth according to time is applied. Lastly, the highly noteworthy (.00) coefficient for the money worth according to time as influenceed by finances of a corporate is stated to be 0.963, with a S.E. of 0.198 and a C.R. of 7.964. The hypothesis H1 is manifested by this strong coefficient, which manifests that finances of corporate procedures have a noteworthy beneficial influence on the comprehension and implementation of the money worth according to time. This link emphasizes how crucial sound management of finance is to helping corporates augmented understand their future cash flows, which in turn help them, make augmented asset choices.

Table 7. Mediating Influence

	Influence	worth	Path Influence
Finances of a corporate → Money worth according to time	Direct Influence	.49	Direct influence stated
Finances of a corporate → Rationing of capital → Money worth according to time	Indirect Influence	.48*.71=.34	Indirect Influence Ensued
	Whole influence	.83	Partial mediation

Source: survey outcomes, 2024

Table 7 presents the analysis of rationing of capital's mediating role in the association among finances of a corporate and the time-based worth of money. This table outlines the direct and indirect influences among various components within the scope of the investigation, giving a comprehensive understanding of their associations. The time-based worth of money is directly influenceed by finances of a corporate to the tune of 0.49. The coefficient demonstrates a strong correlation, implying that sound finances of corporate procedures augment comprehension and use of the money worth according to time. The phrase "Direct influence stated" manifests the consequence of finances of a corporate in influencing how corporates view potential future cash flows and asset prospects. On the other hand, the calculation of the indirect influence of finances of a corporate on the money worth according to time through rationing of capital is as follows: 0.48 times 0.71 equals 0.34. This computation manifests how rationing of capital influences finances of a corporate, which in turn influences the time-based worth of money. The term "Indirect Influence Ensued" emphasizes rationing of capital's function as a moderating element, demonstrating that finances of a corporate's influences are not just direct but also function through this intermediary component. When direct and indirect influences are assimilated, finances of a corporate's overall influence on the money worth according to time comes to 0.83. The entire influence of finances of a corporate on the money worth according to time is manifested by this composite measure, which manifests that the influence is still large even after taking rationing of capital into account. Lastly, the term "Partial mediation" implies that although while rationing of capital mediates the link among money worth according to time and finances of a corporate, the direct influence is still rather noteworthy. This outcome emphasizes how intricate financial decision-making activities are, with both direct and mediated channels assimilated.

DISCUSSION

This investigation looked at the complex interactions among rationing of capital, money worth according to time, and finances of a corporate. It provided noteworthy new information on how financial activities influence how choices are made when reactions are scarce. The outcomes manifest that efficient finances of a corporate tactics strengthen corporates' comprehension of the money worth according to time in addition to improving capital management and similar with alike studies like Birhane et al., 2024; Jabo & Kant, 2023 and Pnigarhi et al., 2023. Medium along with small sized corporates (Small scale corporate firms), who frequently have financial restrictions that might impede their ability to develop and attract asset, should pay particular attention to this connection. The intricacy of these interactions is further manifested by the mediating function of rationing of capital, which implies that although finances of a corporate directly influences the money worth according to time, it also uses rationing of capital to influence asset choices. The necessity for corporates to implement thorough management of finance procedures that take into account both direct and indirect influences on their asset plans is manifested by this dual route.

CONCLUSION

To sum up, this investigation adds to our knowledge of how finances of a corporate procedures influence the application of money worth according to time, especially when rationing of capital is assimilated. Based on empirical evidence, it appears that companies with robust finances of corporate strategies are augmented able to manage capital limitations, which in turn helps them make more informed asset choices that take advantage of the money worth according to time. The noteworthy connections among the constructs that have been uncovered offer a strong starting point for more investigation into the financial decision-making procedures used by Small scale corporate firms. In order to achieve augmented asset outcomes, this investigation manifests the need of combining money worth according to time knowledge with management of finance tools.

MANAGERIAL IMPLICATIONS

This investigation's conclusions have several noteworthy management ramifications. Initially, managers have to give top priority to creating strong finances of a corporate plans that deepen their comprehension of the money worth according to time. This entails putting into practice efficient capital budgeting strategies and financial analysis methodologies that enable precise evaluation of asset prospects. Also, managers may allocate reactions more wisely and augment the financial sustainability of the company by understanding how rationing of capital influences asset choices. The capacity to make choices that manifest long-term development and sustainability may be further augmented for managers through training programs that emphasize financial literacy and the money worth according to time.

PRACTICAL IMPLICATIONS

Practically speaking, this investigation emphasizes how noteworthy it is for corporates—Small scale corporate firms in particular—to implement standardized management of finance procedures. Corporates may more influence manage capital restrictions and maximize their asset plans by incorporating the ideas of finances of a corporate and the money worth according to time into their operational frameworks. In practice, this can entail implementing financial modeling and analytical software tools that make it easier to evaluate a project's feasibility using the money worth according to time. In addition, fostering a culture that prioritizes thorough assessment of asset prospects and strategic financial planning may augment decision-making procedures and optimize resource use.

THEORETICAL IMPLICATIONS

This work has noteworthy theoretical ramifications for the banking industry, especially when it comes to comprehending how rationing of capital, finances of a corporate, and the money worth according to time interact. By proving that rationing of capital acts as a mediating element that influences the link among finances of a corporate and the money worth according to time, this investigation adds to the body of knowledge. Future theoretical frameworks that objective to explain financial decision-making in resource-constrained contexts might benefit from such outcomes. The outcomes also call for a reassessment of current models to take into account the intricacies of capital management and how they influence asset choices.

RECOMMENDATIONS

It is advised that companies augment their finances of corporate procedures by implementing thorough training on capital budgeting tools and the money worth according to time in light of the outcomes. It is advisable to motivate managers to embrace a proactive stance towards financial planning, encompassing periodic evaluations of capital allocation tactics. Firms should also think about putting in place management of finance technologies that make it easier to analyze asset possibilities and take into consideration both direct and indirect influences on financial outcomes. Putting in place a strong governance structure to supervise financial decision-making procedures may help guarantee that assets are in line with the long-term strategic objectives of the company.

FUTURE DIRECTIONS

In more varied settings, future studies ought to investigate the precise activities by which rationing of capital influences the connection among finances of a corporate and the money worth according to time. More in-depth understanding of how these linkages change over time, especially in dynamic economic situations, may be obtained through longitudinal investigation. Also, investigation the influence of outside variables, such market circumstances and legal frameworks, might augment our comprehension of how financial choices are made. The generalizability of the outcomes might be augmented by extending the investigation to assimilate bigger, more diverse samples from various industries, offering a more comprehensive understanding of how finances of corporate procedures influence the money worth according to time.

REFERENCES

Ademosu, A. (2022). The effect of the financial system and its channels on SMALL SCALE CORPORATE FIRMS'access to financing: A Nigerian perspective.

Adula, M., Birbirsa, Z. A., & Kant, S. (2023). The effect of interpersonal, problem solving and technical training skills on performance of Ethiopia textile industry: Continuance, normative and affective commitment as mediators. *Cogent Business & Management, 10*(3), 2286672. Advance online publication. DOI: 10.1080/23311975.2023.2286672

Asefa, K., Kant, D. S., & Debela, K. L. (2023, November). Effect of Transformational Leadership on Organizational Performance: The Mediating Role of Employee Commitment and Expert Systems (AI) Inclusion in Ethiopia. In *2023 International Conference on Communication, Security and Artificial Intelligence (ICCSAI)* (pp. 305-310). IEEE.

Baker, H. K., Kumar, S., & Pattnaik, D. (2021). Twenty-five years of the journal of finances of a corporate: a scientometric analysis. Journal of Finances of a corporate, 66, 101572.

Brealey, R. A., Myers, S. C., & Marcus, A. J. (2023). *Fundamentals of finances of a corporate*. McGraw-Hill.

Cheong, C., & Hoang, H. V. (2021). Macroeconomic factors or firm-specific factors? An examination of the effect on corporate profitability before, during and after the global financial crisis. *Cogent Economics & Finance, 9*(1), 1959703. DOI: 10.1080/23322039.2021.1959703

Coles, J. L., & Li, Z. F. (2023). An empirical assessment of empirical finances of a corporate. *Journal of Financial and Quantitative Analysis, 58*(4), 1391–1430. DOI: 10.1017/S0022109022000448

Dereso, C. W., Kant, S., Muthuraman, M., & Tufa, G. (2023). Effect of Point of Service on Health Department Student's Creativity in Comprehensive Universities of Ethiopia: Moderating Role of Public-Private Partnership and Mediating Role of Work Place Learning. In: Jain, S., Groppe, S., Mihindukulasooriya, N. (eds) Proceedings of the International Health Informatics Conference. Lecture Notes in Electrical Engineering, vol 990. Springer, Singapore. DOI: 10.1007/978-981-19-9090-8_13

Dirman, A. (2020). Financial distress: The effects of profitability, liquidity, leverage, firm size, and free cash flow. International Journal of Business. *Economics and Law*, *22*(1), 17–25.

Durga, P., Godavarthi, D., Kant, S., & Basa, S. S. (2024). Aspect-based drug review classification through a hybrid model with ant colony optimization using deep learning. *Discov Computing*, *27*(1), 19. DOI: 10.1007/s10791-024-09441-w

Graham, J. R. (2022). Presidential address: Finances of a corporate and reality. *The Journal of Finance*, *77*(4), 1975–2049. DOI: 10.1111/jofi.13161

Guyo, D. M., Kero, C. A., & Kant, S. (2025). Is Marketing Intermediaries' Mediation Required for Livestock and Products Marketing to Improve the Economic Status of Pastoralist Communities in Ethiopia? In *AI in Agriculture for Sustainable and Economic Management* (pp. 216-234). CRC Press.

Guyo, D. M., Kant, S., & Kero, C. A. (2023, November). Mediation of Marketing Intermediaries and AI Adoption Between Livestock Products Marketing and Economic Status of Pastoralist in Ethiopia. In *2023 International Conference on Communication, Security and Artificial Intelligence (ICCSAI)* (pp. 311-316). IEEE.

Jabo, D., Borji, B., & Kant, S. (2024, February). Impact of Technical CRM on Ethiopia Bank Human-Computer Interface and Competitive Advantage as Mediators of Performance. In 2024 IEEE International Conference on Computing, Power and Communication Technologies (IC2PCT) (Vol. 5, pp. 679-682). IEEE.

Kant, S., & Adula, M. (2024). AI Learning and Work Attitude Mediation Between Reward and Organizational Support in Ethiopia. In Gomathi Sankar, J., & David, A. (Eds.), *Generative AI for Transformational Management* (pp. 109–136). IGI Global., DOI: 10.4018/979-8-3693-5578-7.ch005

Kant, S., & Adula, M. (2024). Mediated by AI-Based Generative Re-Enforcement Learning and Work Attitude: Are Intrinsic Rewards Transforming Employee Perceived Organizational Support? In Gomathi Sankar, J., & David, A. (Eds.), *Generative AI for Transformational Management* (pp. 83–108). IGI Global., DOI: 10.4018/979-8-3693-5578-7.ch004

Kant, S., & Adula, M. (2024). Human-Machine Interaction in the Metaverse in the Context of Ethiopia. In *Impact and Potential of Machine Learning in the Metaverse* (pp. 196–212). IGI Global., DOI: 10.4018/979-8-3693-5762-0.ch008

Khan, S., & Shoaib, A. (2024). Firm value adjustment speed through financial friction in the presence of earnings management and productivity growth: Evidence from emerging economies. *Humanities & Social Sciences Communications*, *11*(1), 1–17. DOI: 10.1057/s41599-024-03118-x

Li, X., Wang, J., & Yang, C. (2023). Risk prediction in management of finance of listed companies based on optimized BP neural network under digital economy. *Neural Computing & Applications*, *35*(3), 2045–2058. DOI: 10.1007/s00521-022-07377-0

Markonah, M., Salim, A., & Franciska, J. (2020). Effect of profitability, leverage, and liquidity to the firm value. *Dinasti International Journal of Economics. Finance & Accounting*, *1*(1), 83–94.

Mulyungi, J. (2021). Effect Of Short-term Financing Choices On Firm Value Of Non-financial Firms Listed On The Nairobi Securities Exchange, Kenya (Doctoral dissertation, Kca University).

Nyoach, T. D., Lemi, K., Debela, T., & Kant, S. (2024). Does Organizational Commitment Mediate the Association between Employee Association Management and Bank Performance? The Case of Banks in Ethiopia. *International Journal of Organizational Leadership*, *13*(2), 355–376. DOI: 10.33844/ijol.2024.60419

Panigrahi, A., Pati, A., Sahu, B., Das, M. N., Nayak, D. S. K., Sahoo, G., & Kant, S. (2023). En-MinWhale: An ensemble approach based on MRMR and Whale optimization for Cancer diagnosis. *IEEE Access : Practical Innovations, Open Solutions, 11*, 113526–113542. DOI: 10.1109/ACCESS.2023.3318261

Vernimmen, P., Quiry, P., & Le Fur, Y. (2022). *Corporate finance: theory and practice*. John Wiley & Sons.

KEY TERMS AND DEFINITIONS

Capital Rationing: Prioritizing which initiatives to take on becomes necessary when a corporation has limited reactions to spend in projects. This situation is known as capital rationing. Budgetary restrictions or internal regulations may be the cause of this, necessitating that businesses assess and choose investment options that maximize returns on their money.

Corporate Finance: Finance related to corporate is the extent of investment that scrutinizes an firms financing options, investment choices, and structure of capital. The major objective is to maximize shareholder worth through a combination of short- and long-term financial planning and the application of various strategies.

Time Worth of Money: This monetary philosophy conditions that due of the likelihood of upcoming proceeds. These supposition systems the basis of the notions that currency may earn curiosity and that money gains worth with time.

Chapter 8
Enhancing SME Finance in Bangladesh Through an Integrated Online Credit Bureau Platform

Shila Mamtaz
Independent Researcher, Bangladesh

Md. Kamrul Bari
http://orcid.org/0000-0001-5325-2779
Uttara University, Bangladesh

ABSTRACT

The alternative functioning measures against the worldwide financial constraints on SME growth have yet to either be initiated or are being exercised in limited form in the Bangladesh context. The Credit Bureau, one of such measures, is being applied here in a limited form where further technological advancement and sophistication are needed. Given the urge, the study employed a "phenomenological method of qualitative research" with the objective of developing a new pattern or phenomenon of a 'common online platform for credit bureaus' from the essence of earlier experiences both home and abroad in the credit reporting industry. In data collection, it used document analysis and in-depth interviews to supplement the findings. Compiling the existing and new concepts

DOI: 10.4018/979-8-3693-8247-9.ch008

resulting from the research findings, the paper concluded with a 'model proposition'. Thus, the study contributes to the further sophistication of the conventional credit information-sharing mechanism of the country. The research might help develop feasibility studies in the future to assist policy executors in this regard.

1. INTRODUCTION

SMEs are one of the key contributors to economic growth around the world (OECD, 2010; Karadag, 2016). But they receive a disproportionately small share of credit from the financial system across developed and developing countries (Creehan, 2018; Nemoto et al.,2018). Literature shows that the formal financial sector does not provide access to loans for 65 million formal MSMEs (micro and SMEs) in emerging nations, which have unmet financial needs of $5.2 trillion annually (Schumukler, 2017). One of the most prominent factors contributing to this lack of SME finance is information asymmetries among borrowers and lenders (Darvas, 2013; Oztürk & Mrkaic, 2014).

Credit reporting is an institutional response to this problem of information asymmetries. Here, the institutional arrangements that allow creditors to share information are known as credit bureaus and registries (Love & Mylenko, 2003). However, Asian countries are mostly without comprehensive credit bureau coverage (Kwan, 2018). Not being an exception, the SME rating process in Bangladesh also has further development areas (Anwar, 2017).

Further, Bangladesh is currently working towards achieving the Development Vision 2041, for which there is no alternative except deepening innovation-driven and tech-based knowledge and practices (Alam, 2019). Again, the Fourth Industrial Revolution coincides with this. Appreciably sophisticated technology has brought different industry applications to Bangladesh. But in the question of SMEs' limited access to finance, though many countries are successfully addressing the issue by implementing different innovative functioning measures, these measures, including the sophistication of the country's credit bureau, are yet to be reviewed here in Bangladesh.

2. RESEARCH QUESTION, OBJECTIVE, IMPLICATIONS

To address the issues discussed above, a comprehensive literature search was initiated (including the studies of Creehan, 2018; Miller, 2003; World Bank, 2011, 2012, 2016, 2019). The experiences and insights from the study show that a common online platform for credit bureaus can be such a country-specific, innovation-driven measure to ease SME finance in Bangladesh (please refer to Section 4 on the findings from document analysis). This gave birth to the following research questions: 1. How to develop a common online platform for credit bureaus that would have potential impacts or benefits regarding the enhancement of SME finance in Bangladesh; and 2. Would the platform be viable in Bangladesh's present infrastructural setup? As a result, the goal of this paper was set: *to develop a new phenomenon of a common online platform for credit bureaus to improve SME finance in Bangladesh that can be viable in Bangladesh's present infrastructural setup.* Thus, the study indeed contributes to the further sophistication of the conventional information-sharing mechanism used for SME finance and applies technological advancement to its present relevant infrastructural setup in Bangladesh.

The remainder of the paper is organized as follows: Section 3 describes the research design; Section 4 depicts findings from document analysis, including the most followed latest credit reporting guide, in developing concepts for the country-specific new model in the proposition; and Section 5 shows the interview findings in developing further codes and concepts for the model. Section 6 presents the model in the proposition and shows how the model would be viable both from a cost-benefit perspective and the country's present legal setup, and Section 6 gives a concluding remark.

3. RESEARCH DESIGN

The study used the "phenomenological method of qualitative research" (Polkinghorne, 1989) to develop a new pattern or phenomenon of 'common online platforms for credit bureaus,' where the phenomenology method involves studying a small number of subjects (five to twenty-five) through extensive engagement to develop patterns (Creswell, 2009). Accordingly, in-depth interviews with 11 experts in the relevant field (please refer to Appendix 1) were conducted following a document analysis. Thus, two types of data collection methods were involved in developing the pattern: document analysis and in-depth interviews. In-depth interviews were collected as it is useful to obtain detailed information to explore new issues in depth (Opdenakker, 2006).

The non-probability purposive sampling was used for the identification of the interviewees. The reason for choosing purposive sampling is simple. Not all the stakeholders have the necessary knowledge and/or access to relevant information (for example, not all the bank employees of all levels have access to SME information. Some do not even deal with SMEs at all. The same is true for regulators.). A relevant pool of different stakeholder groups was interviewed. Data were sourced from different domains: information providers (agencies), users (banks), regulators (Bangladesh Bank), and academicians (BIBM) (Appendix 1). This helped minimize biases. Primary data was collected through unstructured interviews, as they provide a general understanding of a problem, the scope for important issues to be uncovered, and insights into problem-solving methods (Klenke, 2008), and the interviews were flexible enough to allow an exploration of the under-researched phenomenon (Pedrosa, 2012). Interviews lasted between 30 and 60 minutes. However, input from one domain was compared with the findings from another, and no major inconsistencies were discovered. The number of interviewees was extended until "data saturation," defined as the absence of new information in new data (Boyce & Neale, 2006). An interview guide, including the processes of planning, developing instruments, collecting data, analyzing that data, and disseminating findings (Boyce & Neale, 2006), was consulted. For data analysis, an open coding approach (Galliano, 2013), which involves reading data several times and then creating tentative labels for chunks of data that summarize what is happening, was executed. The way the data were analyzed is described in the next section with reference to the discussion of Table 1 below.

4. FINDINGS FROM THE CONTENT ANALYSIS

Asymmetric information, when borrowers know more about their ability and willingness to repay loans than do lenders (Stiglitz & Weiss, 1981), is alleged to be one of the core issues with the imperfection of the credit market. Lenders are unable to appropriately evaluate borrowers' creditworthiness due to restricted access to comprehensive and timely information, which eventually leads to higher default rates and lower loan availability. Before considering credit applications, lenders in such a situation try to mitigate the consequences of default with collateral, mostly fixed assets like land and buildings.

To overcome these obstacles, credit reporting service providers provide credit reports, which serve the vital purpose of compiling and disseminating accurate credit information. The perception of risk is reduced by a credit report with sufficient credit information, making it easier for a business to acquire finance (Miller, 2003). A credit reporting system in this context refers to the organizations, people, regulations, practices, standards, and tools that enable well-informed decision-making (World Bank, 2011). The requirement for physical collateral is substituted by, or at the very least augmented by, "reputation collateral" under this system. Reputation collateral in the context of credit information sharing refers to situations when historical payment records and other pertinent data gathered by credit bureaus will enable a more precise projection of the borrower's likelihood of payback, which may be utilized when asking for new credit (World Bank, 2016). A whole credit information cycle normally involves gathering, analyzing, creating, storing, and disseminating data. So they can lessen information asymmetry and default rates, which in turn should lead to lower average interest rates, improved competition in the credit market, and eventually increased loan availability.

Fortunately, Bangladesh is one of the few countries (only 30 worldwide) that has both public and private credit registries or bureaus. Here, public credit registries took the form of the CIB (Credit Information Bureau), which is reported by its central bank, the Bangladesh Bank. It reports the total loan exposure and loan status of the company to the banking sector. Only the banking channel has access to the report, and the existence of an adverse report on the company blocks the credit. On the other hand, private credit registries took the form of credit rating agencies, which are eight in number and work under the Securities and Exchange Commission of Bangladesh. Any company's approach is to arrange all financial and credit-related data processing upon payment. This study discovered that small business ratings are not done by rating agencies. As a result, the problem of information asymmetry becomes more acute for SMEs. Apart from this, the study finds that while much of the literature discusses the role of the CB in credit markets, particularly in the market for SMEs, little attention has been paid to institutional responses to ensure service excellence. Accordingly, Bangladesh is ranked 159th out of 190 countries in the World Bank Group's 2018 Doing Business assessment for the criteria 'getting credit', where a significant barrier to obtaining credit is the asymmetry of credit information.

In this connection, while reviewing the global guidelines and best practices in the credit reporting industry, the study found that the "Global Credit Reporting Program," which the International Finance Corporation (IFC) introduced in 2001 and later renamed "Credit Information Solutions" to more accurately reflect its objective, is a combination of analytical and operational work that aims to support the growth of credit bureaus and registries in over 90 countries. Since the program's inception, the World Bank Group has worked to create accommodating credit reporting environments in the countries mentioned above and implement reforms where necessary, taking into account the industry's historical development as well as current trends. In this regard, unquestionably, the World Bank Group's twenty-plus years of experience in developing and modifying credit bureaus and registries around the world have had a significant effect on establishing new credit reporting markets.

In order to aid the member nations in the development of credit reporting systems, the group initially developed a "Credit Bureau Knowledge Guide" (2006) that expounded on the expertise the World Bank Group had amassed over the course of several years of managing the Global Credit Reporting Program. The second edition of the Credit Bureau Knowledge Guide' (2012) incorporated the newly introduced 'General Principles', the first-ever set of universal standards for credit reporting, developed by a task force led by the World Bank and the Bank for International Settlements (BIS). Since the General Principles were released, the task force has been formalized as the International Committee on Credit Reporting (ICCR)[1], and since then, it has worked on developing additional publications to provide guidance on credit reporting.

In its continuation, the latest version is the third edition, the 'Credit Reporting Knowledge Guide' (2019). Like the two earlier editions, the latest version disseminates knowledge on best practices in credit reporting development, based on the experiences of the group. Besides the financial, business, technological, and other operational and practical considerations, the version incorporated a greater emphasis on the impact of new technologies, data, and the development of

In its continuation, the latest version is the third edition, the 'Credit Reporting Knowledge Guide' (2019). Like the two earlier editions, the latest version disseminates knowledge on best practices in credit reporting development based on the experiences of the group. Besides the financial, business, technological, and other operational and practical considerations, the new version incorporated a greater emphasis on the impact of new technologies, data, and the development of new online products and services catering specifically to the needs of borrowers. Indeed, it seeks to align the adoption of disruptive technologies with the core Bali Fintech (financial technology—an innovative approach to delivering financial services in different markets around the world that reflects the actual or perceived inability of traditional lenders to provide optimal financial services to underserved or unserved borrower segments) agenda while ensuring financial sector resilience, addressing risks, and promoting business. The guide basically discusses how new technologies, online-based data, and related new products and models have the potential to transform the credit and credit reporting industries and how the reporting industry is adapting to the rapidly changing technological and mostly online-based fintech environment. Several new case studies of recent developments strengthen the theoretical discussions with practical guidelines to provide practitioners with real examples of how credit reporting systems have developed, showing the challenges they faced and the successes they realized.

Following the guidelines, an effective credit reporting system includes a cycle of collecting, producing, processing, storing, distributing, and using the information to support credit-granting decisions. It involves a number of actors: the users (the creditor companies), regulatory authorities, CRSPs (credit reporting service providers), and data providers. The three types of CRSPs are credit registries, credit bureaus, and commercial credit reporting companies. Active participation by each of these stakeholders is critical to ensuring the effectiveness of the credit reporting system.

Credit registers were, and in many cases still are, utilized as a supervision tool to identify systemic risk within loan portfolios. They primarily function as the internal databases inside a country's central bank. Credit bureaus collect information in a standardized format from a variety of credit providers, including banks, credit card companies, telecommunications and utility companies, retail lenders, and other non-bank financial institutions. Additionally, they gather and disseminate a variety of information that is readily accessible to the general public (such as phone directories, court judgments, and bankruptcy announcements), and/or they make it easier to access databases maintained by other parties (such as collateral registers and identity repositories). Utility bills and other non-traditional sources of information may also provide important information that helps credit bureaus create more thorough credit reports. On the other hand, commercial credit reporting companies are entities that gather information for assessing credit risks, credit scoring purposes, or for business purposes, such as extending trade credits (World Bank, 2011). The businesses then resell the information they have gathered as company credit reports. Data is gathered from banks, vendors, financing firms, company owners, and public records, including tax liens, bankruptcies, and court judgments. In order for a CRSP to run well, data suppliers are also crucial. Potential data sources for CRSPs include any corporate or public organizations that gather consumer data. For instance, a CRSP may have access to databases on court judgments, personal identity records, registries of collateral, or even a Fintech firm that exchanges information with them.

Most importantly, the 'Credit Reporting Knowledge Guide' (2019) itself argues that while following the Guide, the legal framework for credit reporting might differ from country to country, including a combination of credit reporting laws, banking laws, data protection laws, and credit protection laws. Further, the financial world is in a state of constant change. So, it is subject to see how regulators around the world choose to adopt and regulate potentially disruptive innovations while following given guidelines. For instance, in the more decentralized digital world, several new options and models have arisen as alternatives to the traditional centralized models. In credit reporting as well, as the Guide believes, some new models will succeed while others will die out. Again, besides the conventional credit registry CRSPs or credit bureau CRSPs model, the guide allowed for another alternative model of public-private CRSPs. A key indicator is that even the leading service providers in the arena are experimenting and rolling out prototypes for new ways of sharing information, indicating a willingness to embrace disruptive innovation and technology to stay relevant. However, to identify appropriate model CRSPs, they must develop or acquire country-specific, locally adapted, and customized systems that will enable adequate data collection from existing and new data sources.

According to SME Finance Forum[2] (2020), this third edition of the Credit Reporting Knowledge Guide, like the two earlier editions, disseminates knowledge on best practices in credit reporting development based on the experiences of the World Bank Group, which has helped to develop favorable credit information systems and implement reforms in many countries around the world. Business Information Industry Association, BIIA (2020)[3] also depicts that this guide focuses more on the credit needs of individuals and SMEs that stand to benefit most from the development of credit reporting systems.

. However, the *major findings* from the literature are as follows:

1. Credit reporting and information-sharing systems reduce information asymmetry and the loan default rate and increase access to credit for SMEs.
2. The Credit Reporting Knowledge Guide' (2019) is the latest version of the guidelines issued by ICCR, the task force by the World Bank, and BIS. It is said to be the only recognized standard setter and guideline issuer on credit reporting (ICCR, 2026), based on the World Bank Group's twenty-plus years of experience in developing credit reporting systems in more than 90 countries.
3. The guide incorporates the list and role of the required stakeholders including CRSP, Data Providers, and others in credit reporting and information-sharing systems, with a focus on adaptation to concurrent technical advancement

4. The Guide encourages the application of country-specific new models (for different sets of legal, infrastructural, credit reporting laws, banking laws, data protection laws, and existing and adaptable technologies), as even the leading credit reporting service providers are experimenting and rolling out prototypes for new ways of information sharing.

Based on the findings above, a country-specific model is being developed that could be viable for Bangladesh's present regulatory and infrastructural setup. For this, the application of applicable sections from the 'Credit Reporting Knowledge Guide' (2012, 2019) and a phenomenological method of social science research are firmly applied to develop the new concept of a common online platform for credit bureaus.

5. INTERVIEW FINDINGS

This section depicts the interview findings, focusing on the potential impact areas where such a platform can contribute, with a view to adding components to the model. During the interview, in response to the question on the lack of SME finance, entrepreneurs R-1 and R-2 (Annex-1) shared their experiences of loan rejections. To R-1, *"it entails going door to door with banks, which takes a lot of time and effort.* The other respondents, R-8 and R-9, also viewed loan approval as a complex process. From their views, the study drew Figure 1 below and verified it through member checking to give an image of the present complex loan approval process for SMEs in Bangladesh.

Figure 1. Conventional SME Finance Mechanism (drawn by the author)

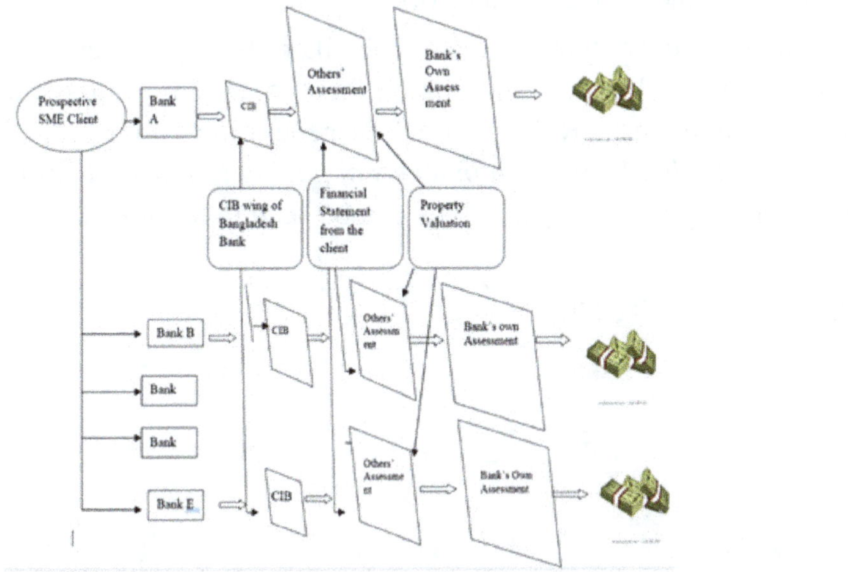

Figure 1 above indicates that, at the present setup, a prospective SME borrower approaches first a bank, say Bank A. At first, the bank collects credit information on the client's exposure and quality from the CIB cell of the Bangladesh Bank. This is shown as the first obstacle or door to be crossed by the SME client. Another phase to pass for bank financing is the assessment made by others than the creditor bank, like reports by clients on their financials or property valuation agencies. If these are found to be favorable, the bankers conduct their own assessment through site visits, market reports, property authentication, and account verification in terms of financial, business, management, security, and credit risk grading. After completion of that, the proposal is presented to the bank's approving authority, which may or may not approve the loan. Then the decision is conveyed to the SME client. The process takes one to two months on average.

The client then goes to another bank's doorstep in case the loan is not approved by the first bank. If any other bank (bank B or bank E) finds it primarily a prospective one, then it goes through the above lengthy process again, while some other banks may find it not creditworthy. As a result, an SME client has to go door to door at banks at a significant level of cost in terms of time, money, and effort.

The study drew the attention of bankers through interviews on the above-mentioned issue. They shared their constraints in assisting SMEs in terms of finance. R-3, from a first-generation bank, opined, *"Most SMEs are not bankable even in terms of having finance. There remains a big vacuum of information"*. This can be seen in the following Figure 2:

Figure 2. SME VACCUAM

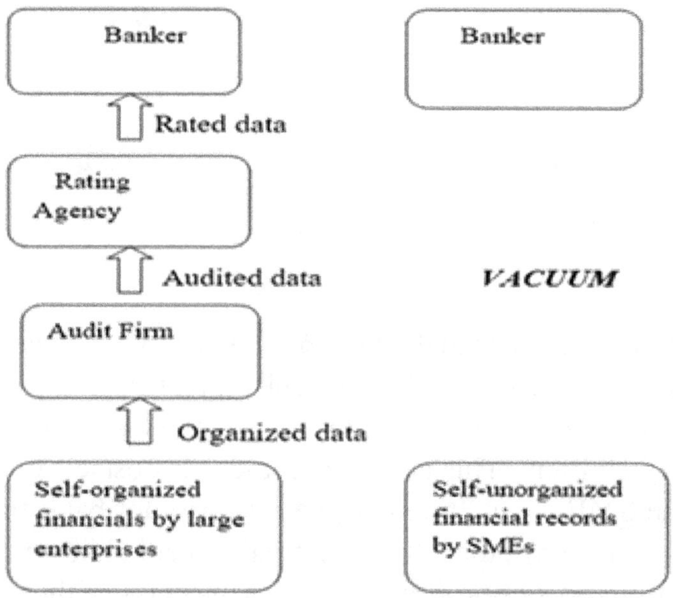

Figure 2 is self-explanatory. For large loans, banks are getting organized, audited, and further rated with ready and dependable data, but the financial data of SMEs is not reliable to work with.

According to the respondents, an integrated, common tech-based platform of information is expected to contribute to filling this vacuum. Respondent R-3 opined in favor of a common digital platform. Respondents R-4 and R-5, from a second- and third-generation bank, respectively, also believe that an online or technologically advanced system is required.

Another finding, as R-6 from a credit rating agency informed the researchers, was that they provide services mainly for large enterprises. R-7, a member from another credit rating agency, thinks they would appreciate initiatives to ensure better financial services in terms of credit reporting to SMEs under regulatory obligations. But R-8, an academician, opposed this. He believes that rating agencies will have a self-profit motive, making their services costly to SMEs. He suggested that an independent nonprofit body work on SME credit data processing and rating. The study had the opportunity to hear regulators' views as well. One of the regulators interviewed, R-10, opined: " *If a client is to go from bank to bank for a loan, if his credit information is made available on a common platform by all banks at the same time, any bank from a total of sixty-two scheduled banks can be interested in a competitive market with all the ready data.*" A different aspect was received from another regulator, R-11. S/he added, *"Any innovation must not be in conflict with Section 46(1) of Chapter 4 of the Bangladesh Bank Order of 1972"*. Following Section 46(1), the shared information shall be treated as confidential and shall not be disclosed except for the purposes of the chapter.

However, as the study categorized and identified patterns in all the interview data, the results were consolidated. Applying the coding method, the unstructured data in the form of quotes and insights from interviews was compared and grouped into distinguishable codes or concepts that are shown in Table 1 below. For instance, following the table, different interviewee respondents were discussing the obligations of the applicant enterprise in going door-to-door to the banks for a loan, the complex process of loan approval in banks, and the SMEs being considered non-bankable in most cases. All of these were grouped under a code referring to the role played by 'a bank'. From the code, a major component (component 2 in Figure 3) of the model was later drawn.

Table 1. Found themes that generate the proposed model's components

Themes	Respondent	Narratives
Credit facilities from a bank	R-1, R-2	Going door to door at banks
	R-9	Loan approval-more complex process
	R3	Non-bankable SME
Common online platform	R-3	Common digital platform
	R-4	Requirement of an online or technologically advanced system
	R-10	Common platform for credit reporting
	R-9	Viable platform shared by all data providers
Data administering	R-7	Financial services under regulatory obligations
	R-9	Consolidation, prompt service, and inclusion purpose
	R-11	Any innovation not in conflict with BB rules
Datacenter wing	R-6	Services to large enterprises are only provided through the credit rating agencies
	R-8	Independent non-profit body on SME data processing and rating
Data content	R-4	Authentication of SME data
	R-5	Content of credit report
	R-8	The self-profit motive of credit rating agencies

In this way, aside from the major findings from the content analysis, the development of some themes or concepts resulted in introducing and/or supporting the components and features of a new model proposed in the study on credit reporting. The model drawn this way is discussed below.

6. PROPOSITION OF THE MODEL FROM THE RESEARCH FINDINGS

In view of the findings from all the data collected through document analysis and an in-depth interview, a proposition from the study is that it has the required policy implications to establish an online common platform for CB. On the platform, information related to SME loan applications would be stored to be shared by financial institutions, which would be the potential providers of finance to the SMEs. The proposed model is as follows:

Figure 3.

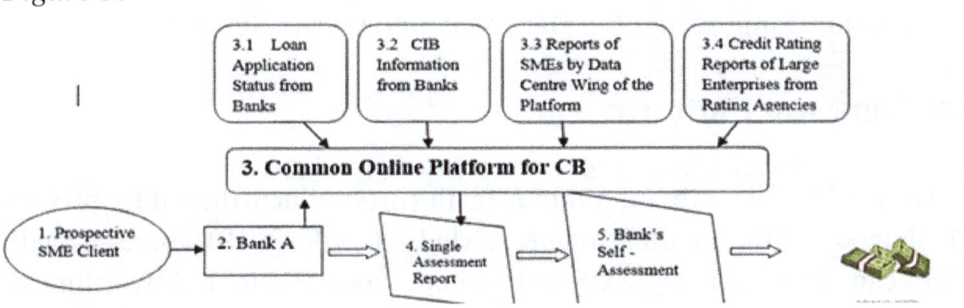

The model shows a comparatively simpler way to finance SME projects. Here are the five major components of the model:

1. A prospective SME loan client applying for a set of loans over a particular time
2. A bank to which the approaching enterprise will apply for the first time
3. The proposed common online platform.
4. A single CB assessment report from the common online platform for a credit bureau.
5. The bank's self-assessment on the loan.

The components would work in such a way that, for a set of loans, a prospective SME client would apply only once to one bank. The bank will immediately do two things. At first, it will post the 'loan application details with status' to the platform under one unique code for one client, and then, on the client's approach or consent, it will receive a 'single CB assessment report' (point 4 in figure 3 and illustrated at point 6.5 below) with proposed 'data content' from the platform. Then the bank will go for its own assessment, as earlier, and convey the financing decision to the client. Clearly, following this loan process, only two components—the platform itself and its single CB assessment report (among the components listed above)—are the only newly added components to the conventional SME finance mechanism, implicating the new model under the proposition. These two new components must have the following distinct features to complete the model:

6.1 Common platform 6.2 Online 6.3 Data center wing
6.4 Data administering 6.5 Data content 6.6 Data Services

6.1 Common Platform

The model will serve as a common platform (similar to the public-private CRSP model of the Credit Rating Knowledge Guide, 2019) where an SME client can show, in a single CB assessment report, their creditworthiness to the entire financial industry. The report will have four data sources:

a. Banking companies, for data on loan application details with status (new posting by banks)
b. Bangladesh Bank CIB report (conventional posting for loan outstanding starting from Tk.1 with the outstanding and loan status that are presently in force)
c. Data Center wing of the platform (new posting on SME rating only)
d. Credit Rating Agencies (posting of large enterprise reports that are already in force)

But only the statutory (by law) data users will have access to the output data or the single CB assessment report (Reference Section 6.5). All of these data sources will use a nationwide single code for a single entity' to easily aggregate all of an enterprise's information under a single code. The trade license or registration number can be used as the code number.

6.2 Online

Section 45 (1) of Bangladesh Bank Order 1972 indicates that a banking company may, in connection with any financial arrangement entered into or proposed to be entered into with any person, make an application to the bank (the central bank) in such form as the bank may specify, requesting that it provide the applicant with such credit information as specified in the application. To avoid disrupting the existing legal framework and simultaneously following the Credit Rating Knowledge Guide, 2019, an SME client will initially approach a banking company for a set of loans under the proposed model. But the difference will be: *Firstly,* an enterprise will have no need to apply for the same set of loan proposals to any other bank, irrespective of its first application's approval. Once an enterprise applies to any bank for a set of loans, the bank would give the 'loan application details with status' information under the unique code of the client to the database of the common platform. *Secondly,* the platform will provide in its portal the following selected short info list (Table 2 below) from the client's complete 'data content' (reference Section 6.5 below):

Table 2. Short Info list for posting the 'loan application details with status' to the platform

Code:
Client Code – Application date - Business area- Business location- Amount Sought- Security value- Contact no.- Time-to-time loan status (sanctioned/ under process/yet to serve)

By searching the portal, any bank branch can find, with a click, prospective SME clients within its jurisdiction. It can contact them further in possible cases. In cases where the parties (a bank and the applicant enterprise) decide to go for formal agreements, they will unquestionably proceed with written consent. However, this will facilitate competition in the present competitive market of 60 scheduled banks and thus boost SME access to finance.

6.3 Data Administering

The platform in the proposed model might fulfill the role of a CRSP following the Guide 2012–2019. As stated, a CRSP is an entity that administers a networked credit information exchange. It enables credit information collection, validation, processing, consolidation, and further disclosure in an organized format to users, as well as value-added services based on such data (Credit Reporting Knowledge Guide, 2nd edition, 2012). The study also found that in credit reporting, a regulator is an authority with statutory powers of supervision and the power to create operational rules and regulations. In a country like China, the central bank acts as both the operator of a CRSP and the regulator of credit information sharing. The proposition places the platform to serve both duties under the jurisdiction of the Bangladesh Bank.

6.4 Data Center Wing for SMEs

Under the provision of enabling credit information collection, processing, and consolidation by CRSP, the platform can also provide a data center wing for SMEs. It will serve the requirements of establishing an independent nonprofit government body (please refer to interview findings) to work on SME data collection, processing, and consolidation. Bangladesh Bank may consider forming a wing as a government or institute on behalf of the country to take the lead in serving the national economy. The cost to the nonprofit wing may be carried out by-

i. Allocation of SME funds, like funds from JICA (the most frequently used fund for SMEs)
ii. Nominal charge from SME clients
iii. Fees from banks on the generation of reports, such as CIB report generation fees.

Bangladesh Bank can serve through its eight branches throughout the country. This might lessen the SME vacuum (please refer to Figure 1).

6.5 Data Content

For the model, it is proposed to do a 'single CB assessment report, which is the complete credit report, including credit history, past payment behavior, mortgage, collateral (if any), asset liability, cash flow, financial statements, and other relevant data. Finally, the data content for a single CIB assessment report, which is the ultimate data output from the platform, might include:

Table 3. 'Single CB assessment report content'- the ultimate data output from the platform

1.	Client Code
2.	Demographic information like- Business area, address, amount sought, Security, Contact
3.	Loan application details with status –with the content of point 6.2 above
4.	CIB data that are presently in force
5.	Credit Rating reports on SMEs from the Data Center Wing (new postings) or Credit Rating Agency reports on large enterprises (that are also present in force)

6.6 Data Services

As value-added services based on credit information are included within CRSP responsibilities (World Bank, 2012), the data can serve any other financial service to promote SME finance. Like Bangladesh, the government took the plan to set up 100 Special Economic Zones across the country to attract more FDI and increase the country's exports (BEZA, 2016). The proposed platform services may be used by the economic zone authorities to obtain the clearance they require from SMEs. It will give confidence to the importers and thus boost exports by the country's SMEs.

7. THE COST-BENEFIT ANALYSIS OF THE MODEL

In this regard, the value proposition from R-9 was more supportive. To him, "*the platform being shared by all the data providers for consolidation, prompt service, and inclusion purposes is expected to be viable and sustainable on its merits.*" However, from the above discussion, the benefits of the proposed model along with their costs can be summarized as follows:

Table 4. Cost Benefit Analysis of the proposed model

Stakeholders	Cost	Benefits
Financier Companies/ Banks	1. A bank is to report the 'loan application details with status' information.	1. Any bank branch can find at a click a list of all the prospective SME clients within its jurisdiction. 2. Data can be gathered from a single source, the platform. 3. The banker will get complete credit reporting in a consolidated 'single CB assessment report'.
SME Loan Clients	--	1. An enterprise will apply only once for a set of loans. 2. Through the platform, an enterprise can demonstrate its creditworthiness to all financier companies in a single report. 3. Loan processing time will be reduced. 4. The clients will not have to go from bank to bank; rather, they will be able to get financing companies at their door. Thus, access to SME finance is expected to increase significantly.
The Industry	1. The central bank will have to serve an additional responsibility of a CRSP.	1. The model will enable the mechanisms for credit information collection, processing, consolidation, and disclosure in an organized form. 2. It will promote perfect competition within banks to serve SME finance. 3. The data can serve any other value-added financial services to promote SME finance. 4. Most importantly, access to SME finance will be enhanced.

8. LEGAL BASIS TO THE MODEL

The legal basis for credit information reporting is given in Bangladesh Bank Order 1972 (President's Order), Chapter IV, "Collection and Furnishing of Credit Information. The study examined all the relevant sections. *Section 45(2)* states that on receipt of an application under clause (1), the bank (Bangladesh Bank) may, as soon as may be, furnish the applicant with such credit information relating to the matters, provided that the information so furnished shall not disclose the names of the banking companies that have submitted such information. Most importantly, *Section 46 (1)* states that any credit information contained in any statement submitted by a banking company or furnished by the bank to any banking company under Article 45 shall be treated as confidential and shall not, except for the purposes of the chapter, be published or otherwise disclosed. *Section 46(2)* states that nothing shall apply to the disclosure by any banking company, with the prior permission of the bank, of any information furnished under Article 44.

From the above observations, the study found that the common online platform model is not controversial under the law, especially on grounds of confidentiality. This can be justified in a way: following Section 45(2), the new model does not need to disclose the names of the banking companies as before. Following Section 46(1), the shared information by the bank (Bangladesh Bank) or any banking company shall be treated as confidential and shall not be disclosed, except for the purposes of Chapter IV, and the model will work only for the purposes of the chapter. Following Section 46(2)(a), nothing shall apply to the disclosure made with the prior permission of the bank (Bangladesh Bank). In required cases, it can be a matter of having permission.

Even after these, the implications of the model can be subject to detailed legal opinions if needed.

9. CONCLUDING REMARKS

Despite being one of the few countries with both public and private credit reporting agencies, Bangladesh has struggled with the adequacy and proper integration of information on enterprises in need of financing. Regarding SMEs, the inconsistency got even higher in the absence of ratings by private credit registries. From the study of widely followed international guidelines and the country's relevant laws, the objective of the study was set to develop a new phenomenon of a common online platform for credit bureaus that can be viable in Bangladesh's present infrastructural setup to improve SME finance in Bangladesh.

Through reviewing the existing credit reporting concepts and developing new ones from the research findings derived from document analysis and an in-depth interview, the phenomenon was eventually developed and brought forward through a model proposition. Thus, the study indeed contributes to the further technological advancement and sophistication of the conventional information-sharing mechanism used for SME finance. Through the study, the proposed model is believed to give a more *simplified, integrated, and all-encompassing solution* to this long-cherished constraint factor of information asymmetry in SME finance. Its implication is expected, from the cost-benefit analysis, to be beneficial to all the stakeholders in the industry. The findings can be extended to other contemporary emerging countries, like Bangladesh. Furthermore, for the researchers, the implementation of the model might be easier than changing fundamental laws and thus more politically palatable. It might help feasibility studies in the future to assist policy executors in bringing in such innovative measures to enhance SME finance.

REFERENCES

Alam, D. S. (2019). Bangladesh: Vision 2041: Alignment with other macro plans. *South Asia Journal*. http://southasiajournal.net/bangladesh-vision-2041

Anwar, S. M. R. (2017). Credit rating for small and medium enterprises: Problems and prospects in Bangladesh. *Journal of Asian Business Strategy*, *6*(11), 234–245. DOI: 10.18488/journal.1006/2016.6.11/1006.11.234.245

Boyce, C., & Neale, P. (2006). *Conducting in-depth interviews: A guide for designing and conducting in-depth interviews for evaluation input.* Monitoring and Evaluation.

Business Information Industry Association. (2020). *World Bank: Credit reporting knowledge guide 2019*. https://www.biia.com/information-world-bank-credit-reporting-knowledge-guide-2019/

Creehan, S. (2018). *How digital innovation can increase small business access to finance in Asia. Asia Focus*. Federal Reserve Bank of San Francisco.

Creswell, J. W. (2009). *Research design: Qualitative, quantitative, and mixed methods approaches* (3rd ed.). SAGE Publications.

Darvas, Z. (2013). *Banking system soundness: Key to SME financing* (Policy Contribution Issue 2013/10). Bruegel.

Finance Forum, S. M. E. (2020). *Credit reporting knowledge guide 2019*. https://www.smefinanceforum.org/post/credit-reporting-knowledge-guide-2019-0

ICCR. (2026). *International Committee on Credit Reporting (ICCR)*. https://www.febis.org/collaborations/iccr/

Karadag, H. (2016). The role of SMEs on economic growth in emerging economies in the post-crisis era: An analysis from Turkey. *Journal of Small Business and Entrepreneurship Development*, *4*(1), 22–31. DOI: 10.15640/jsbed.v4n1a3

Love, I., & Mylenko, N. (2003). *Credit reporting and financing constraints* (Policy Research Working Paper No. 3142). World Bank.

Miller, M. (2003). *Credit reporting systems and the international economy*. MIT Press.

Nemoto, N., Yoshino, N., Okubo, Y., Inaba, D., & Yanagisawa, K. (2018). *Credit risk reduction effect on SME finance through use of information* (ADBI Working Paper Series). Asian Development Bank Institute.

OECD. (2010). *SMEs, entrepreneurship and innovation*. OECD Publishing.

Opdenakker, R. (2006). Advantages of four interview techniques in qualitative research. *Forum Qualitative Sozialforschung / Forum: Qualitative. Social Research*, *7*(4).

Öztürk, B., & Mrkaic, M. M. (2014). *SMEs' access to finance in the euro area: what helps or hampers?* International Monetary Fund.

Pedrosa, A. (2012). Customer integration during innovation development: An exploratory study in the logistics service. *Creativity and Innovation Management*, *21*(3), 263–276. DOI: 10.1111/j.1467-8691.2012.00648.x

Polkinghorne, D. E. (1989). Phenomenological research methods. In Valle, R. S., & Halling, S. (Eds.), *Existential-phenomenological perspectives in psychology: Exploring the breadth of human experience* (pp. 41–60). Plenum Press. DOI: 10.1007/978-1-4615-6989-3_3

Schumukler, S. L. (2017). *Innovative experiences in access to finance: Market friendly roles for the visible hand*. World Bank Publications.

Stiglitz, J. E., & Weiss, A. (1981). Credit rationing in markets with imperfect information. *The American Economic Review*, *71*(3), 393–410.

World Bank. (2011). *General principles for credit reporting*. World Bank.

World Bank. (2012). *Credit reporting knowledge guide* (No. 94160; pp. 1–120). https://documents.worldbank.org/curated/en/873561468320947849/Credit-reporting World Bank. (2016). *Credit registry*. https://www.worldbank.org/en/publication/gfdr/gfdr-2016/background/credit-registry

World Bank. (2019). *Credit reporting knowledge guide 2019*. https://documents.worldbank.org/en/262691559115855583/Credit-Reporting-Knowledge-Guide

ADDITIONAL READING

Asian Development Bank. (2015). *Let's scale up access to SME finance to boost Asia's growth, cross-border trade*. https://www.google.com/search?q=https://www.adb.org/news/features/lets-scale-access-sme-finance-boost-asias-growth-cross-border-trade

Avery, R. B., Calem, P. S., & Canner, G. B. (2004). Credit report accuracy and access to credit. *Federal Reserve Bulletin*, *90*(3), 297–322. DOI: 10.17016/bulletin.2004.90-3-2

Kuwahara, S., Yoshino, N., Sagara, M., & Taghizadeh-Hesary, F. (2015). *Role of the credit risk database in developing SMEs in Japan: Lessons for the rest of Asia* (ADBI Working Paper No. 547). Asian Development Bank Institute.

Ozturk, B., & Mrkaic, M. (2014). *SMEs' access to finance in the euro area: What helps or hampers* (IMF Working Paper No. 14/78). International Monetary Fund.

Simovic, V., Vaskovic, V., & Poznanovic, D. (2011). Performance evaluation of the Serbian Credit Bureau model. *African Journal of Business Management*, *5*(11), 4594–4608.

World Bank. (2012). *Rethinking the role of the state in finance*. World Bank.

KEY TERMS AND DEFINITIONS

Credit Information Bureau (CIB): CIB is a service provided by the Bangladesh Bank, the central Bank of Bangladesh. Its key functions include tracking loans, assessing risk, preventing excessive loans, and providing credit history primarily to the scheduled banks in Bangladesh.

Credit Register: A credit register is a centralized record kept by a financial authority that collects, organizes, and disseminates information on the borrowing and repayment behavior of individuals, businesses, or organizations, allowing lenders and regulators to assess credit risk and track financial stability.

Credit Reporting Service Providers (CRSPs): These are the organizations that collect, store, and share credit-related information about individuals, and/or organizations to the lenders. These organizations compile data related to the borrowers' credit history, loan payment behavior, defaults, and financial obligations and share them with banks, financial institutions, and even the regulators.

Data Administering: Data administering is the process of developing, maintaining, and monitoring the rules, policies, and systems that manage an organization's data, ensuring that information is correct, consistent, secure, and accessible for permitted use.

Data Center: Large volumes of digital data are stored, processed, and managed in data centers, which are specialized facilities with computer systems, servers, storage devices, and networking equipment.

International Committee on Credit Reporting (ICCR): The Bank for International Settlements (BIS) assisted in the creation and coordination of the ICCR, which is a permanent organization of the World Bank. This esteemed council is the only acknowledged international body that establishes guidelines and standards for credit reporting.

SME Finance Forum: The G20 Global Partnership for Financial Inclusion (GPFI) founded the SME Finance Forum in 2012 as a knowledge hub for data, research, and best practices in promoting SME finance. It is a global membership network that unites financial institutions, technology companies, and finance institutions.

ENDNOTES

1 The ICCR is a permanent structure of the World Bank, created and coordinated with support from the Bank for International Settlements (BIS). It counts, currently, with over 30 members, including private sector service providers (credit reporting service providers' associations from Europe, Asia, Eurasia, Africa, and Latin America). This prestigious committee is the only recognized international standard setter and guideline issuer on credit reporting.

2 The SME Finance Forum operates a global membership network that brings together financial institutions, technology companies, and finance institutions, which was established by the G20 Global Partnership for Financial Inclusion (GPFI) in 2012 as a knowledge center for data, research, and best practice in promoting SME finance.

3 The Business Information Industry Association (BIIA) is a trade association that has established one of the largest global networks of business information service providers with over 70 members.

APPENDIX

Table 5. Details of the interviewees with the used codes

Sl.	Respondents	Code	Portfolio
1.	Respondent 1	R-1	SME-1
2.	Respondent 2	R-2	SME-2
3.	Respondent 3	R-3	Vice President, Head of Relationship Banking in a first-generation bank
4.	Respondent 4	R-4	Assistant Vice Presidents of a second-generation private bank
5.	Respondent 5	R-5	Assistant Vice Presidents of a third-generation bank
6.	Respondent 6	R-6	Member of one of the leading credit rating agencies, CRAB
7.	Respondent 7	R-7	Member from another credit rating agency, CRISL
8.	Respondent 8	R-8	Professor at a University.
9.	Respondent 9	R-9	Former Director, BIBM- Bangladesh Institute of Bank Management.
10.	Respondent 10	R-10	One of the General Managers in Bangladesh Bank. Have exposure in policy formulation as worked in the BRPD (Banking Regulations and Policy Dept.) for 20 years.
11.	Respondent 11	R-11	Present Head of CIB, Bangladesh Bank.

Conclusion

The evolution of corporate finance has been effectively captured from different dimensions in this edited text. The authors tried to lay out the newfound realities and frameworks within which the corporate financial managers and the researchers of the discipline are now forced to operate. However, the research initiatives covered in the texts still cannot answer all the questions that an inquisitive mind may ask. Yet, the efforts of the authors of different chapters demand appreciation for bringing up and discussing the issues surrounding the development of an evolved framework of corporate finance in today's world to the students, corporate practitioners, and researchers alike.

The following sections of this chapter offer some future research directions related to different research works covered in this edited volume to motivate potential researchers, students, and corporate practitioners to explore and create additional knowledge in the realm of corporate finance.

The first chapter of the book particularly concentrates on the adoption of Mobile financial services (MFS), a derivative of fintech solutions, focusing on service offerings through mobile devices, in developing economies, and explores user experiences along with their exposures to digital frauds. While the chapter offers valuable insights, further research is essential to address the totality of the concerned topic (which was beyond the scope of the study itself). For example, a detailed look at the fraud typologies; the degree of digital literacy and awareness, along with their combined effect on the susceptibility towards becoming a victim of a financial fraud while interacting with the MFS services; the addition of the impact of trust (as an antecedent and major independent variable) on the perceived effectiveness of the MFS services in developing economies, and the role of perceived security of digitally aware users in moderating or, mediating that relationship; the integration of the perceived securities of the users with their actual experiences of fraud; a comprehensive look at the possible mitigation strategies; the impact of the perceived security related to the MFS solutions, and fraud vulnerabilities on the firm value of the concerned MFS or the parent organization, etc. could only enhance the knowledge of the practitioners and the researchers of the corporate financial domain. In addition, developing a new or implementing the existing service quality scale(s) and user satisfaction of the MFS services, along with some phenomenological exploration of fraud victims and developing case studies on the MFS firms in the targeted economies, could all be a set of meaningful exploration objectives in an emerging economy context.

The second chapter of the book looks at the evolution of green venture capital as a specialized investment vehicle with a specific environmental agenda to support environmentally friendly innovations. The research presented in this chapter specifically examines the conceptual development, nature of investments, financing roles, particular sectoral applications, risks, shortcomings, benefits, and prospects that green venture capital has to offer, specifically in the context of supporting green nascent yet sustainable technology ventures. Despite praiseworthy efforts, this research has some specific gaps necessitating further research initiatives in this field. It is understandable that a single research initiative is never enough to address all of the major aspects associated with a particular discipline. Future researchers in this field, therefore, can explore the possibility of a data-driven framework for assessing investment risks, the effects of green venture capital on the capital structure of the green early-stage innovations, a detailed look at the possibilities of the application of this concept in emerging economy contexts, the revolutionary role that the fintech solutions can play in the context of green venture capital with a special focus on a standardized environmental performance matrices along with the exploration of the interplay of different related independent as well as latent variables in addressing the effect of green venture capital on firm performance, and an overarching impact of green venture capital in economic development along with its interaction(s) with active political economies for offering valuable meaningful knowledge that is currently seems to be absent in the aforementioned contexts.

The third chapter of the text explores how technological advancements (such as artificial intelligence or AI, blockchain, cloud computing) are causing large-scale transformations in the fields of financial management, reporting, and auditing processes, adding to the efficiency of business operation and enhancing transparency as well as accountability of digital finance while creating novel challenges related to regulations, security, and adaptation. Future research in this area could benefit from the exploration of issues such as the regional diversity of the aforementioned transformation, a longitudinal study to see if and how the nature and components of the aforementioned transformation change across time, and the effects that they have on transparency, accountability, risk management and mitigation, and firm efficiency in adding value to the shareholders' wealth.

The fourth chapter of this edited volume argues that the discipline of forensic accounting has evolved enough to integrate investigative skills with advanced technologies and has also played a crucial role in ensuring effective governance practices of the concerned firms, where it is applied. It also indicates how the discipline has gradually gained importance in detecting and preventing fraud. The chapter also discusses how different tools, such as financial statement analysis, data mining, artificial intelligence, digital forensics, etc., can be used in uncovering complex fraud in today's evolved organizational landscape. The chapter further implies that the failure of conventional audit practices has eventually failed to be effective in high-profile scams (such as WorldCom and Enron), offering further rationality for implementing a comprehensive forensic audit integrated with the aforementioned tools. It also establishes a probable use-case for integrating blockchain and big data analytics to fulfill the future needs of forensic accounting to transform its traditional reactive role to a rather proactive role for ensuring fraud prevention, risk management, and regulatory compliance. While the insights shared in this chapter are both interesting and intriguing, further research in the field is essential to shed light on other important dimensions and realities surrounding forensic accounting. For example, future research in the field needs to incorporate empirical studies related to the applications of both machine learning and artificial intelligence in forensic accounting to test their probable efficacy in the real world. The proactive fraud detection model discussed in this chapter also needs to be implemented, and predictive models need to be developed. In addition, these are also to be tested in real-life scenarios for exploring their full potential.

The fifth chapter discusses how the leniency program under India's Competition Act 2001 has evolved and its practical effectiveness from a researcher's lens. This chapter argues that while the concept is progressive in theory, it suffers from significant structural as well as implementation deficiencies. One of the critical findings of this study is that the leniency Plus program's aim was to incentivize disclosure of multiple cartels, but eventually ended up with offering "extra carrots and no sticks", which could further stabilize cartels instead of dismantling them. This study also finds that the effectiveness of the penalty system is hindered by the protracted appellate proceedings, averaging around three years. It recommends that repeat offenders be excluded from immunity, except in exceptional circumstances, and also that India must align its regulatory framework with the global standard to create a truly effective leniency program to enhance corporate financial stability and investor confidence. Despite its invaluable findings and recommendations, the discussion related to the topic can never be considered complete unless the underlying topic is evaluated from every possible dimension. Therefore, additional research is mandatory. A few of the future research directions are covered below:

Additional research in this domain can include a comprehensive empirical study to untangle the mysterious relationship among the features of the leniency programs and cartel detection rate, implementation of a time series analysis to identify the trends of leniency utilization, implement a comprehensive cost-benefit analysis of the leniency program, compare India's leniency program with those from the developed world and compare them based on relevant performance matrices to identify the areas of lapses and concerns.

The sixth chapter of this edited volume looks at a particular contingency created by the COVID-19 pandemic and the way it has reshaped financial planning and analysis (FP&A) during the crisis. The study finds that traditional financial planning and analysis tools are incapable of addressing the rapidly evolving economic realities, forcing corporate firms to adopt dynamic scenario planning, real-time data analysis, and enhanced collaboration (which are effectively more flexible approaches to address the concerns) during uncertain times to ensure the sustenance of corporate resilience. Further research in this field could include (but is not limited to) (a) implementing an empirical validation of the effectiveness of the proposed practices, (b) develop, structure and implement benchmark (and/or relevant frameworks) for FP&A during contingencies and compare the performances of firms across industries, sizes and geographic location for effective comparative analyses of the realities surrounding their overall performance in this dimension, (c) conducting in-depth industry specific case studies to determine the possible industry-specific realities associated with the performance of their respective FP&A performances, (d) offer detailed insights to the readers through SME vs large studies (it is understandable that the type, degree and nature of the applications of the FP&A tools will vary based on the firm size), (e) study the role that an the effectiveness of the applications of advanced technologies in FP&A (for example, AI & ML-based predictive models), (f) investigating the cultural factors of organizations on the adoption and effectiveness of the FP&A practices, etc.

The seventh chapter of the book identifies that corporate finance practices have a significant positive impact on both capital rationing and time value of money (TVM), particularly in the Ethiopian SME context. It further identifies that firms with robust corporate finance strategies are better equipped to navigate capital constraints. It also identifies that effective capital budgeting tools and financial literacy enable SMEs to overcome resource limitations and optimize long-term investment outcomes. However, like all other research initiatives, it could not address all the dimensions of corporate interest surrounding the topic within its given context and scope. Future research in this topic can cover issues such as the temporal dynamics of the topic, which can be addressed through research initiatives tracking how the relationships among corporate finance, TVM, and capital rationing change over time (particularly across different economic cycles); the mediating role of capital rationing across firm lifecycle stages in predicting firm value; covering more developed and least developed economies to see if and how the underlying dynamics changes with the changes of geographic regions and/or the size as well advancements of the economy as a whole; incorporating external environmental and technological developments in the dynamics; etc.

The eighth and final chapter finds that Bangladesh's credit reporting infrastructure suffers a critical constraint despite having both public and private credit bureaus, particularly for SMEs. Content analysis of the World Bank's Credit Reporting Knowledge Guide (2019) and interviews with experts across stakeholder groups (including regulators), the study found that SMEs face a long, complex door-to-door loan approval process for SMEs (which is also often repetitive in nature when a client is rejected a loan by a bank and moves to another for a similar service). To improve the situation and reduce the fund constraints across SMEs in Bangladesh, the study suggests that it is now essential to develop a common online platform that would consolidate credit information from several data sources under a single unique code per enterprise. It also offers a cost-benefit analysis to establish the rationale for proposing the model. Similar research in this context could benefit from looking into (a) empirically testing the proposed model of the study; (b) connecting digital literacy, technology adoption level, and existing technological infrastructure of the country to implement such a solution; (c) exploring the cybersecurity and privacy concerns associated with the implementation of such a centralized online platform; (d) incorporating a comprehensive cost analysis (including opportunity costs) into a quantitative cost model and comparing that with a quantitative benefit model to estimate the net benefit of the proposed model and its impact on firm the values of the SMEs and the banks; (e) implementing global comparative analysis and establish global best practices form an SME dimension, among others.

In concluding remarks, it can be said that this edited volume not only offers novel and interesting dimensions of corporate finance from a global context, but also offers a long list of future research agendas for potential researchers to look into. Therefore, it is reasonable to conclude that this volume is certainly a valuable addition to the body of contemporary corporate finance research in the world.

Compilation of References

Abubaker, Z., Barzinji, Q., Wan, S., Wan sallha, Y., Sofian, M., Rosbi, B., Fairuz, M., Md Salleh, M. F., Abdullah, A., & Barzinji, Z. (2022). *International Journal of Economics, Commerce and Management United Kingdom Licensed under Creative Common THE EFFECT OF FORENSIC ACCOUNTING ON FRAUD PREVENTION, THE MODERATING ROLE INTERNAL CONTROL EFFECTIVENESS.*

Accenture. (2021). *The future of finance: How digital transformation is reshaping corporate finance.* Retrieved from https://www.accenture.com

Ademosu, A. (2022). The effect of the financial system and its channels on SMALL SCALE CORPORATE FIRMS'access to financing: A Nigerian perspective.

Adula, M., Birbirsa, Z. A., & Kant, S. (2023). The effect of interpersonal, problem solving and technical training skills on performance of Ethiopia textile industry: Continuance, normative and affective commitment as mediators. *Cogent Business & Management, 10*(3), 2286672. Advance online publication. DOI: 10.1080/23311975.2023.2286672

Agrawal, R., & Yadav, M. (2024). Enablers for Usage of the Mobile Wallet by Msmes in Rural India: Using the Interpretive Structural Modelling Approach. *Financial Internet Quarterly, 20*(2), 26–40. DOI: 10.2478/fiqf-2024-0010

Ajayi-Nifise, A. O., Olubusola, O., Falaiye, T., Mhlongo, N. Z., & Daraojimba, A. I. (2024). A REVIEW OF U.S. FINANCIAL REPORTING SCANDALS AND THEIR ECONOMIC REPERCUSSIONS: INVESTIGATING THEIR BROADER IMPACT AND PREVENTATIVE MEASURES. *Finance & Accounting Research Journal*, *6*(2), 2. Advance online publication. DOI: 10.51594/farj.v6i2.787

Aksoy, T., & Uzay, S. (2021). Relationship Between Fraud Auditing and Forensic Accounting. In Aksoy, T., & Hacioglu, U. (Eds.), *Auditing Ecosystem and Strategic Accounting in the Digital Era: Global Approaches and New Opportunities* (pp. 127–146). Springer International Publishing., DOI: 10.1007/978-3-030-72628-7_6

Alam, D. S. (2019). Bangladesh: Vision 2041: Alignment with other macro plans. *South Asia Journal*. http://southasiajournal.net/bangladesh-vision-2041

Alhusban, A., Alhusban, A., Haloush, H., Alshurafat, H., Al-Msiedeen, J., Abdel, A., Massadeh, A., & Alhmoud, R. (2020). THE REGULATORY STRUCTURE AND GOVERNANCE OF FORENSIC ACCOUNTANCY IN THE EMERGING MARKET: CHALLENGES AND OPPORTUNITIES. *Journal of Governance and Regulation (Print)*, *9*(4), 149–161. DOI: 10.22495/jgrv9i4art13

Alonso, A. D., Kok, S. K., Bressan, A., O'Shea, M., Sakellarios, N., Koresis, A., & Santoni, L. J. (2020). COVID-19, aftermath, impacts, and hospitality firms: An international perspective. *International Journal of Hospitality Management*, *91*, 102654. DOI: 10.1016/j.ijhm.2020.102654 PMID: 32863526

Alsadah, N., & Al-Sartawi, A. (2023). Forensic Accounting and Cybersecurity: A Literature Review Paper. In Hannoon, A., & Mahmood, A. (Eds.), *Artificial Intelligence, Internet of Things, and Society 5.0* (pp. 235–244). Springer Nature Switzerland., DOI: 10.1007/978-3-031-43300-9_20

Alunni, A. (2019). *Innovation finance and technology transfer: Funding proof-of-concept*. Routledge. DOI: 10.4324/9780429278778

Alzoubi, A. B. (2023). Maximizing internal control effectiveness: The synergy between forensic accounting and corporate governance. *Journal of Financial Reporting and Accounting, ahead-of-print*(ahead-of-print). DOI: 10.1108/JFRA-03-2023-0140

Antwi, B. O., Adelakun, B. O., Fatogun, D. T., & Olaiya, O. P.Bernard Owusu AntwiBeatrice Oyinkansola AdelakunDamilola Temitayo FatogunOmolara Patricia Olaiya. (2024). Enhancing audit accuracy: The role of AI in detecting financial anomalies and fraud. *Finance & Accounting Research Journal*, *6*(6), 6. Advance online publication. DOI: 10.51594/farj.v6i6.1235

Anwar, S. M. R. (2017). Credit rating for small and medium enterprises: Problems and prospects in Bangladesh. *Journal of Asian Business Strategy*, *6*(11), 234–245. DOI: 10.18488/journal.1006/2016.6.11/1006.11.234.245

Asefa, K., Kant, D. S., & Debela, K. L. (2023, November). Effect of Transformational Leadership on Organizational Performance: The Mediating Role of Employee Commitment and Expert Systems (AI) Inclusion in Ethiopia. In *2023 International Conference on Communication, Security and Artificial Intelligence (ICCSAI)* (pp. 305-310). IEEE.

Auburn University. (n.d.). *Center for Ethical Organizational Cultures*. Retrieved from https://harbert.auburn.edu/binaries/documents/center-for-ethical-organizational-cultures/cases/worldcom.pdf

Australian Competition and Consumer Commission. (2020, September 3). Supermarkets authorised to continue cooperating on COVID-19 response. https://www.accc.gov.au/media-release/supermarkets-authorised-to-continue-cooperating-on-covid-19-response

Australian Competition and Consumer Commission. (2023). NYK convicted of criminal cartel conduct and fined $25 million. https://www.accc.gov.au/media-release/nyk-convicted-of-criminal-cartel-conduct-and-fined-25-million

Awolowo, I. (2019). *Financial Statement Fraud: The Need for a Paradigm Shift to Forensic Accounting - ProQuest.* https://www.proquest.com/openview/5543881754fa01cc976e6fae09fb2d8c/1?pq-origsite=gscholar&cbl=51922&diss=y

Bagla, R. K., & Sancheti, V.BAGLA. (2018). Gaps in customer satisfaction with digital wallets: Challenge for sustainability. *Journal of Management Development*, *37*(6), 442–451. DOI: 10.1108/JMD-04-2017-0144

Baker, H. K., Kumar, S., & Pattnaik, D. (2021). Twenty-five years of the journal of finances of a corporate: a scientometric analysis. Journal of Finances of a corporate, 66, 101572.

Bassey, B., Efiong, E., Efiong, J., & Inyang, W., Ashishie, Uklala, P., Ahaneku, R., Nnamdi, R., Igboke, & Patrick, S. (2020). Recent Relevant Legislations for the Regulation of Audit and Accounting Practices in Nigeria. *Test Engineering and Management*, *83*, 27257–27265.

Beck, T., Demirgüç-Kunt, A., & Maksimovic, V. (2008). Financing patterns around the world: Are small firms different? *Journal of Financial Economics*, *89*(3), 467–487. DOI: 10.1016/j.jfineco.2007.10.005

Bhat, S. (2019, May 29). Regulating cartels: Challenges for competition law. CEERA. https://ceerapub.nls.ac.in/regulating-cartels-challenges-for-competition-law/

Bhatt, B. (2011). Financial Management Importance. (From) http://www.blognbuzz.com/financial-management-importance.html. Retrieved 12 April 2012

Bhattacharjea, A., & De, O. (2021, March). India's cartel penalty practices, optimal restitution and deterrence. Institute of Economic Growth. https://iegindia.org/upload/profile_publication/doc-010421_162610WP424fc.pdf

Blum, U., Steinat, N., & Veltins, M. (2008). On the rationale of leniency programs: A game-theoretical analysis. *European Journal of Law and Economics*, *25*(3), 209–229. DOI: 10.1007/s10657-008-9046-x

Bocken, N. M. (2015). Sustainable venture capital–catalyst for sustainable start-up success? *Journal of Cleaner Production, 108*, 647–658. DOI: 10.1016/j.jclepro.2015.05.079

Bondarenko, P. (2024, July 9). Retrieved from Encyclopedia Britannica: https://www.britannica.com/event/Enron-scandal/Downfall-and-bankruptcy

Borrell, J.-R., Jiménez González, J. L., & García Coto, E. (2013). Evaluating antitrust leniency programs. *Journal of Competition Law & Economics, 10*(1), 107–136. DOI: 10.1093/joclec/nht017

Bowers, S. L. (2023). *Accounting and Corporate Finance For Lawyers*. Aspen Publishing.

Boyce, C., & Neale, P. (2006). *Conducting in-depth interviews: A guide for designing and conducting in-depth interviews for evaluation input*. Monitoring and Evaluation.

Braun, V., & Clarke, V. (2006). Using thematic analysis in psychology. *Qualitative Research in Psychology, 3*(2), 77–101. DOI: 10.1191/1478088706qp063oa

Brealey, R. A., Myers, S. C., & Marcus, A. J. (2023). *Fundamentals of finances of a corporate*. McGraw-Hill.

Buell, S. W. (2024). *The Limits of Individual Prosecutions in Deterring Corporate Fraud* (SSRN Scholarly Paper 4733141). https://papers.ssrn.com/abstract=4733141

Buretta, J., & Terzaken, J. (Eds.). (2022). *The cartels and leniency review* (10th ed.). Law Business Research., https://thelawreviews.co.uk/edition/the-cartels-and-leniency-review-edition-10/

Business Information Industry Association. (2020). *World Bank: Credit reporting knowledge guide 2019*. https://www.biia.com/information-world-bank-credit-reporting-knowledge-guide-2019/

Chand, A., & Bala, S. (2023). Title of the article. International Bar Association. https://www.ibanet.org/article/43fb2d60-ac81-4baa-8e35-3d2da5a1762f

Chawla, D., & Joshi, H. (2017). Consumer perspectives about mobile banking adoption in India–a cluster analysis. *International Journal of Bank Marketing*, *35*(4), 616–636. DOI: 10.1108/IJBM-03-2016-0037

Chawla, D., & Joshi, H. (2020). The moderating role of gender and age in the adoption of mobile wallet. *Foresight*, *22*(4), 483–504. DOI: 10.1108/FS-11-2019-0094

Chen, Z., & Rey, P. (2013). On the design of leniency programs. *The Journal of Law & Economics*, *56*(4), 917–943. DOI: 10.1086/674011

Cheong, C., & Hoang, H. V. (2021). Macroeconomic factors or firm-specific factors? An examination of the effect on corporate profitability before, during and after the global financial crisis. *Cogent Economics & Finance*, *9*(1), 1959703. DOI: 10.1080/23322039.2021.1959703

Chien, H.-Y. (2020). Use of Business Analytics in Accounting Firms—Taking Deloitte as an Example. *E3S Web of Conferences, 218*, 03004. DOI: 10.1051/e3sconf/202021803004

Chisty, N., & Ahmmed, S. (2023). The Silent Detectives: Forensic Accountants and Their Battle against Financial Crime. *Asian Accounting and Auditing Advancement*, *14*, 21–30.

Coles, J. L., & Li, Z. F. (2023). An empirical assessment of empirical finances of a corporate. *Journal of Financial and Quantitative Analysis*, *58*(4), 1391–1430. DOI: 10.1017/S0022109022000448

Competition Bureau Canada. (2023). *Immunity and leniency programs under the Competition Act*. Government of Canada. https://ised-isde.canada.ca/site/competition-bureau-canada/en/how-we-foster-competition/education-and-outreach/immunity-and-leniency-programs-under-competition-act

Competition Commission of India. (2016). Suo Motu Case No. 05 of 2016.

Competition Commission of India. (2017). Suo Motu Case No. 06 of 2017

Competition Commission of India. (2023). Draft lesser penalty regulations. https://cci.gov.in/images/stakeholderstopicsconsultations/en/draft-lesser-penalty-regulations1697431514.pdf

Competition Commission of India. (2024). Advocacy booklets. https://www.cci.gov.in/advocacy/publications/advocacy-booklets

Conference on Research on Economic Theory and Econometrics. (2009, June 17). Conference on Research on Economic Theory and Econometrics. https://www2.aueb.gr/conferences/Crete2009/Tinos_program_updated17June.pdf

Corradi, M., & Nowag, J. (Eds.). (2023). *Title of the book*. Cambridge University Press., DOI: 10.1017/9781108899956

Cowling, M., & Liu, W. (2021). Access to Finance for Cleantech Innovation and Investment: Evidence from UK Small-and Medium-Sized Enterprises. *IEEE Transactions on Engineering Management*.

Creehan, S. (2018). *How digital innovation can increase small business access to finance in Asia. Asia Focus*. Federal Reserve Bank of San Francisco.

Creswell, J. W. (2009). *Research design: Qualitative, quantitative, and mixed methods approaches* (3rd ed.). SAGE Publications.

Croce, A., & Bianchini, R. (2022). The role of environmental policies in promoting venture capital investments in cleantech companies. *Review of Corporate Finance*, *2*(3), 587–616. DOI: 10.1561/114.00000024

Cyril Amarchand Mangaldas. (2023, October). Draft lesser penalty regulations: Key takeaways. https://www.cyrilshroff.com/wp-content/uploads/2023/10/CLIENT-ALERT-Draft-Lesser-Penalty-Regulations-Key-Takeaways.pdf

Dahlberg, T., Guo, J., & Ondrus, J. (2015). A critical review of mobile payment research. *Electronic Commerce Research and Applications*, *14*(5), 265–284. DOI: 10.1016/j.elerap.2015.07.006

Daraojimba, R. E., Farayola, O. A., Olatoye, F. O., Mhlongo, N., & Oke, T. T. (2023). FORENSIC ACCOUNTING IN THE DIGITAL AGE: A U.S. PERSPECTIVE: SCRUTINIZING METHODS AND CHALLENGES IN DIGITAL FINANCIAL FRAUD PREVENTION. *Finance & Accounting Research Journal*, *5*(11), 11. Advance online publication. DOI: 10.51594/farj.v5i11.614

Darvas, Z. (2013). *Banking system soundness: Key to SME financing* (Policy Contribution Issue 2013/10). Bruegel.

Das, S., & Mitra, A. (2024). *Advancing lightweight digital trust architectures in the internet of medical things: A multi-dimensional analysis.* In *Lightweight Digital Trust Architectures in the Internet of Medical Things (IoMT)*, 1-14. DOI: 10.4018/979-8-3693-2109-6.ch001

Dass, R., & Pal, S. (2011). A meta analysis on adoption of mobile financial services. *Indian Institute of Management Ahmedabad*, *2*(1), 1–26.

Davies, H., & Green, D. (2013). *Global Financial Regulation: The Essential Guide (Now with a Revised Introduction).* John Wiley & Sons.

De Bellis, M. (2013). Global Financial Standards and Networks: The Global Administrative Law Perspective. *Revista de Derecho Público*, 1–28. DOI: 10.15425/redepub.30.2013.02

Debrah, C., Chan, A. P. C., & Darko, A. (2022). Green finance gap in green buildings: A scoping review and future research needs. *Building and Environment*, *207*, 108443. DOI: 10.1016/j.buildenv.2021.108443

Deloitte. (2020). *Digital transformation in finance: The impact of AI, blockchain, and cloud computing on financial operations*. Deloitte Insights.

Demirel, P., Li, Q. C., Rentocchini, F., & Tamvada, J. P. (2019). Born to be green: New insights into the economics and management of green entrepreneurship. *Small Business Economics*, *52*(4), 759–771. DOI: 10.1007/s11187-017-9933-z

Deo, S. P., & Verma, T. (2023). Leniency and competition law: A closer look. Lexology. https://www.lexology.com/library/detail.aspx?g=aa815dea-0368-431f-a825-bfa6f1adf63f

Department of Justice. (2023). Justice Department applauds passage of the Criminal Antitrust Anti-Retaliation Act. https://www.justice.gov/opa/pr/justice-department-applauds-passage-criminal-antitrust-anti-retaliation-act

Dereso, C. W., Kant, S., Muthuraman, M., & Tufa, G. (2023). Effect of Point of Service on Health Department Student's Creativity in Comprehensive Universities of Ethiopia: Moderating Role of Public-Private Partnership and Mediating Role of Work Place Learning. In: Jain, S., Groppe, S., Mihindukulasooriya, N. (eds) Proceedings of the International Health Informatics Conference. Lecture Notes in Electrical Engineering, vol 990. Springer, Singapore. https://doi.org/DOI: 10.1007/978-981-19-9090-8_13

Dijkstra, P., & Schoonbeek, L. (2009). Amnesty plus and multimarket collusion. Academia.edu. https://www.academia.edu/846411/Amnesty_Plus_and_Multimarket_Collusion

Dirman, A. (2020). Financial distress: The effects of profitability, liquidity, leverage, firm size, and free cash flow. International Journal of Business. *Economics and Law*, *22*(1), 17–25.

Donner, J., & Tellez, C. A. (2008). Mobile banking and economic development: Linking adoption, impact, and use. *Asian Journal of Communication*, *18*(4), 318–332. DOI: 10.1080/01292980802344190

Donovan, K. (2012). Mobile money for financial inclusion. *Information and Communications for Development*, *61*(1), 61–73.

Dugar, S. M.. (2020). *Guide to competition law* (8th ed.).

Durga, P., Godavarthi, D., Kant, S., & Basa, S. S. (2024). Aspect-based drug review classification through a hybrid model with ant colony optimization using deep learning. *Discov Computing*, *27*(1), 19. DOI: 10.1007/s10791-024-09441-w

Efunniyi, A., Obiki-Osafiele, Agu, Adeniran, P., & Abhulimen, A. (2024). *1597-1616 4 Nigeria Inter-bank Settlement System Plc (NIBSS) 5 Zenith General Insurance Company Limited, Nigeria 6 International Association of Computer Analysts and Researchers*. DOI: 10.51594/farj.v6i8.1509

Ellili, N., Nobanee, H., Haddad, A., Alodat, A. Y., & AlShalloudi, M. (2024). Emerging trends in forensic accounting research: Bridging research gaps and prioritizing new frontiers. *Journal of Economic Criminology*, *4*, 100065. DOI: 10.1016/j.jeconc.2024.100065

Enofe, A. O., Okpako, P. O., & Atube, E. N. (2013). The Impact of Forensic Accounting on Fraud Detection. *European Journal of Business and Management*.

Ernst & Young. (2021). *Digital financial transformation: The role of AI and big data in financial decision-making*. Ernst & Young Global.

Etim, U. (2023). Accounting Ratios and False Financial Statements Detection. *Evidence from Nigerian Quoted Companies.*, *3*, 61–75.

European Commission. (2006). Case COMP/C.38.281/B.2, Raw Tobacco Italy, 2006/901/EC. https://eur-lex.europa.eu/legal-content/EN/TXT/PDF/?uri=CELEX:32006D0901

Ezrachi, A., & Kindl, J. (2011). Criminalization of cartel activity – A desirable goal for India's competition regime? *NLSI Review*, *23*(1), 9–28.

Field, A. (2013). *Discovering statistics using IBM SPSS statistics* (4th ed.). SAGE Publications.

Finance Forum, S. M. E. (2020). *Credit reporting knowledge guide 2019*. https://www.smefinanceforum.org/post/credit-reporting-knowledge-guide-2019-0

Florea, R., & Florea, R. (2023, July 1). *Forensic Accounting—Key Tool in Detecting and Preventing Fraud and Financial Crimes. | EBSCOhost*. https://openurl.ebsco.com/contentitem/gcd:174676915?sid=ebsco:plink:crawler&id=ebsco:gcd:174676915

Fowler, F. J. (2014). *Survey research methods* (5th ed.). SAGE Publications.

Friedman, M. (2002). *Capitalism and freedom*. University of Chicago Press. DOI: 10.7208/chicago/9780226264189.001.0001

Gangwani, M. (2020). Suitability of forensic accounting in uncovering bank frauds in India: An opinion survey. *Journal of Financial Crime*, *28*(1), 284–299. DOI: 10.1108/JFC-07-2020-0126

George, B. (2021). *Fraudulent Accounting and the Downfall of WorldCom*. University of Carolina.

Government of Canada. (1985). *Canadian Competition Act* (RSC 1985, c 19). Section 64(1).

Graham, J. R. (2022). Presidential address: Finances of a corporate and reality. *The Journal of Finance*, *77*(4), 1975–2049. DOI: 10.1111/jofi.13161

Gulapalli, E. K., Morand, C. L., & Wolski, G. E. (2017). Merger and Acquisition Transaction Disputes. In *Litigation Services Handbook* (pp. 1–35). John Wiley & Sons, Ltd., DOI: 10.1002/9781119363194.ch24

Guyo, D. M., Kero, C. A., & Kant, S. (2025). Is Marketing Intermediaries' Mediation Required for Livestock and Products Marketing to Improve the Economic Status of Pastoralist Communities in Ethiopia? In *AI in Agriculture for Sustainable and Economic Management* (pp. 216-234). CRC Press.

Guyo, D. M., Kant, S., & Kero, C. A. (2023, November). Mediation of Marketing Intermediaries and AI Adoption Between Livestock Products Marketing and Economic Status of Pastoralist in Ethiopia. In *2023 International Conference on Communication, Security and Artificial Intelligence (ICCSAI)* (pp. 311-316). IEEE.

Hasan, M. (2024, January 28). Changing landscape of mobile money in Bangladesh. Retrieved November 6, 2024, from The Daily Star website: https://www.thedailystar.net/supplements/mfs-and-financial-inclusion-bangladesh/news/changing-landscape-mobile-money-bangladesh-3530006

Henriques, J., Caldeira, F., Cruz, T., & Simões, P. (2024). A Survey on Forensics and Compliance Auditing for Critical Infrastructure Protection. *IEEE Access, 12*, 2409–2444. IEEE Access. DOI: 10.1109/ACCESS.2023.3348552

Holtslag, M., Chevrollier, N., & Nijhof, A. (2021). Impact investing and sustainable market transformations: The role of venture capital funds. *Business Ethics, the Environment & Responsibility, 30*(4), 522–537. DOI: 10.1111/beer.12371

Honigsberg, C. (2020). *Forensic Accounting | Annual Reviews*. https://www.annualreviews.org/content/journals/10.1146/annurev-lawsocsci-020320-022159

Hossain, M. Z. (2023). *Emerging Trends in Forensic Accounting: Data Analytics, Cyber Forensic Accounting, Cryptocurrencies, and Blockchain Technology for Fraud Investigation and Prevention* (SSRN Scholarly Paper 4450488). DOI: 10.2139/ssrn.4450488

Hussain, S., Gupta, S., & Bhardwaj, S. (2024). Determinants inhibiting digital payment system adoption: An Indian perspective. *Qualitative Research in Financial Markets*. Retrieved from https://www.emerald.com/insight/content/doi/10.1108/QRFM-09-2023-0223/full/html

Hutchinson, B., Dekker, S., & Rae, A. (2024). How audits fail according to accident investigations: A counterfactual logic analysis. *Process Safety Progress, 43*(3), 441–454. DOI: 10.1002/prs.12579

ICCR. (2026). *International Committee on Credit Reporting (ICCR)*. https://www.febis.org/collaborations/iccr/

In Re: Alleged anti-competitive conduct by Maruti Suzuki India Limited (MSIL) in implementing discount control policy vis-a-vis dealers, Suo Moto Case No. 01 of 2019.

In Re: Cartelisation by Broadcasting Service Providers by Rigging the Bids Submitted in Response to the Tenders Floated by Sports Broadcasters, Case No. 02 of 2013.

In Re: Cartelisation in industrial and automotive bearings, Suo Motu Case No. 05 of 2017.

In Re: Cartelisation in respect of Zinc Carbon Dry Cell Batteries Market in India, Suo Moto Case No. 02 of 2016 & Case Nos. 02 & 03 of 2017.

In Re: Cartelization in Respect of Tenders floated by Indian Railways for supply of Brushless DC Fans, Suo Moto Case No. 03 of 2014, at 7.11.

In Re: Chief Materials Manager, South Eastern Railway, Reference Case No. 03 of 2016.

Infobank. (1994). Banking law, capital market, corporate finance/mergers and acquisitions, competition - EC, competition - UK, employment, environmental law, financial services, information technology, and more. *Business Law Review, 15*(10), 262–284. DOI: 10.54648/BULA1994077

Iyer, P., Davari, A., & Mukherjee, A.IYER. (2018). Investigating the effectiveness of retailers' mobile applications in determining customer satisfaction and repatronage intentions? A congruency perspective. *Journal of Retailing and Consumer Services*, *44*, 235–243. DOI: 10.1016/j.jretconser.2018.07.017

Izedonmi, F., & Ibadin, P. O. (2012). Forensic Accounting and Financial Crimes: Adopting the Inference, Relevance and Logic Solution Approach. *African Research Review*, *6*(4), 4. Advance online publication. DOI: 10.4314/afrrev.v6i4.9

Jabo, D., Borji, B., & Kant, S. (2024, February). Impact of Technical CRM on Ethiopia Bank Human-Computer Interface and Competitive Advantage as Mediators of Performance. In 2024 IEEE International Conference on Computing, Power and Communication Technologies (IC2PCT) (Vol. 5, pp. 679-682). IEEE.

Jack, W., & Suri, T. (2011). *Mobile money: The economics of M-PESA*. National Bureau of Economic Research. Retrieved from National Bureau of Economic Research website: https://www.nber.org/papers/w16721

Javaid, H. A. (2024). Improving Fraud Detection and Risk Assessment in Financial Service using Predictive Analytics and Data Mining. *Integrated Journal of Science and Technology, 1*(8). https://ijstindex.com/index.php/ijst/article/view/63

Kang, G. (Grace). (2024, April 1). *We Learn from History: Earnings Management and Business Scandals in the Early of 2000s. | EBSCOhost.* DOI: 10.31966/jabminternational.v31i1.945

Kanthi, K. & Kumar, K. (2015). "A Study on Investment preferences and behavior of individual investors in Coimbatore City", Bonfring International Journal Industrial engineering and Management Science, Vol 5 (4), pp 170-174

Kant, S., & Adula, M. (2024). AI Learning and Work Attitude Mediation Between Reward and Organizational Support in Ethiopia. In Gomathi Sankar, J., & David, A. (Eds.), *Generative AI for Transformational Management* (pp. 109–136). IGI Global., DOI: 10.4018/979-8-3693-5578-7.ch005

Kant, S., & Adula, M. (2024). Human-Machine Interaction in the Metaverse in the Context of Ethiopia. In *Impact and Potential of Machine Learning in the Metaverse* (pp. 196–212). IGI Global., DOI: 10.4018/979-8-3693-5762-0.ch008

Kapoor, A., Sindwani, R., & Goel, M. (2024). Assessing inhibitors to adoption of m-wallet: A BWM approach. *International Journal of Business Excellence*, *32*(4), 433–455. DOI: 10.1504/IJBEX.2024.137567

Karabayır, M. (2019). *Forensic Accounting: Development and Practices Around the World* (pp. 47–62).

Karadag, H. (2016). The role of SMEs on economic growth in emerging economies in the post-crisis era: An analysis from Turkey. *Journal of Small Business and Entrepreneurship Development*, *4*(1), 22–31. DOI: 10.15640/jsbed.v4n1a3

Kashyap, P. (2020). Digital transformation and financial reporting: The future of corporate finance. *Journal of Financial Management*, *45*(2), 215–230.

Kaur, R., & Tanwar, A. (2024), "Role of Green Investment on Economic Aspects of Sustainable Development", Taneja, S., Kumar, P., Reepu, Balusamy, B., Sood, K. and Grima, S. (Ed.) *Sustainability Development through Green Economics (Contemporary Studies in Economic and Financial Analysis, Vol. 114)*, Emerald Publishing Limited, Leeds, pp. 91-106. DOI: 10.1108/S1569-375920240000114006

Khan, A. (2023, October 3). Competition Commission of India publishes the draft lesser penalty regulations. Mondaq. https://www.mondaq.com/india/cartels-monopolies/1380552/competition-commission-of-india-publishes-the-draft-lesser-penalty-regulations

Khan, S., & Shoaib, A. (2024). Firm value adjustment speed through financial friction in the presence of earnings management and productivity growth: Evidence from emerging economies. *Humanities & Social Sciences Communications, 11*(1), 1–17. DOI: 10.1057/s41599-024-03118-x

Kothari, C. R. (2004). *Research methodology: Methods and techniques* (2nd ed.). New Age International.

Kranacher, M.-J., & Riley, R. (2019). *Forensic Accounting and Fraud Examination*. John Wiley & Sons.

Krishnan, S., & Shashidhar, N. (2021). *Interplay of Digital Forensics in eDiscovery*.

Kshetri, N. (2013). *Cybercrime and cybersecurity in the global south*. Springer. Retrieved from https://books.google.com/books?hl=en&lr=&id=SepWfACNTgQC&oi=fnd&pg=PP1&dq=Kshetri,+N.+(2016).+Cybercrime+and+cybersecurity+in+the+global+South.+Palgrave+Macmillan.&ots=BFIGqbCHZW&sig=vssMzKotSTeNFvnwJPssIoTUFW0

Kshetri, N. (2021). Blockchain's roles in meeting key supply chain management objectives. *International Journal of Information Management, 39*, 80–89. DOI: 10.1016/j.ijinfomgt.2017.12.005

Lefouili, Y., & Roux, C. (2012). Leniency programs for multimarket firms: The effect of amnesty plus on cartel formation. *International Journal of Industrial Organization, 30*(6), 624–634. DOI: 10.1016/j.ijindorg.2012.04.004

Lerner, J., & Nanda, R. (2020). Venture capital's role in financing innovation: What we know and how much we still need to learn. *The Journal of Economic Perspectives, 34*(3), 237–261. DOI: 10.1257/jep.34.3.237

Lin, L. (2022). Venture capital in the rise of sustainable investment. *European Business Organization Law Review, 23*(1), 187–216. DOI: 10.1007/s40804-021-00238-8

Liu, Y., Wang, M., Huang, D., Huang, Q., Yang, H., & Li, Z. (2019). The impact of mobility, risk, and cost on the users' intention to adopt mobile payments. *Information Systems and e-Business Management, 17*(2-4), 319–342. DOI: 10.1007/s10257-019-00449-0

Li, X., Wang, J., & Yang, C. (2023). Risk prediction in management of finance of listed companies based on optimized BP neural network under digital economy. *Neural Computing & Applications, 35*(3), 2045–2058. DOI: 10.1007/s00521-022-07377-0

Love, I., & Mylenko, N. (2003). *Credit reporting and financing constraints* (Policy Research Working Paper No. 3142). World Bank.

Lupo, M. F. (2023). *The Importance and Evolution of Forensic Accounting* [Doctoral Thesis, Universita degli studi di Salerno]. http://elea.unisa.it/xmlui/handle/10556/7266

Malek, K., Maine, E., & McCarthy, I. P. (2014). A typology of clean technology commercialization accelerators. *Journal of Engineering and Technology Management, 32*, 26–39. DOI: 10.1016/j.jengtecman.2013.10.006

Marcella, A. J. (2021). *Cyber Forensics: Examining Emerging and Hybrid Technologies*. CRC Press. DOI: 10.1201/9781003057888

Markonah, M., Salim, A., & Franciska, J. (2020). Effect of profitability, leverage, and liquidity to the firm value. *Dinasti International Journal of Economics. Finance & Accounting*, *1*(1), 83–94.

Marra, A., Antonelli, P., & Pozzi, C. (2017). Emerging green-tech specializations and clusters–A network analysis on technological innovation at the metropolitan level. *Renewable & Sustainable Energy Reviews*, *67*, 1037–1046. DOI: 10.1016/j.rser.2016.09.086

Martyniszyn, M. (2015). Leniency (amnesty) plus: A building block or a Trojan horse? *Journal of Antitrust Enforcement*, *3*(3), 391–409. DOI: 10.1093/jaenfo/jnv005

Matar, D. O. (2023). The role of forensic accounting strategies in reducing financial and administrative corruption cases. *American Academic & Scholarly Research Journal, 14*(3), Article 3. https://aasrc.org/aasrj/index.php/aasrj/article/view/2198

Maulidi, A., & Ansell, J. (2021). Tackling practical issues in fraud control: A practice-based study. *Journal of Financial Crime*, *28*(2), 493–512. DOI: 10.1108/JFC-07-2020-0150

Mayock, C., & Meirsch, G. (2023). Leniency. European Commission. https://competition-policy.ec.europa.eu/cartels/leniency_en

Mehta, P. S. (2003). Competition policy in developing countries: An Asia-Pacific perspective. Asia Pacific Economic Cooperation Bulletin, 79(2002/03), 1–25.

Mehta, U. S., & Pati, S. (2016, January). Designing effective leniency programme for India: Need of the hour. CUTS International. https://cuts-ccier.org/wp-content/uploads/2019/01/Designing_Effective_Leniency_Programme_for_India-Need_of_the_Hour.pdf

Miller, M. (2003). *Credit reporting systems and the international economy*. MIT Press.

Miller, N. H. (2009). Strategic leniency and cartel enforcement. *The American Economic Review*, *99*(3), 750–768. DOI: 10.1257/aer.99.3.750

Mitra, A., & Jain, V. (2024). *Development and application of machine learning algorithms for sentiment analysis in digital manufacturing: A pathway for enhanced customer feedback*. In *Emerging Technologies in Digital Manufacturing and Smart Factories*, 26-38.

Mitra, A., & Sachdeva, P. (2023). Decoding the Twitter sentiment using artificial intelligence tools: A study on Tokyo Olympics 2020. *Lecture Notes in Networks and Systems*, *757*, 539–554. DOI: 10.1007/978-981-99-5166-6_37

Mohin, P. V., & Chinni, N. (2022). Impact of Covid-19 on Personal Financial Planning: An empirical study of different professions. *Central European Management Journal*, *30*(4), 1509–1521.

Mulyungi, J. (2021). Effect Of Short-term Financing Choices On Firm Value Of Non-financial Firms Listed On The Nairobi Securities Exchange, Kenya (Doctoral dissertation, Kca University).

Nagrik Chetna Manch v. Fortified Securities Solutions, Case No. 5 of 2015.

Nakitende, M. G., Rafay, A., & Waseem, M. (2024). Frauds in Business Organizations: A Comprehensive Overview. In *Research Anthology on Business Law, Policy, and Social Responsibility* (pp. 848–865). IGI Global. DOI: 10.4018/979-8-3693-2045-7.ch045

Nemoto, N., Yoshino, N., Okubo, Y., Inaba, D., & Yanagisawa, K. (2018). *Credit risk reduction effect on SME finance through use of information* (ADBI Working Paper Series). Asian Development Bank Institute.

Newman, C. L., Wachter, K., & White, A.NEWMAN. (2018). Bricks or clicks? Understanding consumer usage of retail mobile apps. *Journal of Services Marketing*, *32*(2), 211–222. DOI: 10.1108/JSM-08-2016-0289

Ngoc, N. M., Tien, N. H., & Anh, D. B. H. (2020). Opportunities and challenges for real estate brokers in post Covid-19 period. *Journal of Science and Technology*, *170*(10), 203–208.

Nigrini, M. J. (2020). *Forensic Analytics: Methods and Techniques for Forensic Accounting Investigations*. John Wiley & Sons.

Nyoach, T. D., Lemi, K., Debela, T., & Kant, S. (2024). Does Organizational Commitment Mediate the Association between Employee Association Management and Bank Performance? The Case of Banks in Ethiopia. *International Journal of Organizational Leadership, 13*(2), 355–376. DOI: 10.33844/ijol.2024.60419

OECD. (2010). *SMEs, entrepreneurship and innovation*. OECD Publishing.

Official Journal of the European Union. (2006). Notice on leniency in cartel cases, OJ C 298/17, L353/48.

Official Journal of the European Union. (2006). Notice on leniency in cartel cases, OJ C 298/17, L353/49.

Official Journal of the European Union. (2006). Notice on leniency in cartel cases, OJ C 298/17.

Olatoye, A. O., Ojeyinka, A. G., Adenuga, O., Olusola, T. A., & Egho, E. (2024). MANAGER USAGE OF FORENSIC ACCOUNTING AND FRAUD DETECTION IN LAGOS STATE. *SAPIENTIA FOUNDATION JOURNAL OF EDUCATION, SCIENCES AND GENDER STUDIES, 6*(1), Article 1. http://www.sfjesgs.com/index.php/SFJESGS/article/view/505

Oliveira, T., Thomas, M., Baptista, G., & Campos, F. (2016). Mobile payment: Understanding the determinants of customer adoption and intention to recommend the technology. *Computers in Human Behavior, 61*, 404–414. DOI: 10.1016/j.chb.2016.03.030

Olufemi, B., Bello, O., Olufemi, K., & Author, C. (2024). *Artificial intelligence in fraud prevention: Exploring techniques and applications challenges and opportunities. 5*, 1505–1520. DOI: 10.51594/csitrj.v5i6.1252

Opdenakker, R. (2006). Advantages of four interview techniques in qualitative research. *Forum Qualitative Sozialforschung / Forum: Qualitative. Social Research, 7*(4).

Orlandi, A. (2021). The emergence of double-entry bookkeeping in Tuscan firms of the thirteenth and fourteenth centuries. *Accounting History, 26*(4), 534–551. DOI: 10.1177/10323732211032298

Özkul, F. U., & Pamukçu, A. (2012). Fraud Detection and Forensic Accounting. In Çaliyurt, K., & Idowu, S. O. (Eds.), *Emerging Fraud: Fraud Cases from Emerging Economies* (pp. 19–41). Springer., DOI: 10.1007/978-3-642-20826-3_2

Öztürk, B., & Mrkaic, M. M. (2014). *SMEs' access to finance in the euro area: what helps or hampers?* International Monetary Fund.

Palepu, K., & Healy, P. (2003). The Fall of Enron. *The Journal of Economic Perspectives*, •••, 3–26.

Panigrahi, A., Pati, A., Sahu, B., Das, M. N., Nayak, D. S. K., Sahoo, G., & Kant, S. (2023). En-MinWhale: An ensemble approach based on MRMR and Whale optimization for Cancer diagnosis. *IEEE Access : Practical Innovations, Open Solutions*, *11*, 113526–113542. DOI: 10.1109/ACCESS.2023.3318261

Patel, N. (2024). Auditor Independence: Moving toward Harmonization or Simplication? *Southern California Law Review*, *97*, 495.

Pedrosa, A. (2012). Customer integration during innovation development: An exploratory study in the logistics service. *Creativity and Innovation Management*, *21*(3), 263–276. DOI: 10.1111/j.1467-8691.2012.00648.x

Polina, S., Taukebay, S., & Gaukhar, S. (2024). *Window Dressing and Misleading of Investors Based on Lehman Brothers Case*. Analysis From Different Perspectives.

Polkinghorne, D. E. (1989). Phenomenological research methods. In Valle, R. S., & Halling, S. (Eds.), *Existential-phenomenological perspectives in psychology: Exploring the breadth of human experience* (pp. 41–60). Plenum Press. DOI: 10.1007/978-1-4615-6989-3_3

Polzin, F., Sanders, M., & Täube, F. (2017). A diverse and resilient financial system for investments in the energy transition. *Current Opinion in Environmental Sustainability*, *28*, 24–32. DOI: 10.1016/j.cosust.2017.07.004

Prasad, G. C. (2021, March 26). Probing cartels a challenge in digital age, says CCI chief. Mint. https://www.livemint.com/market/mark-to-market/probing-cartels-a-challenge-in-digital-age-cci-11616756956947.html

PwC. (2020). *The role of digital technologies in reshaping corporate financial practices.* PwC Global Financial Report.

RAKESTRAW, T. L., EUNNI, R. V. & KASUGANTI, R. R. (2013). The mobile apps industry: A case study. *Journal of Business Cases and Applications*, *9*, 1.

Ramolobe, K., Pillay, S., & Ngcamu, B. (2023). *Towards an Inclusive Society: Promoting Disability Inclusion in Local Government Municipalities.*

Rana, N. P., Dwivedi, Y. K., Lal, B., Williams, M. D., & Clement, M. (2017). Citizens' adoption of an electronic government system: Towards a unified view. *Information Systems Frontiers*, *19*(3), 549–568. DOI: 10.1007/s10796-015-9613-y

Rehman, A., & Hashim, F. (2021). Can forensic accounting impact sustainable corporate governance? *Corporate Governance (Bradford)*, *21*(1), 212–227. DOI: 10.1108/CG-06-2020-0269

Rifani, R. A., & Hasan, H. (2022). Disclosure of Fraud Through Forensic Accounting, Audit Investigation and Auditor Professionalism. *Jurnal Economic Resource*, *5*(2), 2. Advance online publication. DOI: 10.57178/jer.v5i2.364

Robertson, N., McDonald, H., Leckie, C., & McQuilken, L.ROBERTSON. (2016). Examining customer evaluations across different self-service technologies. *Journal of Services Marketing*, *30*(1), 88–102. DOI: 10.1108/JSM-07-2014-0263

Rogers, E. M. (2003). *Diffusion of innovations* (5th ed.). Free Press.

Rohilla, A. (2024). Strengthening Financial Resilience: A Holistic Approach to Combatting Fraud. *Indian Journal of Economics and Finance*, *4*(1), 20–23. DOI: 10.54105/ijef.A2566.04010524

Roszkowska, P. (2021). Fintech in financial reporting and audit for fraud prevention and safeguarding equity investments. *Journal of Accounting & Organizational Change*, *17*(2), 164–196. DOI: 10.1108/JAOC-09-2019-0098

Roy, A. Chandler. (2016). *Questions of ethics and etiquette in the Society of Accountants in Edinburgh, 1853–1951—Roy A Chandler, 2017*. https://journals.sagepub.com/doi/abs/10.1177/1032373216675912

Salzgitter v. Commission, Case T-308/00, ECLI:EU:T:2004:199 (General Court of the European Union, 2004).

Sandeepan, N., & Fatima, M. (2021, May 5). Leniency regime in India: The CCI's consistently inconsistent approach. The Times of India, 1.

Sangeetha, M., Hoti, A., Bansal, R., Hasan, M. F., Gajjar, K., & Srivastava, K. (2022). Facilitating artificial intelligence supply chain analytics through finance management during the pandemic crises. *Materials Today: Proceedings*, *56*, 2092–2095. DOI: 10.1016/j.matpr.2021.11.418

Sanz-Prieto, I., de-la-Fuente-Valentín, L., & Rios-Aguilar, S. (2021). Technical Due Diligence as a Methodology for Assessing Risks in Start-up Ecosystems. In ICEIS (2) (pp. 421-428). DOI: 10.5220/0010521704210428

Savu, A.-C., & Bolcu, L. D. (2021). Implementation of judicial accounting expertise in the digital context. *Revista de Studii Financiare*, *6*(11), 109–121. DOI: 10.55654/JFS.2021.6.11.08

Schumukler, S. L. (2017). *Innovative experiences in access to finance: Market friendly roles for the visible hand*. World Bank Publications.

Shaharuddin, N. S., Zain, Z. M., & Ahmad, S. F. S. (2021). Financial planning determinants among working adults during Covid 19 pandemic. *International Journal of Academic Research in Accounting Finance and Management Sciences*, *11*(1), 285–304. DOI: 10.6007/IJARAFMS/v11-i1/8998

SHAHID IQBAL, M., UL HASSAN, M. & HABIBAH, U. (2018). Impact of self-service technology (SST) service quality on customer loyalty and behavioral intention: The mediating role of customer satisfaction. *Cogent Business & Management*, *5*, 1.

Shaikh, A. A., & Karjaluoto, H. (2015). Mobile banking adoption: A literature review. *Telematics and Informatics*, *32*(1), 129–142. DOI: 10.1016/j.tele.2014.05.003

Shankar, A., & Kumari, P. (2019). A study of factors affecting mobile governance (mGov) adoption intention in India using an extension of the technology acceptance model (TAM). *South Asian Journal of Management*, *26*(4), 71–94.

Shbeilat, M., & Alqatamin, R. (2022). Challenges and forward-looking roles of forensic accounting in combating money laundering: Evidence from the developing market. *Journal of Governance and Regulation*, *11*(3), 103–120. DOI: 10.22495/jgrv11i3art10

Singh, N., Nair, V., & Oberoi, P. (2018, August 13). Evolving leniency regime under the Indian competition law. Oxford Law Faculty. https://www.law.ox.ac.uk/business-law-blog/blog/2018/08/evolving-leniency-regime-under-indian-competition-law

Singh, I., Singh, J., & Baruah, A. (2020). Income and Employment Changes Under COVID-19 Lockdown: A Study of Urban Punjab. *Millennial Asia*, *11*(3), 391–412. DOI: 10.1177/0976399620957630

Slade, E. L., Dwivedi, Y. K., Piercy, N. C., & Williams, M. D.SLADE. (2015). Modeling consumers' adoption intentions of remote mobile payments in the United Kingdom: Extending UTAUT with innovativeness, risk, and trust. *Psychology and Marketing*, *32*(8), 860–873. DOI: 10.1002/mar.20823

Slade, E., Williams, M., Dwivedi, Y., & Piercy, N. (2015). Exploring consumer adoption of proximity mobile payments. *Journal of Strategic Marketing*, *23*(3), 209–223. DOI: 10.1080/0965254X.2014.914075

Smith, J. A. (2015). *Qualitative psychology: A practical guide to research methods* (3rd ed.). SAGE Publications.

Solomon, J. (2020). *Corporate Governance and Accountability*. John Wiley & Sons.

Stiglitz, J. E., & Weiss, A. (1981). Credit rationing in markets with imperfect information. *The American Economic Review*, *71*(3), 393–410.

Tanwar, S. (2022). Introduction to Blockchain Technology. In Tanwar, S. (Ed.), *Blockchain Technology: From Theory to Practice* (pp. 1–41). Springer Nature., DOI: 10.1007/978-981-19-1488-1_1

Taşkın, D. (2021). Financing Strategies for New Product Development and Innovation. Engines of Economic Prosperity: Creating Innovation and Economic Opportunities through Entrepreneurship, 79-92. Andersson, T. L. (2020). Tesla: a sequence of belief (Doctoral dissertation).

Thakur, R. (2013). Customer Adoption of Mobile Payment Services by Professionals across two Cities in India: An Empirical Study Using Modified Technology Acceptance Model. *Business Perspectives and Research*, *1*(2), 17–30. DOI: 10.1177/2278533720130203

The Competition Commission of India (Lesser Penalty) Regulations. 2009, Reg. 4(a) (India).

The Competition Commission of India (Lesser Penalty) Regulations. 2009, Reg. 4(b) (India).

The Competition Commission of India (Lesser Penalty) Regulations. 2009, Reg. 4(c)(i) (India).

The Competition Commission of India (Lesser Penalty) Regulations. 2009, Reg. 4(c)(ii) (India).

The Competition Commission of India (Lesser Penalty) Regulations. 2009, Reg. 5(1) (India).

The Competition Commission of India (Lesser Penalty) Regulations. 2009, Reg. 5(2) (India).

The Competition Commission of India (Lesser Penalty) Regulations. 2009, Reg. 5(4) (India).

The Competition Commission of India (Lesser Penalty) Regulations. 2009, Reg. 5(8) (India).

Thomas, N. S. (2024). *The Applications of Data Mining Techniques in Detecting Occupational Fraud: A Qualitative Review of Forensic Accounting Practices*. https://esource.dbs.ie/items/caa8d886-fb6e-4bc6-b4e3-5c7d455e7134

Tiptur, S., & Tripathi, P. (2021, December). Cartel leniency program in India: Why no race here? National Law School of India University. https://nls.ac.in/resources/cartel-leniency-program-in-india-why-no-race-here/

Tran, T., Do, H., Vu, T., & Do, N. (2020). The factors affecting green investment for sustainable development. *Decision Science Letters*, *9*(3), 365–386. DOI: 10.5267/j.dsl.2020.4.002

Trehan, M. A., & Shah, P. (2024). An Impact Of Forensic Accounting Training On Strengthening Banking Fraud Controls. *Educational Administration: Theory and Practice*, *30*(1), 1. Advance online publication. DOI: 10.53555/kuey.v30i1.5494

U.S. Department of Justice. (1993). Corporate leniency policy.

U.S. v. Bridgestone Corporation, No. 4:11CR00651-001 (S.D. Tex. Oct. 07, 2011). https://www.justice.gov/atr/case-document/file/489816/download

Ugochukwu, J. N. (2021). EFFECTIVE DEPLOY OF DIGITAL FORENSIC TECHNIQUES AND THE SUSTENANCE OF MATERIAL MISSTATEMENT-FREE FINANCIAL REPORTING IN NIGERIA. [JARE]. *Journal of Academic Research in Economics*, *13*(3), 442–470.

Umanhonlen, F. O., P, O. J., & Osikhenaogiedu, K. (2020). Combating economic and financial crimes in nigeria: The role of the forensic accountant. *Journal of Management and Science*, *10*(4), 4. Advance online publication. DOI: 10.26524/jms.10.7

UNCTAD. (1959, November 25). U.N. UNCTAD.

Upadhyay, N., Upadhyay, S., Abed, S. S., & Dwivedi, Y. K. (2022). Consumer adoption of mobile payment services during COVID-19: Extending meta-UTAUT with perceived severity and self-efficacy. *International Journal of Bank Marketing*, *40*(5), 960–991. DOI: 10.1108/IJBM-06-2021-0262

Verma, A., & Singh, V. (2024). International Journal of Research Publication and Reviews THE USE OF DATA ANALYTICS IN FORENSIC ACCOUNTING: A REVIEW OF CURRENT TRENDS AND TECHNIQUES. *International Journal of Research Publication and Reviews*, *5*, 4197–4203.

Verma, S., & Gustafsson, A. (2020). Investigating the emerging COVID-19 research trends in the field of business and management: A bibliometric analysis approach. *Journal of Business Research*, *118*, 253–261. DOI: 10.1016/j.jbusres.2020.06.057 PMID: 32834211

Vernimmen, P., Quiry, P., & Le Fur, Y. (2022). *Corporate finance: theory and practice*. John Wiley & Sons.

Vial, G. (2019). Understanding digital transformation: A review and a research agenda. *The Journal of Strategic Information Systems*, *28*(2), 118–144. DOI: 10.1016/j.jsis.2019.01.003

Villacé-Molinero, T., Fernández-Muñoz, J. J., Orea-Giner, A., & Fuentes-Moraleda, L. (2021). Understanding the new post-COVID-19 risk scenario: Outlooks and challenges for a new era of tourism. *Tourism Management*, *86*, 104324. DOI: 10.1016/j.tourman.2021.104324 PMID: 36540617

Waleed Hilal, S. Gadsden, A., & Yawney, J. (2022). *Financial Fraud: A Review of Anomaly Detection Techniques and Recent Advances—ScienceDirect*. https://www.sciencedirect.com/science/article/pii/S0957417421017164

Whish, R., & Bailey, D. (2012). *Competition law* (7th ed.).

Wils, W. P. J. (2013). Antitrust compliance programmes and optimal antitrust enforcement. *Journal of Antitrust Enforcement*, *1*(1), 52–76. DOI: 10.1093/jaenfo/jns006

World Bank. (2011). *General principles for credit reporting*. World Bank.

World Bank. (2012). *Credit reporting knowledge guide* (No. 94160; pp. 1–120). https://documents.worldbank.org/curated/en/873561468320947849/Credit-reporting World Bank. (2016). *Credit registry*. https://www.worldbank.org/en/publication/gfdr/gfdr-2016/background/credit-registry

World Bank. (2019). *Credit reporting knowledge guide 2019*. https://documents.worldbank.org/en/262691559115855583/Credit-Reporting-Knowledge-Guide

Xede, J., Dak-Adzaklo, C. S. P., Ofosu, E., & Adza, S. W. D. (2023). Competition laws, external financing and investment. *Journal of International Financial Markets, Institutions and Money*, *82*, 101700. DOI: 10.1016/j.intfin.2022.101700

Zayed, L. M. M., Nour, M. I., Al Attar, K., Almubaideen, H., & Abdelaziz, G. A. M. (2024). Role of Artificial Intelligence (AI) in Accounting Information Systems in Detecting Fraud. In Musleh Al-Sartawi, A. M. A., & Nour, A. I. (Eds.), *Artificial Intelligence and Economic Sustainability in the Era of Industrial Revolution 5.0* (pp. 397–409). Springer Nature Switzerland., DOI: 10.1007/978-3-031-56586-1_30

Zhou, T. (2012). Understanding users' initial trust in mobile banking: An elaboration likelihood perspective. *Computers in Human Behavior*, *28*(4), 1518–1525. DOI: 10.1016/j.chb.2012.03.021

About the Contributors

Md. Kamrul Bari, FIPA FFA, is a doctoral researcher in finance at IBA, University of Dhaka, and an associate professor (adjunct) at Uttara University in Dhaka, Bangladesh. With 20 years of experience across academia and industry, he bridges corporate practice and academic theory through his works at the Dhaka Chamber (DCCI), multinational corporations, and consulting engagements. His professional accounting credentials from IPA Australia enrich his international insights. An internationally published researcher on capital markets and corporate finance, he is ranked among the top 18% of WoS reviewers and is a former Deputy Editor-in-Chief of an international journal.

***

Md. Khaled Amin is an assistant professor of marketing in the faculty of business administration at American International University-Bangladesh. Before joining that school, Mr. Amin worked as a senior lecturer for Daffodil International University and as a lecturer for Northern University Bangladesh. Mr. Amin also worked as a part-time faculty member for universities such as Zhejiang Shuren University, Zhejiang Gongshang University, and Uttara University. He holds a master's degree and a bachelor's degree in business administration with a concentration in marketing from American International University-Bangladesh and completed his doctorate in management science with a concentration in marketing and innovation management at Zhejiang Gongshang University, China. He also holds a Postgraduate Diploma in

Higher Education Teaching (PGDipHET) with a concentration in Higher Education Teaching, which he obtained from Bangladesh University of Professionals (BUP), Dhaka, Bangladesh. His academic research interest encompasses a broad spectrum of areas such as consumer psychology, e-commerce and social media, e-learning, and technology and innovation.

Richa Diwakar is a doctoral research scholar at Amity College of Commerce and Finance, Amity University Uttar Pradesh, Noida. Her area of research is in the field of forensic accounting.

Jitin Gambhir is known for his engaging teaching style, dedication to student mentorship and administration with over 16 years of experience in reputed universities and institutes. A professional with a strong academic background, contributed to develop academic concepts and ethical standards among students to help them grow professionally in the competititve environment. An administrator with a versatile experience on various positions.

Anwesha Ghosh is an Assistant Professor at Amity Law School, Amity University Mumbai. Prior to this, she served as an Assistant Professor at Amity University Kolkata and at the Rajiv Gandhi National University of Law (RGNUL), Patiala. She was also a UGC-sponsored Senior Research Fellow (SRF) at the Central University of Punjab, where she submitted her Ph.D. thesis on gender diversity in Indian corporate boards. A University Gold Medalist in both LL.B. and LL.M., she has additionally received an Endowment Medal for Corporate and Commercial Laws. Dr. Ghosh has held research positions at GNLU and KIIT University, contributing to projects on HIV-affected children and the criminal justice system's response to rape. Her academic work has been published in UGC CARE and Scopus-indexed journals, and she is the author of An Introspection of Corporate Criminal Liability in India. She has presented at international conferences in Thailand and Turkiye as a panel speaker, earning best paper awards for her research on women's leadership and LGBTQ+ inclusion. With expertise in Corporate Law, mergers, and financial regulations, Dr. Ghosh also has a keen scholarly interest in women's rights, environmental law, and the evolving intersections between artificial intelligence and law.

She actively mentors students, judges moot courts, and serves as a resource person in national and international legal seminars.

Vishal Jain is presently working as an Associate Professor at Department of Computer Science and Engineering, School of Engineering and Technology, Sharda University, Greater Noida, U. P. India. Before that, he has worked for several years as an Associate Professor at Bharati Vidyapeeth's Institute of Computer Applications and Management (BVICAM), New Delhi. He has more than 14 years of experience in the academics. He obtained Ph.D (CSE), M.Tech (CSE), MBA (HR), MCA, MCP and CCNA. He has authored more than 90 research papers in reputed conferences and journals, including Web of Science and Scopus. He has authored and edited more than 30 books with various reputed publishers, including Elsevier, Springer, Apple Academic Press, CRC, Taylor and Francis Group, Scrivener, Wiley, Emerald, NOVA Science and IGI-Global. His research areas include information retrieval, semantic web, ontology engineering, data mining, ad hoc networks, and sensor networks. He received a Young Active Member Award for the year 2012–13 from the Computer Society of India, Best Faculty Award for the year 2017 and Best Researcher Award for the year 2019 from BVICAM, New Delhi.

Kavita Joshi is a Doctoral Research Scholar at the Amity College of Commerce and Finance, Amity University Noida. She is pursuing her research in the area of microfinance and digitalization of financial sector.

Manjit Kour is working as Professor at University Business School at Chandigarh University. She holds a PhD in Business Management from IK Gujral Punjab Technical University, India. She has a good research record with several research papers published in reputed journals. She is an editorial board member and reviewer of many reputed journals including Scopus and ABDC-indexed journals. Her areas of interest include sustainability, green practices, Fintech, online marketing trends and business ethics.

Divyansha Kumar is an Assistant Professor of Marketing and Operations at Chitkara University, Punjab. With over 10 years of experience in the development sector, IT industry, and academia, she has previously held roles at Amity University, Mohali, and Symbiosis University, Pune. She contributed to social empowerment projects through Project KHEL and gained insights into technology-driven solutions at Accenture Services Pvt Ltd. Her research, focused on sustainable business practices and contemporary challenges, has been published in Scopus-indexed and UGC-care-listed journals. She is also active in national and international conferences.

Shila Mamtaz, DBA, is an expert in debt finance with a focus on fintech finance. She currently accomplished a doctorate on "Leveraging FinTech to Enhance Access to Finance for Small Enterprises in Bangladesh" from IBA, University of Dhaka, on February 4, 2024. Before that, she served at a renowned BFI of Bangladesh for more than 7 years as a relationship manager on bank finance. Thus, she has been recognised for her substantive contribution as an adept researcher and practised banker in the debt finance arena.

Archan Mitra is an Assistant Professor at School of Media Studies (SOMS) at Presidency University, Bangalore. He is the author of two book "Cases for Classroom Media and Entertainment Business" and "Multiverse and Media", he also has other several edited books to his credit. He has done his doctorate from Visva-Bharati Santiniketan, West Bengal in the field of "environmental informatics and communication for sustainability". In addition to that he is a certified Science Communicator and Journalism from Indian Science Communication Society (ISCOS), certified Corporate Trainer with Amity Institute of Training and Development, Certified Social Media Network Analyst. He has a strong interest in environmental communication. He was awarded certificate of merit by PRSI, Kolkata Chapter and Medal of Honor by Journalistic Club of Kolkata. He was working as a research assistant with the World Bank's "Environmental Capacity Building in Southeast Asia" project at IIM Kashipur. He was instrumental in launching the World Bank's Green MBA MOOC, he has also assisted in the research project on Uttarakhand disaster mitigation by ICSSR, the leading research on Uttarakhand disaster.

Vichayanan Rattanawiboonsom is an Associate Professor at Naresuan University in Thailand. Currently, she is working as the Dean of the Faculty of Business Economics and Communications at Naresuan University, Thailand. Her research interests include tourism, foreign direct investment, technology transfer, and economic growth. She has conducted studies on topics such as the motivational factors for adopting augmented reality applications in tourism and the relationship between foreign direct investment, technology transfer, and economic growth in the Lower Northern Region of Thailand. Dr. Rattanawiboonsom has also presented her research at conferences and has been involved in the academic community.

Ankit Srivastava is an Assistant Professor of Law at RGNUL, Punjab, and Co-Coordinator of the PhD program. He is a member of the Network for Indian Competition Experts at the Competition Commission of India. With 8 years of teaching and research experience, Dr. Srivastava has previously worked at Amity University Lucknow, NLU Jodhpur, and DNLU Jabalpur. He holds a PhD from NLU Jodhpur, an LLM from NLU Delhi, and a BALLB from Symbiosis Law School Noida. He has directed research projects funded by ICSSR and CCI and serves as Faculty Editor for multiple RGNUL law reviews. An executive member of various RGNUL research centers, he has published 22 papers and presented 11. He has delivered lectures at several government organizations and international universities. His research interests include Competition Law, Corporate Law, Consumer Law, Contract Law, and Research Methodology.

Ritu Wadhwa is Ph.D in Corporate Finance. She is Associate Professor at Amity Business School, Amity University, Noida (U.P.) India. She has more than 21 years of teaching and research experience. She has done MBA (Finance) from GGS Indraprastha University. She has 16 national and 5 international papers to her credit. Also, she has written two books titled "Strategic Financial Management" and "Project Planning Appraisal & Control". Her research Interest area is corporate finance, sustainable finance, financial frauds and international financial reporting standards.

Index

A

B

C

D

F

G

I

L

M

P

S

T

V

www.ingramcontent.com/pod-product-compliance
Lightning Source LLC
LaVergne TN
LVHW080857300926
849162LV00003B/457